Tabular Modeling with SQL Server 2016 Analysis Services Cookbook

Expert tabular modeling techniques for building and deploying cutting-edge business analytical reporting solutions

Derek Wilson

BIRMINGHAM - MUMBAI

Tabular Modeling with SQL Server 2016 Analysis Services Cookbook

First published: January 2017

Production reference: 1200117

Published by Packt Publishing Ltd.
Livery Place
35 Livery Street
Birmingham
B3 2PB, UK.
ISBN 978-1-78646-861-1

www.packtpub.com

Credits

Author

Derek Wilson

Reviewer

Dave Wentzel

Commissioning Editor

Wilson D'souza

Acquisition Editors

Malaika Monteiro

Vinay Argekar

Content Development Editor

Sumeet Sawant

Technical Editor

Sneha Hanchate

Copy Editor

Safis Editing

Laxmi Subramanian

Project Coordinator

Shweta H Birwatkar

Proofreader

Safis Editing

Indexer

Tejal Daruwale Soni

Graphics

Disha Haria

Production Coordinator

Arvindkumar Gupta

About the Author

Derek Wilson is a data management, business intelligence and predictive analytics practitioner. He has been working with Microsoft SQL Server since version 6.5 and with Analysis Services since its initial version. In his current role he responsible for the overall architecture, strategy, and delivery of Business Intelligence, analytics, and predictive solutions. In this role, he is focused on transforming how companies leverage data to gain new insights about their customers and operations to drive revenue and decrease expenses. He has over 17 years of experience in information technology leading and driving architectural solutions across enterprises. Over his career, he has been part of IT services, business units, and consulting organizations, which provides him with a unique perspective on how to communicate the value of technology to business leaders. He is a local chapter leader for the Houston SQL PASS Organization. You can connect with him on his blog at www.derekewilson.com or www.cdoadvisors.com.

I would like to thank my wife, Jessica and my children Jakob and Allison for their support and understanding as I wrote this book. I would also like to thank Dave Wentzel for reviewing and providing feedback to improve the content of this book.

About the Reviewer

Dave Wentzel is a Data Solutions Architect for Microsoft. He helps customers with their Azure Digital Transformation, focused on data science, big data, and SQL Server. After working with customers, he provides feedback and learnings to the product groups at Microsoft to make better solutions. Dave has been working with SQL Server for many years, and with MDX and SSAS since they were in their infancy. Dave shares his experiences at `http://davewentzel.com`. He's always looking for new customers. Would you like to engage?

www.PacktPub.com

For support files and downloads related to your book, please visit www.PacktPub.com.

Did you know that Packt offers eBook versions of every book published, with PDF and ePub files available? You can upgrade to the eBook version at www.PacktPub.com and as a print book customer, you are entitled to a discount on the eBook copy. Get in touch with us at service@packtpub.com for more details.

At www.PacktPub.com, you can also read a collection of free technical articles, sign up for a range of free newsletters and receive exclusive discounts and offers on Packt books and eBooks.

https://www.packtpub.com/mapt

Get the most in-demand software skills with Mapt. Mapt gives you full access to all Packt books and video courses, as well as industry-leading tools to help you plan your personal development and advance your career.

Why subscribe?

- Fully searchable across every book published by Packt
- Copy and paste, print, and bookmark content
- On demand and accessible via a web browser

Customer Feedback

Thank you for purchasing this Packt book. We take our commitment to improving our content and products to meet your needs seriously--that's why your feedback is so valuable. Whatever your feelings about your purchase, please consider leaving a review on this book's Amazon page. Not only will this help us, more importantly it will also help others in the community to make an informed decision about the resources that they invest in to learn.

You can also review for us on a regular basis by joining our reviewers' club. **If you're interested in joining, or would like to learn more about the benefits we offer, please contact us**: customerreviews@packtpub.com.

Table of Contents

Preface

Data has always been a key success of any business. Thanks to advances in software, processing and storage technology data is now more abundant than ever. Businesses can collect and store data from internal systems and mash up external data to new insights about their business. One of the challenges is wrangling the data into a manner that is useful to your organization. Microsoft's SQL Server Analysis Services running in tabular mode allows you to quickly model your data to build business intelligence solutions that will enable your organization to make better decisions.

This book is designed to walk you through the necessary steps to learn the fundamentals of tabular modeling. It uses a public dataset that recorded all crashed in the State of Iowa. Using this dataset, you will design, build, and modify a tabular model. If you are an experienced developer this book can be a great reference to fill gaps in areas, you may not have used. Each recipe can stand alone and show you how to implement a specific feature. If you are a new business intelligence developer and have never used Analysis Services. Start from the beginning of the book and walk through the recipes. Each chapter is designed to build on the knowledge learned in the prior chapters. If you follow all of the recipes in the book you will build a complete solution to help further your understanding from collecting data, modeling, enhancing and visualizing information. You should then be comfortable transferring your knowledge from the examples and recipes in this book and apply the concepts to your own business data and challenges.

What this book covers

Chapter 1, *Introduction to Microsoft Analysis Services Tabular Mode*, introduces SQL Server 2016 and Microsoft's Business Intelligence. You will learn about tabular modeling and the basic concepts that are used to build a solution. You will also review the new features that were released in SQL Server 2016.

Chapter 2, *Setting up a Tabular Mode Environment*, shows you how to install and configure SQL Server Analysis Services in tabular mode. In addition, you will install and configure Visual Studio 2015 and SQL Server Data Tools. Once setup you will learn how to configure your tabular model project.

Chapter 3, *Tabular Model Building*, begins your foundational knowledge of tabular mode. You will begin by adding data to a model, create relationships between tables and then create a calculated column and measure. Finally, you round out the model with hierarchies and folders and deploy the model to the server.

Chapter 4, *Working in Tabular Models*, expands on the initial model and shows how to make modifications to existing and deployed model. In addition, you will learn how to create and modify Key Performance Indicators (KPIs).

Chapter 5, *Administration of Tabular Models*, examines how to manage and modify your model's properties. You will learn about perspectives, data partitions, user roles, and server properties.

Chapter 6, *In-Memory Versus DirectQuery Mode*, shows examples of the two choices in data storage and processing options. You then learn how to configure DirectQuery mode and the advantages and limitations of its use.

Chapter 7, *Securing Tabular Models*, details the different ways to implement security in a tabular model using both row level and dynamic security. The recipes in this chapter show how to create and modify security on your model.

Chapter 8, *Combining Tabular Models with Excel*, explores the various ways to leverage Microsoft Excel when designing and building a tabular model. You will explore data in Excel directly from Visual Studio when building a solution. In addition, you will connect to your model from Excel and use Power View and Power Pivot to explore the model.

Chapter 9, *DAX Syntax and Calculations*, explains the basics of Data Analysis Expressions (DAX) and how DAX is used to enhance a tabular model. Recipes are given on several of the more commonly used DAX formulas and how to filter data in your queries.

Chapter 10, *Working with Dates and Time Intelligence*, details how to create and define a Date table that the model will use for date and time based functions. Then you will explore common date functions to enhance your model to make it easy for your users to leverage the model.

Chapter 11, *Using Power BI for Analysis*, shows how to connect to the completed model and create reports. Recipes in this chapter detail how to create and modify visualizations and bring them together to create a dashboard.

What you need for this book

To run the recipes in this book you will need the following software:

- Virtual Machine Software
- Windows Server 2012
- SQL Server 2016 Developer Edition
- Microsoft Excel 2016
- Microsoft Power BI Desktop

Who this book is for

This book was written primarily for developers who want to better understand how to build BI solutions using Microsoft SQL Server Analysis Services running in tabular mode. If you are a new to Analysis Services running in tabular mode. This book will walk you through developing a complete BI solution. If you are an experienced BI developer, then you can use this book as a reference to review what you already know or skip ahead to the recipes that you need additional information to implement. If you are a business user you can use this book to better understand how to leverage Excel and Power BI to build business solutions.

Sections

In this book, you will find several headings that appear frequently (Getting ready, How to do it, How it works, There's more, and See also).

To give clear instructions on how to complete a recipe, we use these sections as follows:

Getting ready

This section tells you what to expect in the recipe, and describes how to set up any software or any preliminary settings required for the recipe.

How to do it...

This section contains the steps required to follow the recipe.

How it works...

This section usually consists of a detailed explanation of what happened in the previous section.

There's more...

This section consists of additional information about the recipe in order to make the reader more knowledgeable about the recipe.

See also

This section provides helpful links to other useful information for the recipe.

Conventions

In this book, you will find a number of text styles that distinguish between different kinds of information. Here are some examples of these styles and an explanation of their meaning.

Code words in text, database table names, folder names, filenames, file extensions, pathnames, dummy URLs, user input, and Twitter handles are shown as follows: "Create a new user for JIRA in the database and grant the user access to the jiradb database we just created using the following command:"

A block of code is set as follows:

```
Total_Fatalities_GT2_MajorInjuries := SUMX(
FILTER(CRASH_DATA_T, CRASH_DATA_T[MAJINJURY]>2),
CRASH_DATA_T[FATALITIES]
)
```

Any command-line input or output is written as follows:

```
mysql -u root -p
```

New terms and **important words** are shown in bold. Words that you see on the screen, for example, in menus or dialog boxes, appear in the text like this: "Select **System info** from the **Administration** panel."

Warnings or important notes appear in a box like this.

Tips and tricks appear like this.

Reader feedback

Feedback from our readers is always welcome. Let us know what you think about this book-what you liked or disliked. Reader feedback is important for us as it helps us develop titles that you will really get the most out of.

To send us general feedback, simply e-mail feedback@packtpub.com, and mention the book's title in the subject of your message.

If there is a topic that you have expertise in and you are interested in either writing or contributing to a book, see our author guide at www.packtpub.com/authors.

Customer support

Now that you are the proud owner of a Packt book, we have a number of things to help you to get the most from your purchase.

Downloading the example code

You can download the example code files for this book from your account at http://www.packtpub.com. If you purchased this book elsewhere, you can visit http://www.packtpub.com/support and register to have the files e-mailed directly to you.

You can download the code files by following these steps:

1. Log in or register to our website using your e-mail address and password.
2. Hover the mouse pointer on the **SUPPORT** tab at the top.
3. Click on **Code Downloads & Errata**.
4. Enter the name of the book in the **Search** box.
5. Select the book for which you're looking to download the code files.
6. Choose from the drop-down menu where you purchased this book from.
7. Click on **Code Download**.

You can also download the code files by clicking on the **Code Files** button on the book's webpage at the Packt Publishing website. This page can be accessed by entering the book's name in the **Search** box. Please note that you need to be logged in to your Packt account.

Once the file is downloaded, please make sure that you unzip or extract the folder using the latest version of:

- WinRAR / 7-Zip for Windows
- Zipeg / iZip / UnRarX for Mac
- 7-Zip / PeaZip for Linux

The code bundle for the book is also hosted on GitHub at https://github.com/PacktPublishing/Tabular-Modeling-with-SQL-Server-2016-Analysis-Services-Cookbook. We also have other code bundles from our rich catalog of books and videos available at https://github.com/PacktPublishing/. Check them out!

Downloading the color images of this book

We also provide you with a PDF file that has color images of the screenshots/diagrams used in this book. The color images will help you better understand the changes in the output. You can download this file from https://www.packtpub.com/sites/default/files/downloads/TabularModelingwithSQLServer2016AnalysisServicesCookbook_ColorImages.pdf.

Errata

Although we have taken every care to ensure the accuracy of our content, mistakes do happen. If you find a mistake in one of our books-maybe a mistake in the text or the code-we would be grateful if you could report this to us. By doing so, you can save other readers from frustration and help us improve subsequent versions of this book. If you find any errata, please report them by visiting http://www.packtpub.com/submit-errata, selecting your book, clicking on the **Errata Submission Form** link, and entering the details of your errata. Once your errata are verified, your submission will be accepted and the errata will be uploaded to our website or added to any list of existing errata under the Errata section of that title.

To view the previously submitted errata, go to https://www.packtpub.com/books/content/support and enter the name of the book in the search field. The required information will appear under the **Errata** section.

Piracy

Piracy of copyrighted material on the Internet is an ongoing problem across all media. At Packt, we take the protection of our copyright and licenses very seriously. If you come across any illegal copies of our works in any form on the Internet, please provide us with the location address or website name immediately so that we can pursue a remedy.

Please contact us at copyright@packtpub.com with a link to the suspected pirated material.

We appreciate your help in protecting our authors and our ability to bring you valuable content.

Questions

If you have a problem with any aspect of this book, you can contact us at questions@packtpub.com, and we will do our best to address the problem.

1
Introduction to Microsoft Analysis Services Tabular Mode

In this chapter, we will cover the following recipes:

- Learning about Microsoft Business Intelligence and SQL Server 2016
- Understanding tabular mode
- Learning what's new in SQL Server 2016 tabular mode
- Importing sample datasets
- Understanding basic concepts

Introduction

Microsoft continues to add and enhance the business intelligence offerings that are included with SQL Server. With the release of SQL Server 2012, Microsoft added Tabular Mode for Analysis services as a deployment option. Unlike traditional multidimensional Analysis Services models that write to disk and require special model design and implementation, tabular models are created using basic relational data models. Then, using in-memory technology, the model is deployed to RAM for faster access to the data. Microsoft has created a new query language to interact with the Tabular model named Data Analysis Expressions, or DAX for short. For new BI developers' tabular models can be an easier way to get started with delivering business results.

For experienced developers, Tabular models can offer an additional method to develop BI solutions. You can develop robust completed solutions or quickly develop prototypes without investing heavily in ETL or Star Schema designs.

In order to take advantage of this technology you need to understand the basics of tabular models and how they work. This chapter focuses on the background you need to get started with designing and deploying tabular models.

After reading this section, you will understand what tabular mode in SQL Server Analysis Services is. You will also learn the basic components required to create a tabular model and how to import data into your first project.

Every tabular model begins with data that you import into your project. This chapter teaches you the skills required to get started by importing a list of states in the United States and a short list of famous United States landmarks. By using these two small tables and their data, you will learn all of the core components of tabular modeling. Later you will use a much larger sample dataset from the state of Iowa to build a complete tabular model solution.

Learning about Microsoft Business Intelligence and SQL Server 2016

In SQL Server 2016, Microsoft has added many new features to the Business Intelligence stack. The Microsoft BI Stack refers to the components most used with creating data insights. These include Reporting Services, Analysis Services, and Integration Services.

Reporting Services is a standalone enterprise reporting platform. It can connect to a wide variety of data sources that allow you to create rich and powerful reports for your users.

Analysis Services includes traditional OLAP solutions as well as the newer tabular mode version. With Analysis Services you can create analytical solutions that enable your users to quickly explore the data without writing code. In addition, you can add custom calculations to create KPI's, trends, and show period over period growth to the values in the model.

Integration Services is an enterprise data integration solution. You can design and build robust ETL solutions that move data across your enterprise. In addition, you can add steps to transform, clean, or analyze the data while it is being moved to improve the data for your users.

Business intelligence projects are primarily concerned with turning raw data into business information. Source systems store and collect data to process transaction such as making an online purchase. Business intelligence systems look to gather individual transactions and present the data to business users to improve the operations of a business. BI solutions can be created for any industry. In financial industries you can monitor cash flow, expenses, and revenue. You can also create KPIs that let you know when critical metrics are hit or missed. For marketing, you can combine data from various systems, both internal and external, such as Twitter or Facebook to create a comprehensive view of customer interactions. This can help you know how well your marketing campaigns are working and which ones are most effective. In retail industries you can build solutions to track customer purchases and changes in customer patterns over time. For example, questions such as how many users made purchases over the last seven days, or what is the average purchase price per customer are typical BI questions.

This book focuses on Analysis Services, specifically the Tabular Mode engine. Developers can leverage this engine to create high-performing BI solutions that provide valuable data to your business users.

Understanding tabular mode

Microsoft SQL Server Analysis Services can be deployed in two ways, multidimensional mode or tabular mode. Tabular mode is the newest way to build and deploy BI solutions and it requires installation of the Analysis Services engine in Tabular mode within your SQL Server Installation. Once installed you design and build Tabular models in SQL Server Data Tools (SSDT). SSDT is installed inside Visual Studio and allows for a complete development experience within a single tool. You can design, build, and refactor your database solutions. When development is complete you deploy from your desktop SSDT solution to the Tabular model server. Once deployed your users are able to connect to the models and can explore and leverage the data.

Tabular models are deployed in memory or in **DirectQuery** mode and deliver fast access to the data from a variety of client tools.

Learning what's new in SQL Server 2016 tabular mode

The release of SQL Server 2016 includes a variety of enhancements for Tabular mode in the areas of modeling, instance management, scripting, DAX, and developer interfaces. These changes continue to make designing and building Tabular modes easier to provide better value to your business.

Modeling

Modeling is where you start with tabular mode. All users will connect to the server and access the data provided from a model. As a designer, you will spend most of your time inside the Tabular Model adding data, creating relationships, and custom calculations. With the SQL Server 2016 release, tabular models have a compatibility level of 1,200.

If you have used prior editions of SQL Server to build Tabular Models you will notice right away the designer is much faster in this release. When modeling in SQL Server Data Tools, you will notice that the performance of tabular models has been improved. Design changes will occur faster than previous versions, such as creating a relationship or copying a table. Also included now is the ability to create folders to organize your model for better end user navigation. This enables you to group your data into logical folders such as Sales, Regions, Gross, Net, and so on, and it also helps your users know where to go for data instead of a long list of values.

If you need the ability to store multiple definitions for a name or a description to account for different languages, this ability is handled under the **Translation** tab of the model. For instance, you could store *Customer Name* in English and provide a variety of cultural translations as required.

In this release, you can now deploy to a variety of environments, as you have been able to do with multidimensional modeling. Developers can develop and deploy to a test environment. Then if you need to deploy to a UAT environment on a different server, you can do that by leveraging the configuration manager.

Instance management

After setting up and configuring tabular mode on a server that is known as an instance, you can have multiple instances running on the same server provided you have enough hardware to run all instances. Each instance can have different properties, security, and configurations based on your needs.

An SQL Server 2016 Tabular mode instance can now run prior versions of tabular services. This allows for compatibility level 1,100 and 1,103 models to be run without the requirement of upgrading the model to the current release and redeploying the model to the instance.

Scripting

Microsoft continues to add functionality to improve the ability to write scripts for tabular models. Scripting allows you to write code that will perform actions instead of using the visual design tools such as SSDT or SQL Server Management Studio.

PowerShell cmdlets are able to be used, such as `Invoke-ProcessAsDatabase` and `Invoke-ProcessTable` cmdlet.

DAX

DAX is the language that you will use the most inside tabular models. New in this release is an improved formula editor. When creating formulas inside the formula bar functions, fields and measures are color coded. The intelligence function inspects your formula as you create it to let you know any known errors. In line comments can now be added to help document your function by using //. The creation of DAX measures no longer requires the measure to be complete. You can now save incomplete DAX measures in your model and complete them at a later time.

Importing sample datasets

For the examples in this chapter you will import two sets of data to create tables inside the model. This first table is a list of all states in the United States plus the District of Columbia. The second data set is a short list of famous landmarks.

 These examples are available at `https://github.com/derekewilson/SSA S_2016_Tabular_Model`.

Getting ready

This example assumes you have a working tabular mode server and SQL Server Data Tools installed.

How to do it...

1. Open Visual Studio, select **File** and then **New Project**.
2. On the next screen select **Analysis Services Tabular Project** to create a new Analysis Service tabular project.

3. Select **Model** from the menu and **Import from Data Source**.

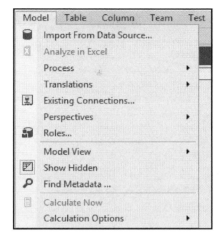

4. Select **Excel File** from the bottom of the **Table Import Wizard** and click **Next**.

5. Browse to the location of the US States.xlsx file. Check the **Use first row as column headers** box.

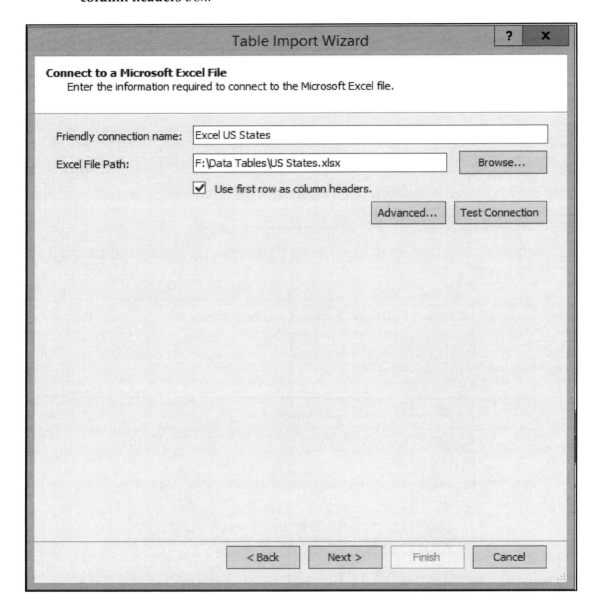

6. Select the **Service Account** to specify a user that has access to the data source. Click **Next**.

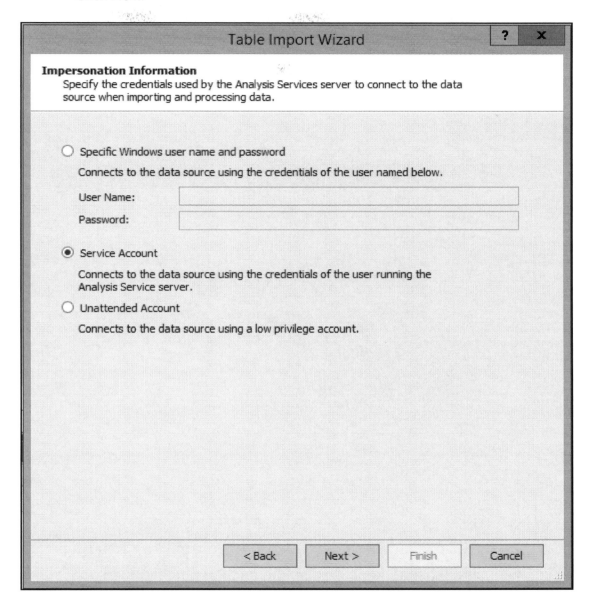

[17]

7. Review the **Source Table** information and click **Finish**.

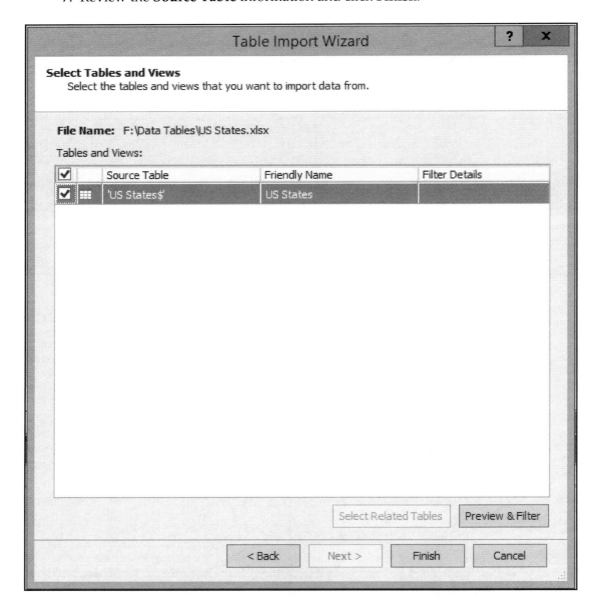

8. Click **Close** after successfully importing the data.

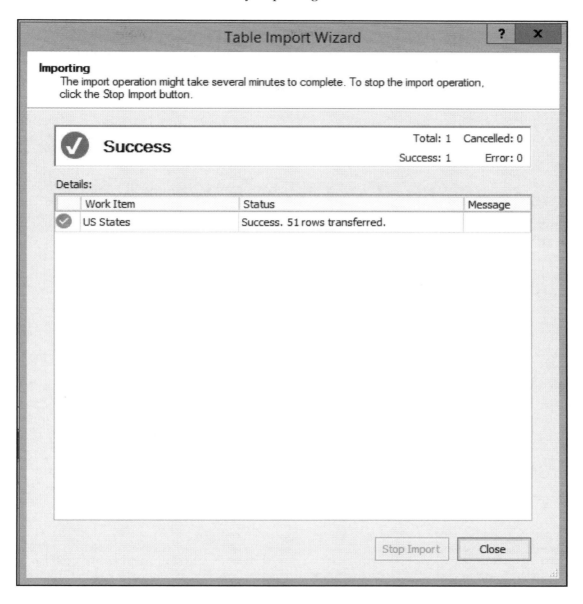

9. Now repeat steps 4-8 and import into the data the `Famous Landmarks.csv` file.

How it works...

Let's review what was done in the previous steps for this first recipe. In steps 1 and 2 we created a new Tabular Model project and selected the option to import data. Then in steps 3 and 4 we selected the source data type of Excel and chose the file to import that included a list of the States in the USA. During step 5 we selected how the data source can be accessed via user security. In step 6, we reviewed the import process and started loading the data. In step 7 we were able to see that the data was successfully imported. Then you repeated the process to import the Famous Landmarks file. You now have two data tables loaded into your model that Tabular mode can use.

Understanding basic concepts

Tabular models are built using four main principles: tables, measures, columns, and relationships:

Tables

Tables contain the columns and rows of data that you are using to populate your Tabular data model. Data can be added from a variety of source systems. Examples include relational database structures such as tables or views, Analysis Services cubes, or text files. The tabular mode engine does not require you to transform data into special schema structures such as Star or Snowflake schemas. By leveraging the tabular model engine you can connect directly to data and transform it in the model designer if needed. This enables quicker model design and iterations without the need to invest in design and building data transformations and load processes. You can share the model with users to ensure the business need is being met. In addition to performing time calculations you will have to create and configure a table known to be a *Date Table*.

Using the model designer, you can view tables as either a diagram or a grid design view. The grid designer view shows the data in the table similar to viewing the data as an Excel file. This view is where you will create new DAX calculations and review the data.

When using the grid designer view, you see a data model of the table that displays the table and column names. Using this mode enables you to create hierarchies on a table and relationships between tables.

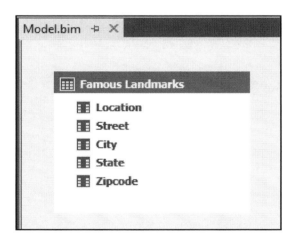

Columns

Every table will contain columns that store the data that make up your model. When you import data into your table, the designer inspects each column to automatically determine the type of data in the column and assign it a data type. In SQL Server 2016, the following data types are allowed:

1. Currency.
2. Date.
3. Decimal Number.
4. Text.
5. True / False.
6. Whole Number.

Measures

In order to perform calculations in Tabular mode you must create measures using Data Analysis Expressions, also known as DAX. Adding measures to your data improves the usefulness of the information to your business users. For instance, adding a calculation to perform period over period growth to a tabular model would allow all users to leverage the same calculation and result. Otherwise, you may have users creating calculations outside of the model that use different logic.

Relationships

As you build more complex models that contain many tables, relationships are the method to determine how data in one table relates to data in another table by linking columns. When adding a relationship to a Tabular Model, the column data must be the same. For example, if you create a relationship between an address table and a state table containing the master data of all 50 United States plus the District of Columbia, the columns used to link would have to match the data.

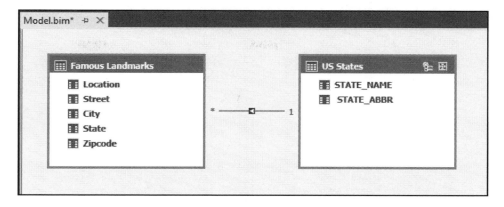

Once you know what columns and tables you want to link together you then must determine the type of relationship to establish. In the Tabular Model designer, you can create two types of relationships:

- One-to-one
- One-to-many

Continuing on our previous example will demonstrate the differences in the types of relationships. Every address can have one state and is a one-to-one relationship. However, every state can have multiple addresses and is an example of a one-to-many relationship.

When building relationships there are rules that are enforced in the model designer; first, each column can only be used in a single relationship. You cannot reuse a column that is already established in a relationship. The second rule is there can be only one active relationship between tables.

Hierarchies

Much like how relationships define how tables are joined together and related, hierarchies define how data between columns is related. You add hierarchies to your model to make it easier for your business users to leverage the data. The classic example of a well formed hierarchy is a **Calendar** hierarchy built on a date table. The top of the calendar is the highest unit of measure and the bottom of the hierarchy is the lowest unit of measure. Therefore, you could have a **Calendar** hierarchy that is defined as **Year** | **Quarter** | **Month** | **Day**. Given this hierarchy users could navigate the model starting at **Year** and then drill down into the next lower level (**Quarter**), and then ultimately down to the day to get more detail based on their needs.

2
Setting up a Tabular Mode Environment

In this chapter, we will cover the following recipes:

- Installing and configuring a development environment
- Installing Visual Studio 2015
- Installing SQL Server Data Tools (SSDT)
- Configuring a workspace server
- Configuring SSAS project properties

Introduction

This chapter will show you how to install and configure SQL Server Analysis Services in tabular mode on a Windows Server 2012 R2. At the end of this chapter, you will have a server set up and configured to leverage for a development environment. As part of the installation, you will install the SQL Database engine to be used later as a data source for the tabular model. Once installed, you will set up the development software on the same server that will allow you to create models. Finally, you will create a project and learn how to configure the workspace server and project settings that allow you to deploy the project to a server.

This setup assumes you have the operating system installed and running with an account with administrator privileges. On this server is where you will begin to learn how tabular mode works, how to interact with data in the model, and how to set up deployment options.

Installing and configuring a development environment

Getting ready

Create a virtual machine running Windows Server 2012 R2 with important updates installed. You can download and install SQL Server Developer Edition for free from Microsoft. Also, make sure you have an account set up with administrative privileges that you will use for the installation and configuration of SQL Server 2016 tabular mode. In my examples, I have a user named `Admin` set up as a local administrator.

How to do it...

1. Launch SQL Server Developer Edition from your virtual machine drive to begin the installation process in the **SQL Server Installation Center** window.

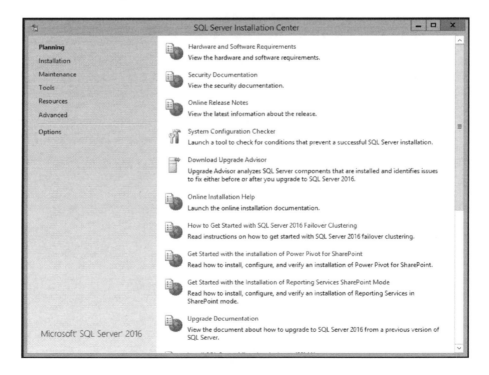

2. Select **Installation** to bring up the options for installing components. Then choose **New SQL Server stand-alone installation or add features to an existing installation**.

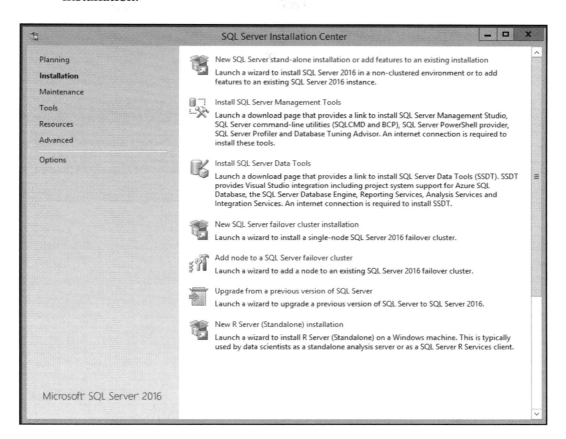

3. The next screen is where you enter your product key if you have one. Since we are using the developer edition, no product key is needed. Click **Next**.

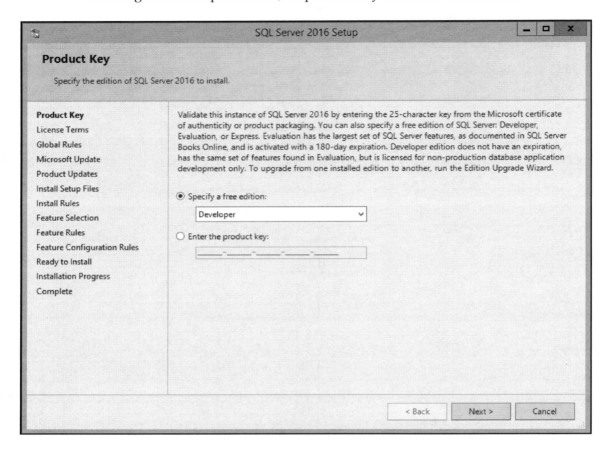

4. Next you need to review and accept the license terms for the software. Review the license terms and click on the checkbox next to **I accept the license terms**, and then click **Next**.

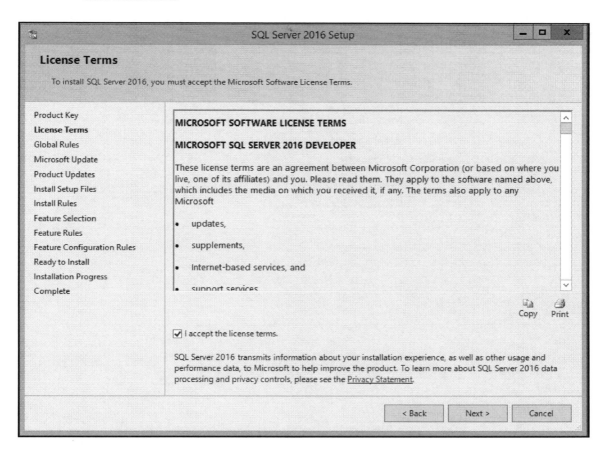

5. The next screen allows you to have **Microsoft Update** automatically check for updates for SQL Server. Depending upon your environment, you may want to turn this on, but for now let's keep it off. Click **Next**.

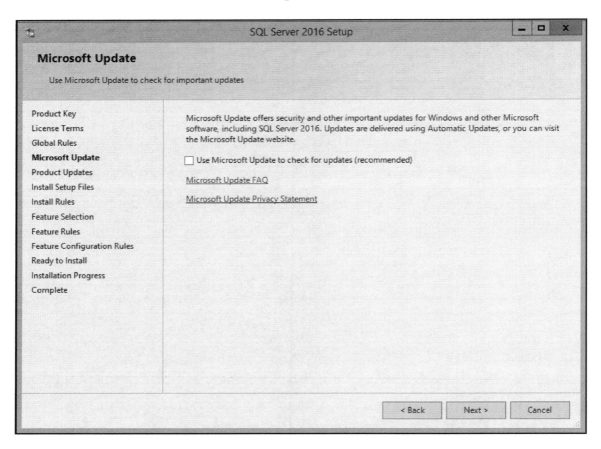

6. Now we are ready to install the features required for our development environment. You can always go back and add additional features later. For our development server we will need **Database Engine Services** and **Analysis Services**. Check both of those boxes and then click **Next**.

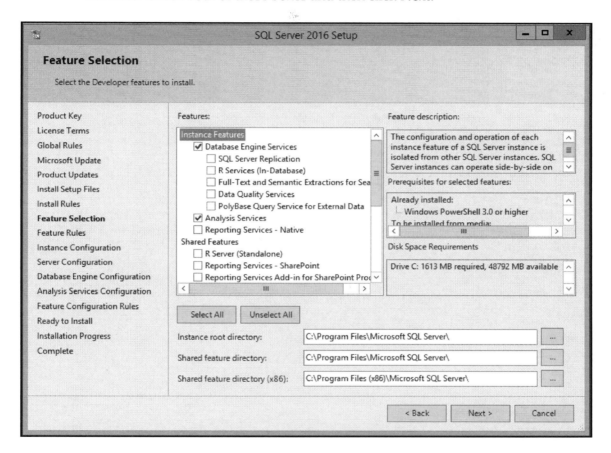

7. Now you can name the instance of the database if you want to use something other than the default instance. This is useful if you will be running more than one database engine on a server. For this development environment, we will only have one instance, so we will use the default. Click **Next**.

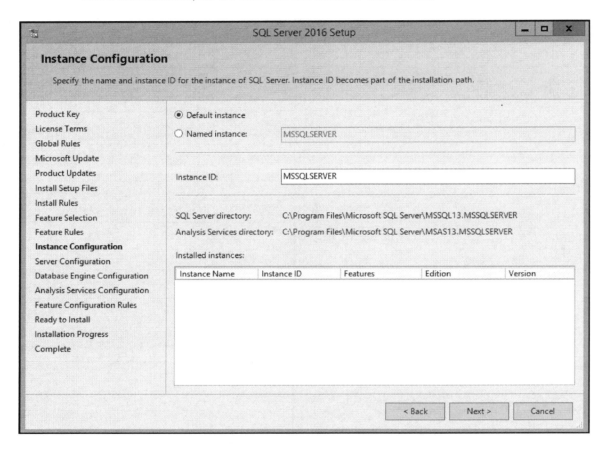

8. The next settings are for the services that will be installed and the accounts that will be enabled to run them. In a production environment you would have specific accounts set up. For this environment, we will keep them as the default values. Click **Next**.

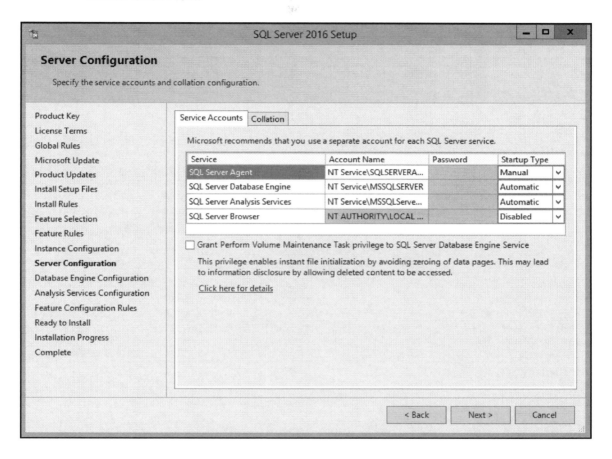

9. Since we selected the Database Engine in step 6. This screen enables us to configure how the SQL Database will be installed. First, change the **Authentication Mode** radio button to **Mixed Mode**. Then enter a password for your server system administrator (sa) account such as `P@ssword`. Secondly, add the current Windows account to be an Administrator on the server by clicking **Add Current User**. Then click **Next**.

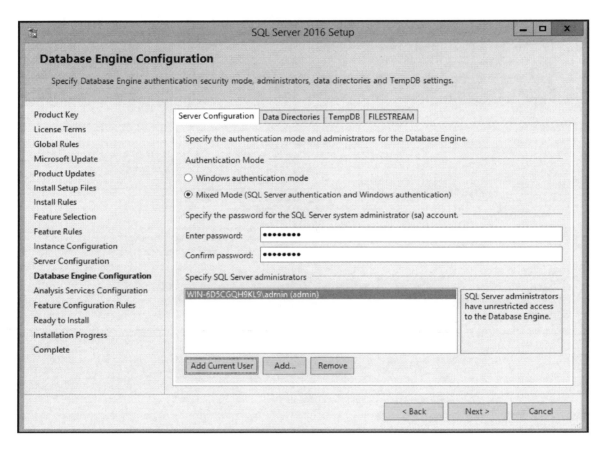

10. Now we are ready to configure **Analysis Services Configuration** in tabular mode. Select the radio button next to **Tabular Mode** and click on the **Add Current User** button to make the local windows account an Administrator. Review on the **Data Directory** tab, that is where you can define where the data is stored if you need to customize your setup. Click **Next**.

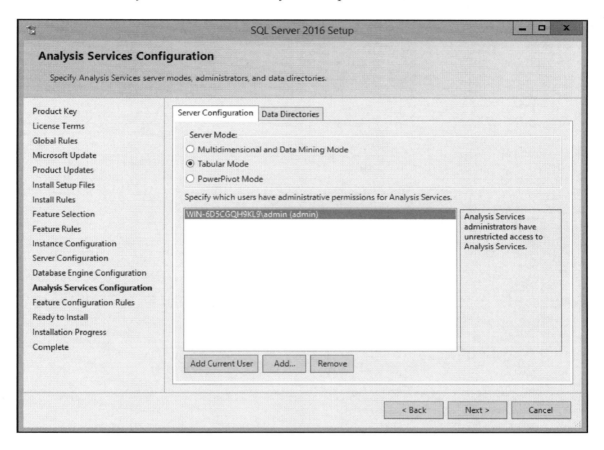

11. Everything is now ready for installation. The **Ready to Install** window allows you to review all of the settings that we just configured. We are ready to click on **Install** to begin the process.

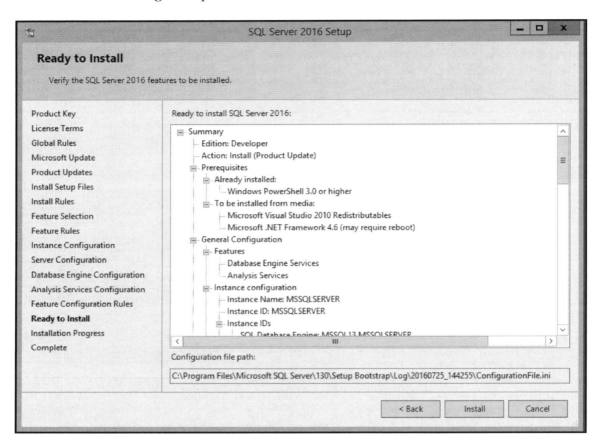

12. Once completed, you will be prompted to restart your server. Click **OK** and then **Close**. From the operating system, select **Restart** to reboot your server.

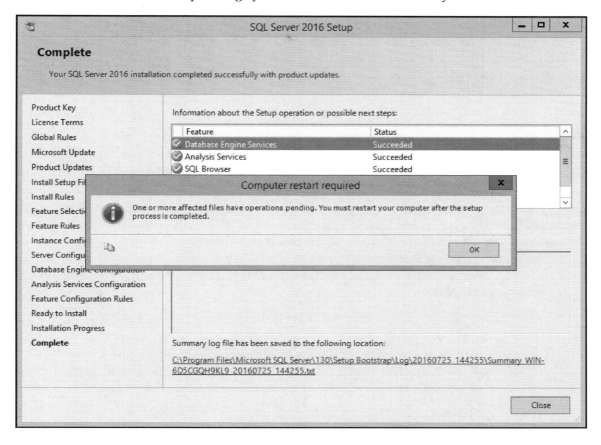

How it works...

This recipe showed you step-by-step instructions to install the SQL Database Engine and Analysis Services in tabular mode. You then configured the services that run the Database Engine and Analysis Services. Next you created a local SQL server account that will have administrative rights to SQL Server and Analysis Services. Upon completion you have a working development server.

Installing Visual Studio 2015

Visual Studio 2015 is the base software that you will use to leverage the **SQL Server Data Tools** (**SSDT**) components. SSDT contains the templates that you use to design and develop your Tabular Models. If you already have Visual Studio installed then you can install SSDT with Visual Studio. To continue with your development environment setup, this recipe will show you how to install Visual Studio and the basic database components of SSDT together. The base components of SSDT only install the SQL Server Database template.

Getting ready

Login to the development server with your local Admin account. Then download the free Visual Studio Community edition at
`https://www.visualstudio.com/en-us/products/visual-studio-community-vs.aspx`.

Once completed, open the file to begin installation.

How to do it...

1. Select the **Custom** radio button to select the features required for SSDT. Then click **Next**.

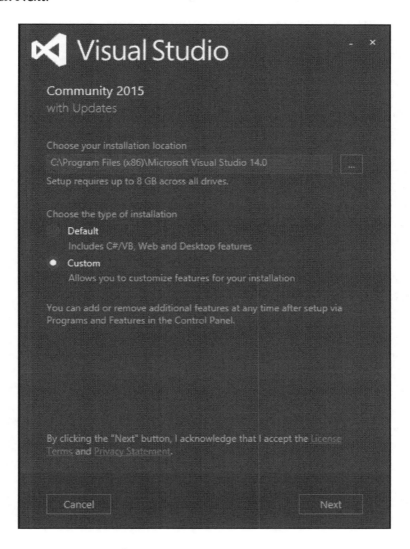

2. Once you reach the **Select Features** window, select **Microsoft SQL Server Data Tools** and then click **Next**.

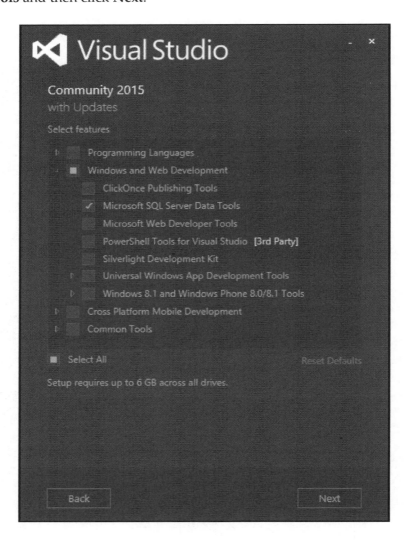

3. On the next screen review the selected features and then click **Install**.

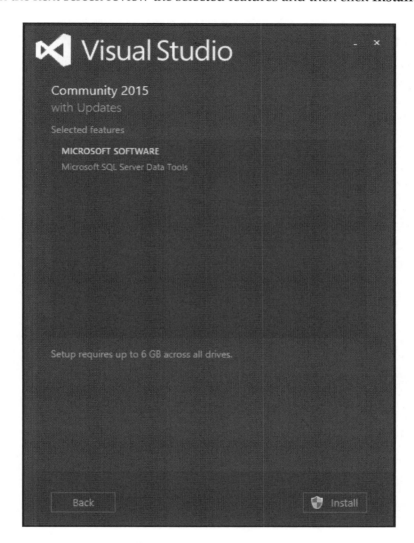

4. Once successfully completed you will need to restart your server.

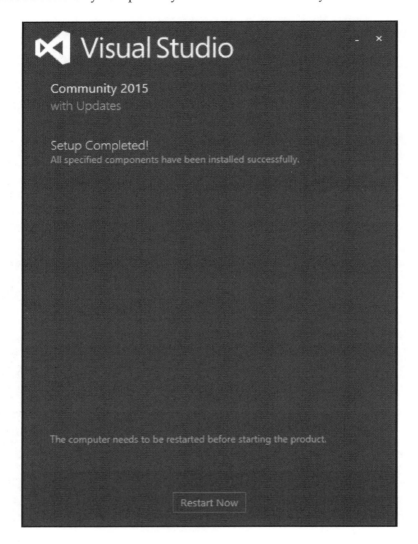

How it works...

This recipe showed you how to download and install Visual Studio 2015. Then using the custom configuration option you installed the database templates for SQL Server Data Tools. Visual Studio is now ready to have the remaining SQL templates installed.

Installing SQL Server Data Tools (SSDT)

Once Visual Studio is installed the next step is to add SQL Server Data Tools (SSDT). SSDT is the environment that you will use to create your tabular model. You will use it to import your data, design your model, add DAX calculations, and finally deploy your model to the server.

Getting ready

Once Visual Studio is installed, you can now install the remaining pieces of SSDT. This recipe shows the steps required to install the templates for Analysis Services, Reporting Services, and Integration Services.

How to do it...

1. From the SQL Server installation disk, select the **installation** tab and then click on **Install SQL Server Data Tools** to open a web browser with the link to download the software.

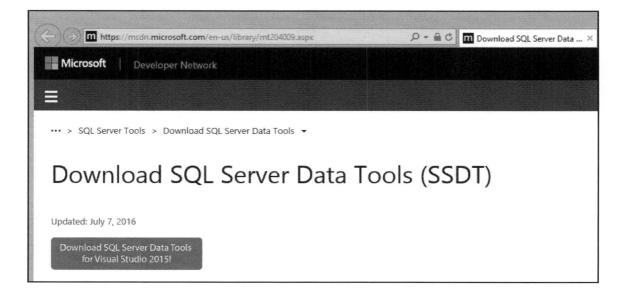

2. Select **Download SQL Server Data Tools for Visual Studio 2015!** and save the file. On the next screen select your language to install and run the **SSDTSetup.exe** program.

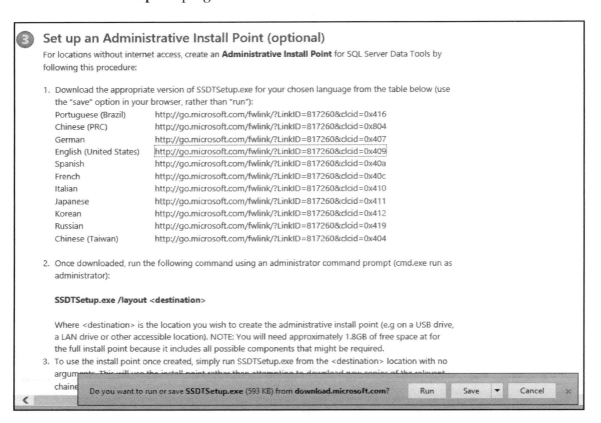

3. On the next window you can select which features of SSDT to install. In this case, keep them all checked and select **Next**.

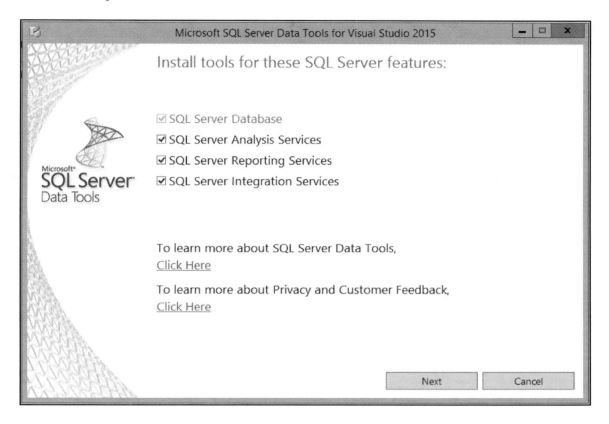

Install tools for these SQL Server features:

☑ SQL Server Database
☑ SQL Server Analysis Services
☑ SQL Server Reporting Services
☑ SQL Server Integration Services

To learn more about SQL Server Data Tools,
Click Here

To learn more about Privacy and Customer Feedback,
Click Here

Next   Cancel

4. In the final step, check the checkbox for **I Agree to the license terms and conditions** and then click **Install**.

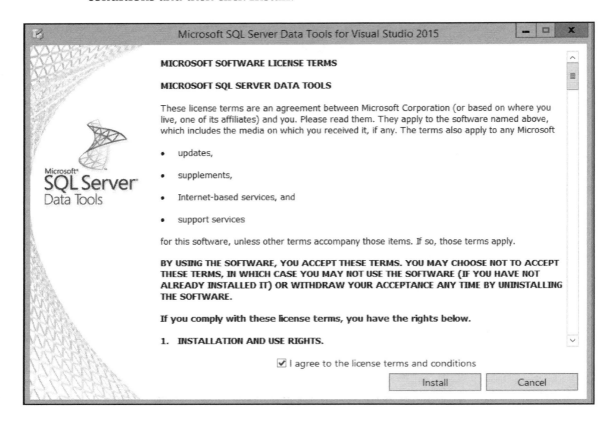

How it works...

This recipe installed the remaining templates for SSDT into Visual Studio. These templates allow you to create Analysis Services, Reporting Services, and Integration Services projects.

Interacting with SQL Server Data Tools

After the installation of Visual Studio and SSDT you will need to set up your environment settings. These setting are chosen the first time you start Visual Studio. However, they can be changed later in the **Options** section of the **Tools** menu. Once set, each new project will use the options selected.

Getting ready

Now that Visual Studio and SSDT have been installed, this section will review how to access SSDT and use it to create a tabular model project.

How to do it...

1. Open **Visual Studio 2015**.

2. On the next screen, sign in if you have an account or select **Not now, maybe later** if you do not, and then select the color scheme you want to use.

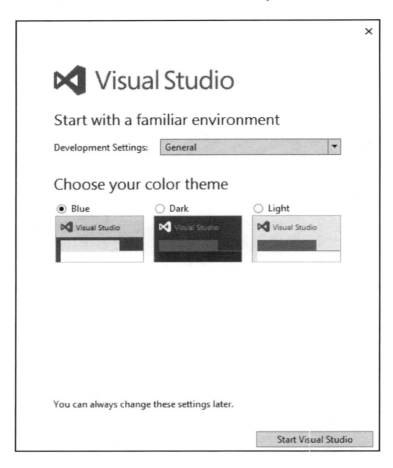

3. You are now at the base screen for Visual Studio projects. Select **New Project...**

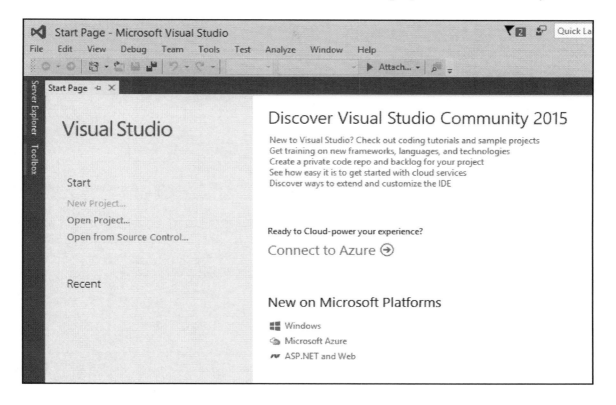

4. You will now be presented with the **New Project** window. From here expand **Business Intelligence**. Here you will see the choices for the features you installed. To create a new Tabular Mode project, select **Analysis Services**. Type `Chapter2_model` in the **Name:** box and click **OK** to create the project.

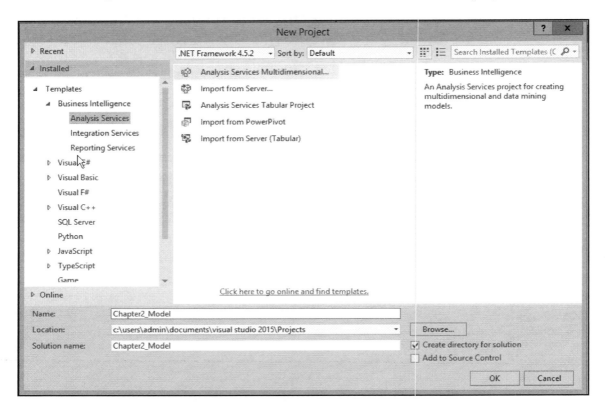

How it works...

This recipe showed you how to create a new Analysis Services Tabular Project in Visual Studio. You can now begin to design tabular models.

Configuring a workspace server

Getting ready

This recipe connects your development environment to the Tabular Model workspace server. If a workspace server has not been configured for a project, you will be prompted to configure it after creating a project.

How to do it...

1. When prompted, enter the server address of the development Tabular server. For our setup we will use **localhost**. Next, set **Compatibility level** to **SQL Server 2016 RTM (1200)** and click **OK**.

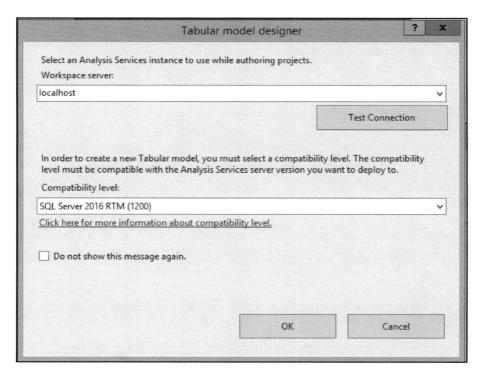

2. Your tabular model designer will now open.

How it works...

The workspace server specifies what Analysis Services will be used to host the workspace database while you are creating models. For authoring it is recommended to use a local Analysis Services instance instead of a remote instance.

There's more...

If you need to change your workspace server after a project has been created, you can change the setting by accessing **Tools** | **Options** | **Analysis Services Tabular Designers**.

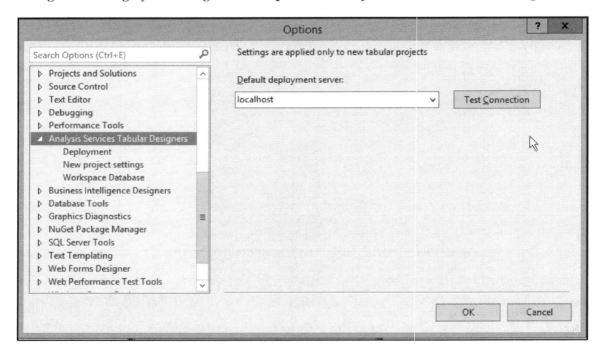

Configuring SSAS project properties

The SSAS project properties are where you set up different environments for your model to use. You design and build your model on the workspace server. When ready for deployment you will select the configuration and server to deploy your solution.

Getting ready

The final step to getting your development environment ready is to configure Visual Studio. In this recipe, you will configure the project properties that will allow you to deploy your model to the Analysis Services service.

How to do it...

1. Click on **Project** to find the properties at the bottom of the page. In this case, **Chapter2_Model Properties...**

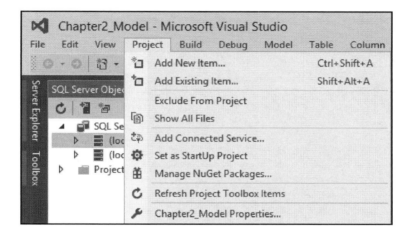

2. On the **Chapter2_Model Properties** pages, change the **Server** to the name of your development server. It defaults to **localhost** so we can click **OK** without changing the value.

How it works...

The project properties area is where you define where the model you design will be deployed. You can create multiple areas such as Development, UAT, and Production. Then, for each area define the server names.

3
Tabular Model Building

In this chapter, we will cover the following recipes:

- Adding new data to a tabular model
- Adding a calculated column
- Adding a measure to a tabular model
- Changing model views
- Renaming columns
- Defining a date table
- Creating hierarchies
- Understanding and building relationships
- Creating and organizing display folders
- Deploying your first model
- Browsing your model with SQL Server Management Studio
- Browsing your model with Microsoft Excel

Introduction

In this chapter, you will build your first tabular model, deploy it to the Analysis Server, and then view the results with SQL Server Management Studio and Microsoft Excel. Instead of using the standard sample databases such as AdventureWorks, you will download a public dataset and then create a simple dimensional model. Once the model is completed, you will learn how to deploy the data. The recipes in this chapter cover all of the basics required to get a working model built. Each recipe builds upon information to complete the model. They should be done in order to get the best understanding.

Tabular modeling allows you to quickly take de-normalized data and turn it into a working dimensional model that makes it easy for your users to leverage. By transforming the data and creating user-friendly fields you will be able to create an easy to use reporting database. All of the recipes in this chapter are built using public vehicle crash data from the state of Iowa. Upon completion of these recipes you will have your first working model and know how to interact with the data.

Adding new data to a tabular model

In this recipe, you will download external data and then add it into the model. The data is freely available from the state of Iowa and is a list of all crashes recorded by date. It includes many columns of data that you will use to build a model in the remaining chapters.

Getting ready

Depending upon your setup you may need to install Microsoft Access Database Engine 2010 Redistributable in order to enable importing data from Excel. For this recipe you will be using data vehicle crash data provided by the state of Iowa. Download the `csv` file of the data here: `https://data.iowa.gov/api/views/bew5-k5dr/rows.csv?accessType=DOWNLOAD`. Once downloaded, open the `csv` in Excel and save it as `Iowa_Crash_Data.xlsx`. There are several fields in the file that will be used to create and enhance the model:

- **CRASH_KEY** – UNIQUE RECORD IDENTIFIER
- **CRASH_DATE** – DATE OF CRASH
- **FATALITIES** – NUMBER OF FATALITIES
- **MAJINJURY** – NUMBER OF MAJOR INJURIES
- **MININJURY** – NUMBER OF MINOR INJURIES
- **POSSINJURY** – NUMBER OF POSSIBLE INJURIES
- **UNKINJURY** – NUMBER OF UNKOWN INJURIES
- **VEHICLES** – NUMBER OF VEHICLES INVOLVED
- **CRCOMNNR** – MANNER OF CRASH
- **MAJCSE** – MAJOR CAUSE
- **ECNTCRC** – CONTRIBUTING CIRCUMSTANCES – ENVIRONMENT
- **LIGHT** – LIGHT CONDITIONS

- **CSRFCND** – SURFACE CONDITIONS
- **WEATHER** – WEATHER CONDITIONS
- **PAVED** – PAVED (1,0)
- **CSEV** – CRASH SEVERITY
- **PROPDMG** – AMOUNT OF PROPERTY DAMAGE

How to do it...

1. Create a new Analysis Services tabular model project and name it `Chapter3_Model`. Then select **Model | Import From Data Source** to bring up the Table Import Wizard window. Scroll to the bottom and select **Excel File**, browse to your **Iowa_Crash_Data** file, check **Use first row as column headers,** and then click **Next**.

2. On the next screen, enter a username and password that has administrator privileges and click **Next**. On the next screen review the **Source Table** and **Friendly Name** and then click **Finish** to begin the import process.

3. Once all records are imported you will be back at the grid view of your project.

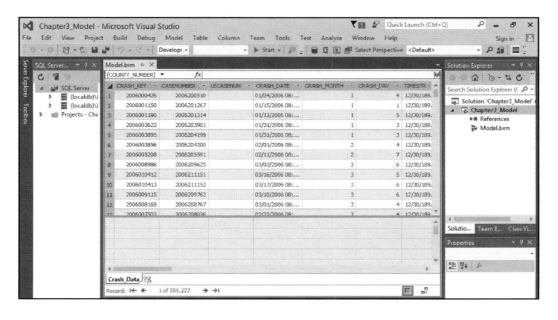

How it works...

In this recipe, you downloaded a public data set and saved it on your local machine. You then imported the data into your tabular model project. You provided a username and password for an account that has permissions to be able to access the crash data. Finally, the data was imported and loaded inside your project model to be extended and enhanced in the following recipes.

Adding a calculated column

Calculations contain code that is applied to all rows in your data. You will create calculations to make the data easier for your users to use. In this recipe, you will add a function to create a new date column to your model.

Getting ready

The data that was imported has the **CRASH_DATE** column formatted as a text field. In order to use this field for calculations, you need the **CRASH_DATE** column to be formatted as a date data type. You can create a new column and use the built-in functions to achieve this result.

How to do it...

1. From the design mode view on the **Crash_Data** tab, scroll to the end of the columns until you see **Add Column**.

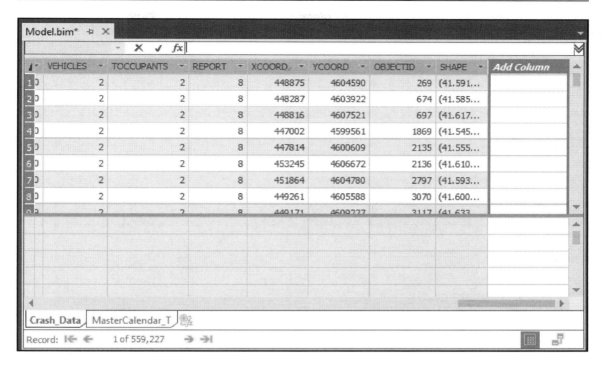

2. Next you need to create a new column based on the **CRASH_DATE** column that is formatted as a date data type. This new column will be used later to create a relationship with the calendar table. Select **Add Column** and in the function box enter:

```
=LEFT(Crash_Data[CRASH_DATE],10)
```

3. Press *Enter*.

4. The formula will run and the column is renamed to **Calculated Column 1**.

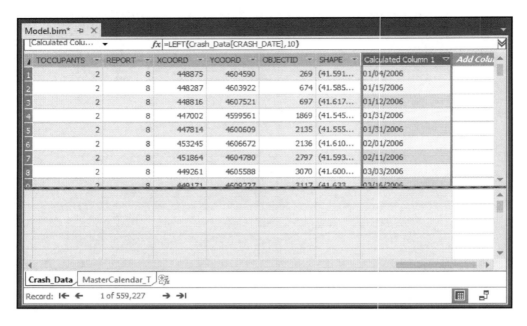

5. Now rename the column to a helpful name and set the data type. Select **Calculated Column 1** and then in the properties window change the following settings. **Column Name** from **Calculated Column 1** to **Crash_Date_fx**, and **Data Type** from **Auto(Text)** to **Date**.

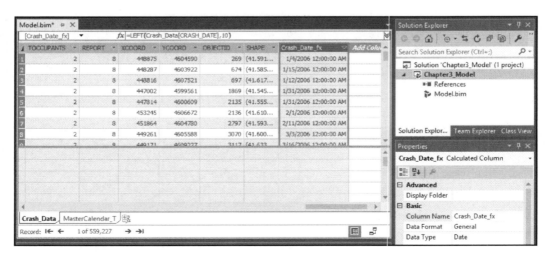

How it works...

When you add a new column to the model each row gets a value based on the logic for the column. In this recipe, you added a new column, created a formula, and then renamed the column. The formula works by retrieving the first 10 characters from the **CRASH_DATE** column to find the calendar date. For example, in row 1 the date you need is **01/04/2006**, everything after the tenth character is ignored. Then you used the properties of the column to set the data type as a date. Your model now has a properly formatted date column.

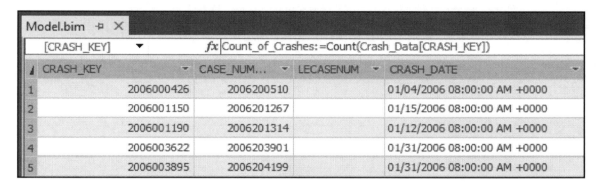

Adding a measure to a tabular model

Measures are what your model uses for calculations against the rows and columns based on the formula. Once a measure has been created in the model, users will be able to add it to their reports. For this recipe you will create one measure that counts the number of rows in the **CRASH_DATE** table. Measures are added to the measure grid area of the grid view in your model.

How to do it...

1. Open your project to the **CRASH_DATE** grid view. You will create the function in the cell highlighted in the following screenshot:

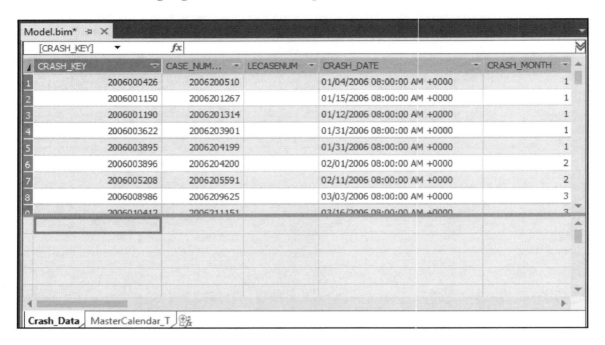

2. Left-click on the highlighted cell and enter the following in the function bar

```
Count_of_Crashs:=COUNT(Crash_Data[CRASH_KEY])
```

3. Press *Enter* to calculate your function.

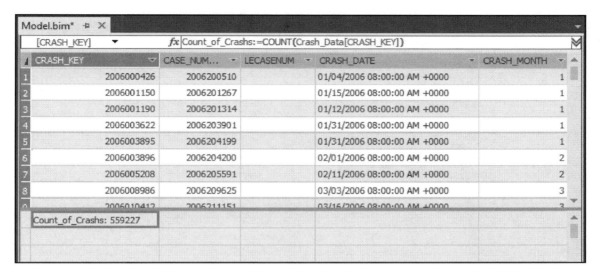

How it works...

In this recipe, you entered a DAX formula into the measure grid area that counts the rows. The formula currently shows the total number of rows in your table of 559,227. However, as you continue to add the following recipes, the formula will dynamically count the number of records at various levels of the model.

Changing model views

As you continue to design and build models, you will need to change the model view to allow you to perform different tasks. There are two views that you can choose in your **Model Grid**: **DataView** and **Diagram View**. Data Views are where you inspect the data and add DAX calculations. Diagram View is where you change column names, add relationships, and add hierarches.

How to do it...

1. Open your **Chapter3_Model**, and then select **Model | Model View**. This exposes the two views you can choose.
2. Select **Diagram View** to switch to enable modeling options.

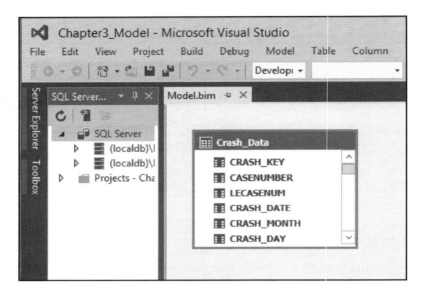

How it works...

The model views are how you interact and work with your tabular model. You used the **Model** menu to change your view from **Grid** to **Diagram**.

There's more...

The other option to quickly change the view is using the icons at the bottom right corner of the model designer. Hover and click on the two different icons to switch between the views.

Here is the Grid view:

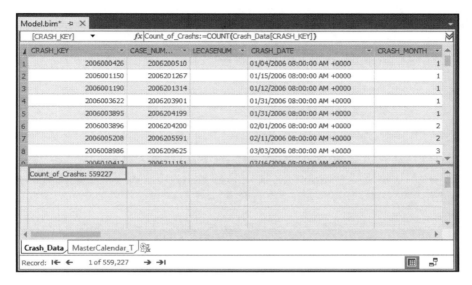

Grid or Data View

This is how the Diagram view looks:

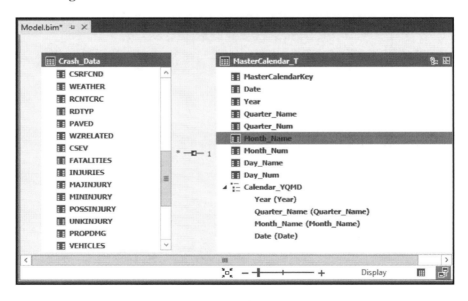

Diagram View

Renaming columns

Often, when you find data to use in a model, the columns have names that you will want to change. The end users of the model need to easily be able to determine what is in the data that you are presenting. This recipe shows you how to change a column name from the diagram view of the model.

How to do it...

1. Change your model view from the Grid view to the Diagram view.
2. Right-click on the column you want to rename. In this example, **CASENUMBER** to bring up the options and select **Rename**.

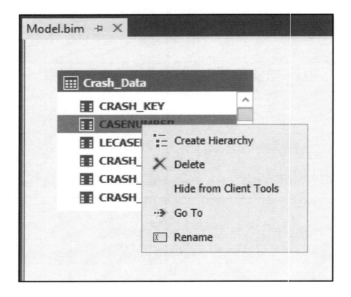

3. **CASENUMBER** is now highlighted, change the name to **CASE_NUMBER** and hit **Enter**.

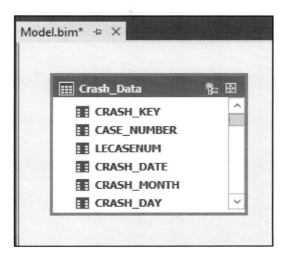

How it works...

The model designer allows for editing of column names. You selected the column to rename and then changed the name by adding an underscore.

Defining a date table

Tabular models require a table to be designated as a date table in order for DAX calculations to perform correctly. A date table can be unique for each solution and be simple or complex as your business needs require.

Getting ready

For this recipe, you will need to create a date table in your SQL Server database called **MasterCalendar_T**. The script that you run will create this table and populate it with data from **1/1/2006** to **12/13/2016**. Once created you are ready to add the **MasterCalendar_T** table to your model and designate it as a date table.

First, create the table in an SQL Server database to store the calendar information:

```
CREATE TABLE [dbo].[MasterCalendar_T](
  [MasterCalendarKey] [int] NULL,
  [Date] [date] NULL,
  [Year] [int] NULL,
  [Quarter_Name] [varchar](2) NULL,
  [Quarter_Num] [int] NULL,
  [Month_Name] [nvarchar](30) NULL,
  [Month_Num] [int] NULL,
  [Day_Name] [nvarchar](30) NULL,
  [Day_Num] [int] NULL
) ON [PRIMARY]
```

Next, populate the table with data from January 1st 2000 to December 31, 2016. This script will load the data into your table:

```
declare @start_date date, @end_date date

set @start_date = '01/01/2000'
set @end_date = '12/31/2016'

WHILE (@start_date<=@end_date)
BEGIN

INSERT INTO MasterCalendar_T2
SELECT
[MasterCalendarKey]=CONVERT(int,CONVERT(VARCHAR(15), @start_date, 112)),
[Date]= @start_date,
[Year] = DATEPART(YEAR,@start_date),
[Quarter_Name] = 'Q'+ cast(DATEPART(QUARTER, @start_date) as char(1)),
[Quarter_Num] = DATEPART(QUARTER, @start_date),
[Month_Name] = DATENAME(MONTH, @start_date),
[Month_Num] = DATEPART(MONTH, @start_date),
[Day_Name]= DATENAME(WEEKDAY, @start_date),
[Day_Num]= DATEPART(day, @start_date)

SET @start_date =DATEADD(dd, 1, @start_date)

END
```

How to do it...

1. Change your model view to the design view. Click on **Model | Import from Data Source** and select **Microsoft SQL Server**. Then click **Next**.
2. Enter your SQL **Server name** and authentication method and select your database name. Click **Next**.

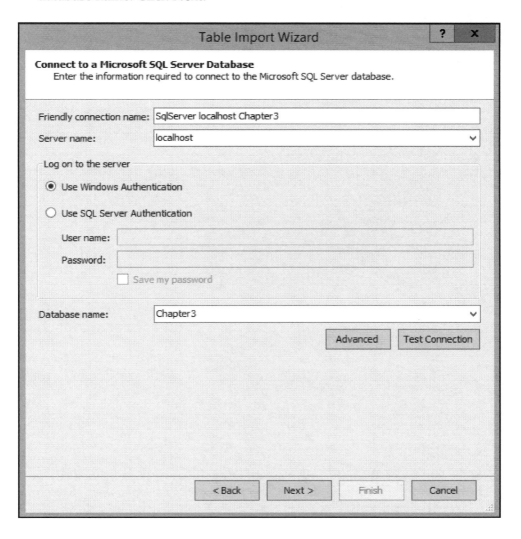

3. Now select the **Impersonation Information** and enter a **User Name** and **Password** that has access to the table you created and then click **Next**.

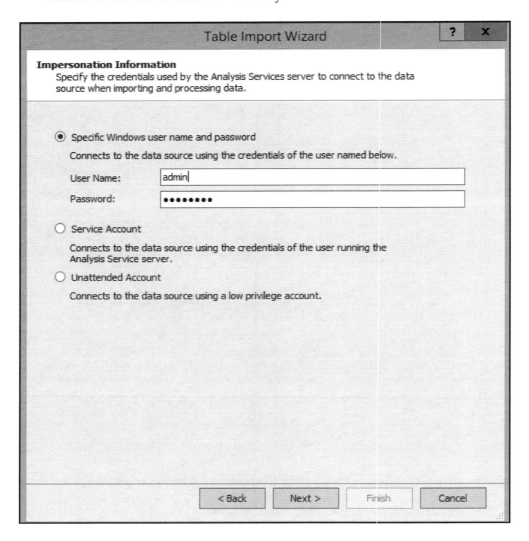

4. Since you know the table and need all of the data, you can leave the default radio button for **Select from a list of tables and views to choose the data to import**. Then click **Next**.

5. Select the **MasterCalendar_T** table and click **Finish**.

6. Once imported you will see 4,018 rows transferred and then click **Close**. You now have two tables imported into your model.

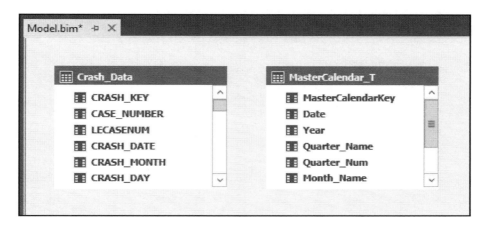

7. To designate the **MasterCalendar_T** table as the date table, left-click on it and then select **Table** from the menu, **Date | Mark as Date Table**.

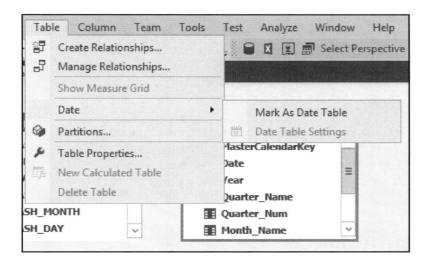

8. On the next screen, select **Date** as the column and then click **OK**.

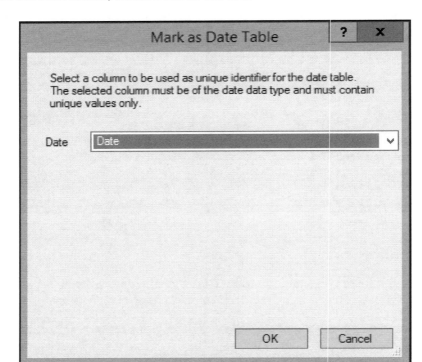

How it works...

In this recipe, you executed a T-SQL script to create a table named **MasterCalendar_T** to store calendar date information. Then you imported the data into your model and designated the table as the date table. The date table allows your DAX calculations to perform date-based functions on your data such as period over period or lag.

Creating hierarchies

Now that you have created and imported a table that contains date information, you need to establish how the data in the **MasterCalendar_T**

table is related. This recipe shows you how to create the standard **Year** | **Quarter** | **Month** | **Day** hierarchy.

How to do it...

1. Left-click on the **MasterCalendar_T** to select the table, then right-click to bring up the menu of options, and select **Create Hierarchy**.

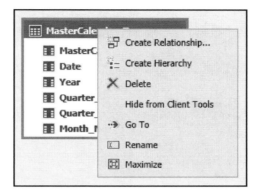

2. On the new virtual column that was added to your table, you will add the columns required to build the hierarchy.

3. Select each column one by one and drag to the **Hierarchy1** name. When completed you will see your completed hierarchy.

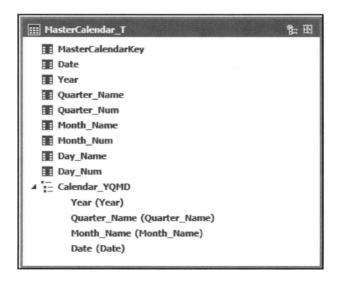

4. Next, right-click on **Hierarchy1** and then select **Rename** and change the name to **Calendar_YQMD**. This identifies the hierarchy as a regular calendar and tells your users what values are available in the hierarchy.

5. Next, you need to define the sort order of the calendar for the hierarchy. Sort order is set on the property of the base columns. On the **Quarter_Name** column change the **Sort By Column** to **Quarter_Num**, and on the **Month_Name** change the **Sort By Column** to **Month_Num**.

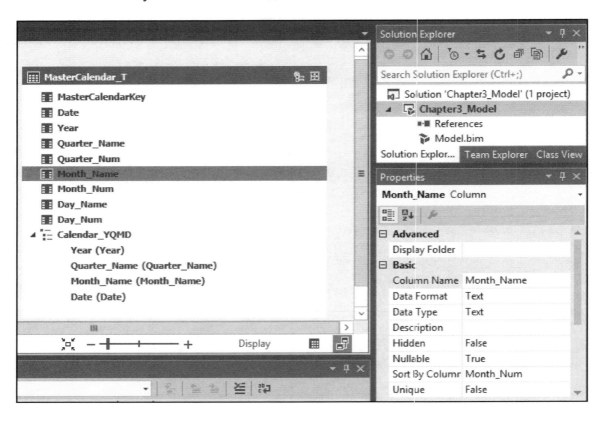

How it works...

This recipe created a new hierarchy in the **MasterCalendar_T** table. For your hierarchy you added the four columns required to create a calendar year hierarchy that has **Year to Quarter** to **Month to Date**. This hierarchy will be exposed in the client tools to allow for easy browsing for your users.

Understanding and building relationships

As you add tables to your model, you will need to build the relationships that tell the tabular model which tables and fields are related to each other. These relationships enable the calculations that you create to perform correctly. In this recipe, you will create a relationship between the **MasterCalendar_T** table and the **Crash_Data** table.

Getting ready

Before starting this recipe make sure you have loaded the Iowa crash data and the **MasterCalendar_T** table into you model. This recipe shows you how to create a relationship between the two tables.

How to do it...

1. Left-click the **Crash_Date_fx** column from the **CRASH_DATE** table and then drag it to the **Date** column in the **MasterCalendar_T** table.

2. Since **MasterCalendar_T** is designated as a **Date** table, the model made the relationship be one-to-many from the **MasterCalendar_T** to the **Crash_Data** table.

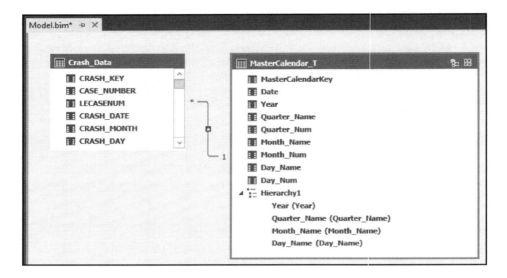

3. Double-click on the relationship arrow that was added to bring up the **Edit Relationship** window. This window allows you to modify any relationship and see the details of what was created. It is showing the relationship that you want, so you can close it by clicking **Cancel**.

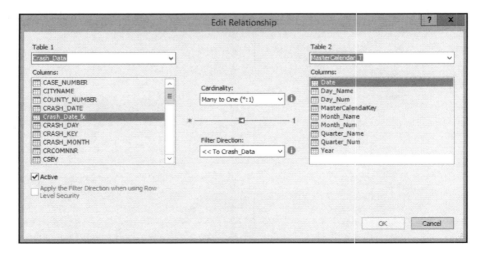

How it works...

This recipe created a link between the **Crash_Data** table and the **MasterCalendar_T** table. The **MasterCalendar_T** table contains only one row for each date and the **Crash_Data** table can contain one too many rows for each date. For example, if there are multiple crashes reported on the same date.

Creating and organizing display folders

As the number of measures increases in your model, you will want to organize them into logical groupings that make it easier to use in the reporting tools. This recipe shows you how to create a group for the data that relates to the injury columns.

Getting ready

Switch back to the diagram view to see the table layout and columns.

How to do it...

1. You are going to create a folder to hold all injury related fields to make it easier for the users to find this information. Select the **Crash_Data** table and then scroll down and left-click the **INJURIES** column.
2. On the properties window type **Injuries_Folder** into the **Display Folder** field.

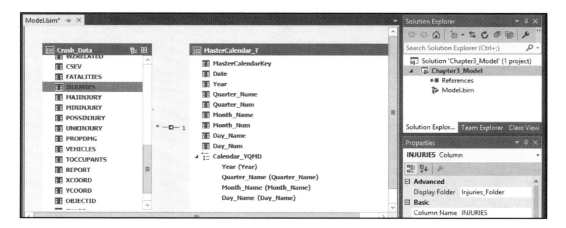

3. Now you are going to add four additional columns to the same folder. Hold down shift and then select **MAJINJURY**, **MININJURY**, **POSSINJURY**, and **UNKINJURY**. In the **Display Folder** property, type **Injuries_Folder**.

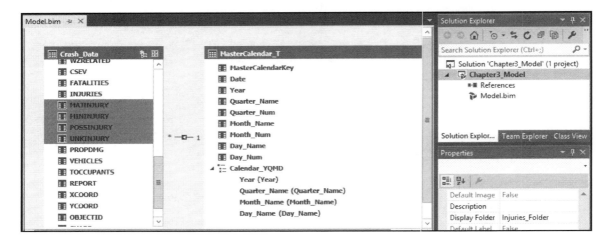

How it works...

A display folder is created in this recipe to store the injury related fields. First you selected an individual column and then typed in the name of the folder. Then you added four fields by selecting them together and typing in the same folder name. Once this model is deployed, your users will be able to see these columns grouped into a folder in the **Crash_Data** dimension.

Deploying your first model

Deployment of your model is the final step to getting the data accessible to your users for reporting. You have designed and built your model in Visual Studio. In order for others to see and use it, you need to push the design and data to the Analysis Services server.

Getting ready

If you have completed all of the steps then you are ready to deploy your model to the server. From here your users will access the data you provide.

How to do it...

1. Select **Build** from the menu and then select **Build Solution**.

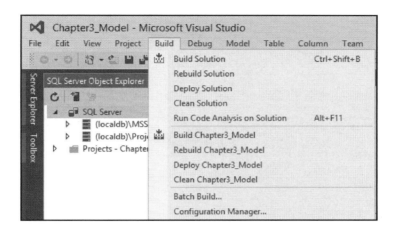

2. If everything is okay, you will get a message that shows the build succeeded.

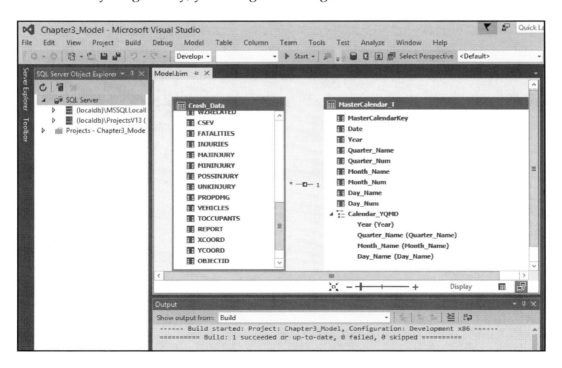

3. Next click **Build** again and then **Deploy** solution. Enter your username and password and click **OK**.

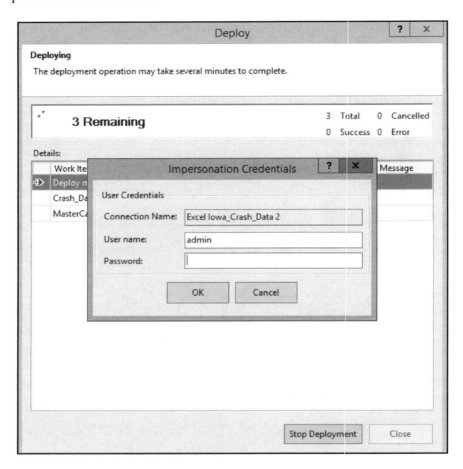

4. All of the data will now be imported. Once completed successfully, you will have data on your server, and you can then click **Close**.

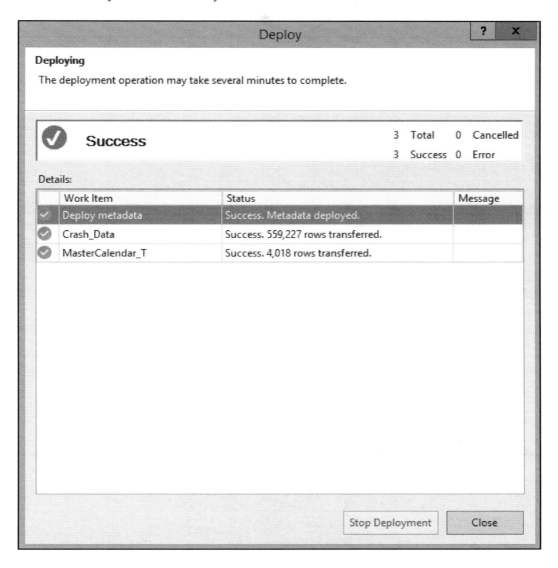

How it works...

The deployment process moves the model from your local project to the Analysis Services server for users to interact with the information. First you built your model to ensure there were no known errors or issues with the formulas or data types. Then you deployed the model to the server using a user that has permissions to deploy to the server. Upon completion your first model is now ready to be viewed.

Browsing your model with SQL Server Management Studio

As a developer, you will want to explore the model prior to releasing it for use. SQL Server Management Studio provides you with a way to browse the model and ensure everything is performing as expected. This recipe shows you how to connect to the model and explore dimensions and measures.

How to do it...

1. Open SQL Server Management Studio and select **Analysis Services...** from the connect drop-down box.

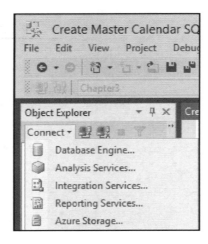

2. Type in your Analysis Services server name and click **Connect**.

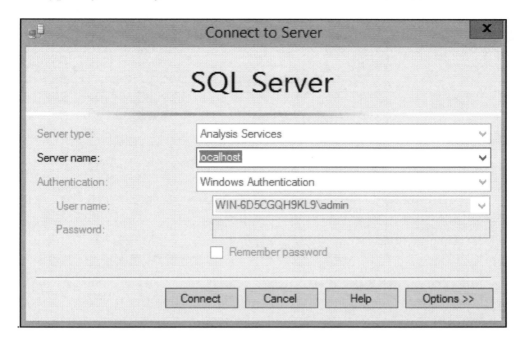

3. Expand the Analysis Services server to show the **Databases** and **Tables** under **Chapter3_Model** to validate that the tables were published to the server.

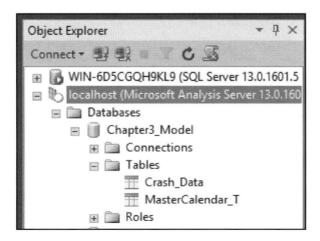

4. Right-click on the **Chapter3_Model** database and then select **Browse...** to open the model browser.

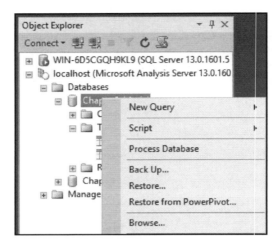

5. From the **Model[Browse]** window expand the **Crash_Data** dimension to find **Injuries_Folder** and then click the + sign to view the five columns you added.

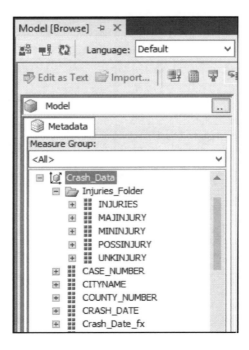

6. Click on the – sign on **Crash_Data** to close the dimension. Then click on the + sign on **MasterCalendar_T** to review the hierarchy you created.

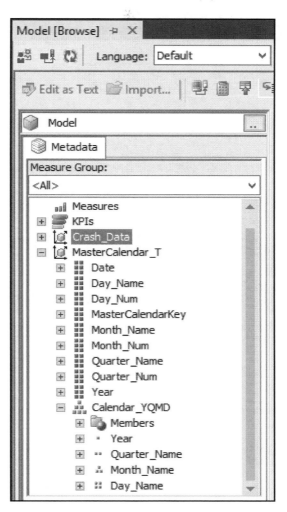

7. Expand **Measures** | **Crash_Data** and drag **Count_of_Crashes** to the area on the right. The total count of records is shown.

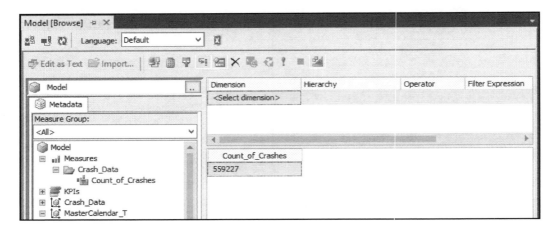

8. To see the total **Count_of_Crashes** by **Year**, expand the **Calendar_YQMD** hierarchy and drag **Year** to the design area on the left side of **Count_of_Crashes**.

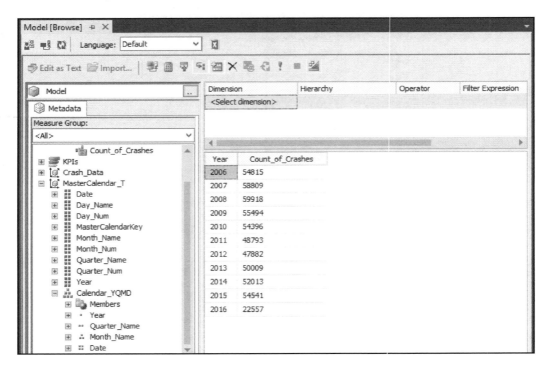

9. To see the number of crashes by **COUNTY_NUMBER**, expand the **Crash_Data** dimension and then drag the **COUNTY_NUMBER** between **Year** and **Count_of_Crashes**.

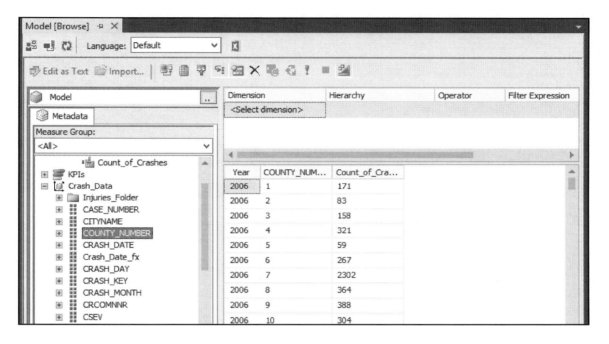

10. To see only the crashes that occur in **COUNTY_NUMBER 7**, drag
COUNTY_NUMBER to the **Dimension** area and set the **Operator** to = 7.

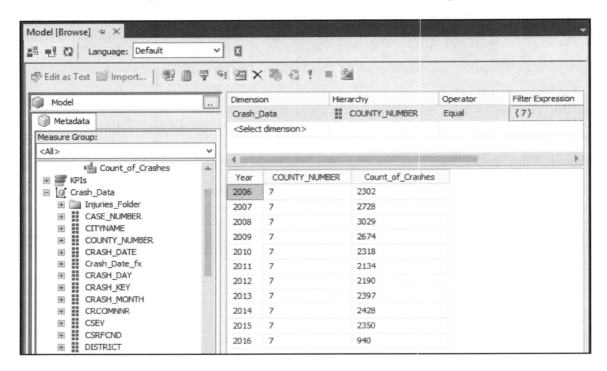

How it works...

In this recipe, you connected to Analysis Services tabular mode to explore the data. Using
SQL Server Management Studio you browsed the measures, dimensions, and hierarchies
that were created in this chapter. By adding the measure on the viewer and then adding
dimensions you can view how the DAX calculation is summarizing the data at each level of
the hierarchy.

Browsing your model with Microsoft Excel

Most users will want to use Microsoft Excel to interact with the data and perform analysis.
By using Excel you can create many types of interactions with the data in the model. This
recipe shows you how to connect to the model and build a Power View report.

How to do it...

1. Open Microsoft Excel and create a new workbook.
2. Click on the **Data** ribbon and then select **Get External Data | From Other Sources | From Analysis Services**.

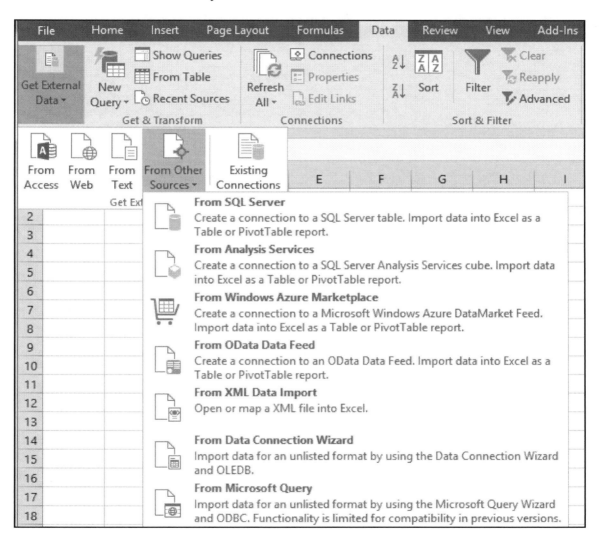

3. Enter your Analysis Services **Server** name and **Log on credentials** on the next window.

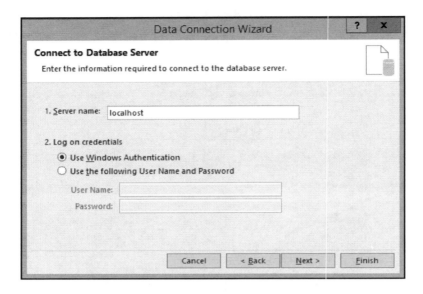

4. Select **Chapter3_Model** from the drop-down list and click **Next**.

5. On the next screen click **Finish**.

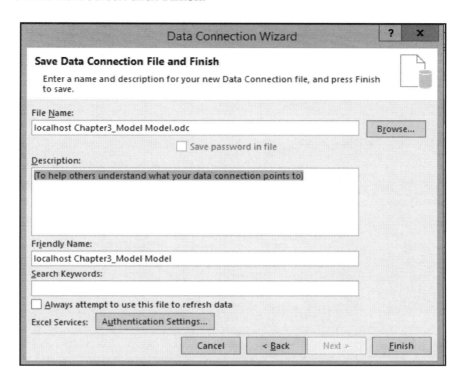

6. Now you can **Select how you want to view the data in Excel**. If you have installed **Power View Report**, select it and select **OK**.

7. After connecting to the data you will have a new **Power View** sheet in Excel.

8. Select **Year** from the **MasterCalendar_TCalendar_YQMD** hierarchy and drag it to the design surface. Then drag the **CRASH_KEY** from the **Crash_Data** table and change the aggregation to **Count** in the **FIELDS** area.

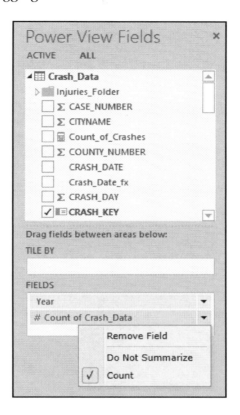

How it works...

You connected to the Analysis Service tabular model using the **data** tab in Microsoft Excel. You then connected to the model that was deployed. By choosing the **Power View** option, Excel opened a new worksheet in **Power View** mode. By dragging and dropping the fields from the **Power View** fields window you were able to interact with the data you published earlier.

4
Working in Tabular Models

In this chapter, we will cover the following recipes:

- Opening an existing model
- Importing data
- Modifying model relationships
- Modifying model measures
- Modifying model columns
- Modifying model hierarchies
- Creating a calculated table
- Creating key performance indicators (KPIs)
- Modifying key performance indicators (KPIs)
- Deploying a modified model

Introduction

This chapter will focus on how to modify and enhance the model built in the previous chapter. After building a model, we will need to maintain and enhance the model as the business users update or change their requirements. We will begin by adding additional tables to the model that contain the descriptive data columns for several code columns. Then we will create relationships between these new tables and the existing data tables.

Once the new data is loaded into the model, we will modify various pieces of the model, including adding a new key performance indicator.

Next, we will perform calculations to see how to create and modify measures and columns.

Opening an existing model

For this recipe, we will open the model created and deployed in Chapter 3. To make modifications to your deployed models, we will need to open the model in the Visual Studio designer.

How to do it...

1. Open your solution from Chapter 3 in Visual Studio, by navigating to **File** | **Open** | **Project/Solution**.

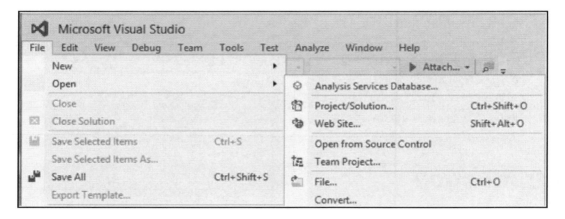

2. Then select the folder and solution, Chapter3_Model, and select **Open**.
3. Your solution is now open and ready for modification.

How it works...

Visual Studio stores the model as a project inside of a solution. In Chapter 3, *Tabular Model Building*, we created a new project and saved it as Chapter3_Model. To make modifications to the model, we open it in Visual Studio. This brings up the design windows necessary to perform the upcoming recipes.

Importing data

The crash data has many columns that store the data in codes. In order to make this data useful for reporting, we need to add description columns. In this section, we will create four code tables by importing data into a SQL Server database. Then, we will add the tables to your existing model.

Getting ready

In the Chapter 3 database on your SQL Server, run the following scripts to create the four tables and populate them with the reference data:

1. Create the Major Cause of **Accident Reference Data** table:

```
CREATE TABLE [dbo].[MAJCSE_T](
   [MAJCSE] [int] NULL,
   [MAJOR_CAUSE] [varchar](50) NULL
) ON [PRIMARY]
```

2. Then, populate the table with data:

```
INSERT INTO MAJCSE_T
VALUES
(20, 'Overall/rollover'),
(21, 'Jackknife'),
(31, 'Animal'),
(32, 'Non-motorist'),
(33, 'Vehicle in Traffic'),
(35, 'Parked motor vehicle'),
(37, 'Railway vehicle'),
(40, 'Collision with bridge'),
(41, 'Collision with bridge pier'),
(43, 'Collision with curb'),
(44, 'Collision with ditch'),
(47, 'Collision culvert'),
```

```
(48, 'Collision Guardrail - face'),
(50, 'Collision traffic barrier'),
(53, 'impact with Attenuator'),
(54, 'Collision with utility pole'),
(55, 'Collision with traffic sign'),
(59, 'Collision with mailbox'),
(60, 'Collision with Tree'),
(70, 'Fire'),
(71, 'Immersion'),
(72, 'Hit and Run'),
(99, 'Unknown')
```

3. Create the table to store the lighting conditions at the time of the crash:

```
CREATE TABLE [dbo].[LIGHT_T](
   [LIGHT] [int] NULL,
   [LIGHT_CONDITION] [varchar](30) NULL
) ON [PRIMARY]
```

4. Now, populate the data that shows the descriptions for the codes:

```
INSERT INTO LIGHT_T
VALUES
(1, 'Daylight'),
(2, 'Dusk'),
(3, 'Dawn'),
(4, 'Dark, roadway lighted'),
(5, 'Dark, roadway not lighted'),
(6, 'Dark, unknown lighting'),
(9, 'Unknown')
```

5. Create the table to store the road conditions:

```
CREATE TABLE [dbo].[CSRFCND_T](
   [CSRFCND] [int] NULL,
   [SURFACE_CONDITION] [varchar](50) NULL
) ON [PRIMARY]
```

6. Now populate the road condition descriptions:

```
INSERT INTO CSRFCND_T
VALUES
(1, 'Dry'),
(2, 'Wet'),
(3, 'Ice'),
(4, 'Snow'),
(5, 'Slush'),
(6, 'Sand, Mud'),
(7, 'Water'),
(99, 'Unknown')
```

7. Finally, create the weather table:

```
CREATE TABLE [dbo].[WEATHER_T](
  [WEATHER] [int] NULL,
  [WEATHER_CONDITION] [varchar](30) NULL
) ON [PRIMARY]
```

8. Then populate the weather condition descriptions.

```
INSERT INTO WEATHER_T
VALUES
(1, 'Clear'),
(2, 'Partly Cloudy'),
(3, 'Cloudy'),
(5, 'Mist'),
(6, 'Rain'),
(7, 'Sleet, hail, freezing rain'),
(9, 'Severe winds'),
(10, 'Blowing Sand'),
(99, 'Unknown')
```

You now have the tables and data required to complete the recipes in this chapter.

How to do it...

1. From your open model, change to the Diagram view in **Model.bim** folder.
2. Navigate to **Model | Import from Data Source**, and then select Microsoft SQL Server on the **Table Import Wizard**, and click on **Next**.
3. Set your **Server Name** to Localhost and change the **Database name** to **Chapter3** and click on **Next**.
4. Enter your admin account username and password and click on **Next**.

5. You want to select from a list of tables the four tables that were created at the beginning of this recipe.

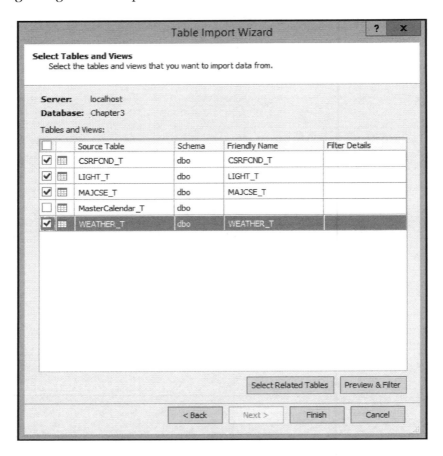

6. Click on **Finish** to import the data.

How it works...

This recipe opens the **Table Import Wizard** and allows us to select the four new tables that are to be added to the existing model. The data is then imported into your tabular model workspace. Once imported, the data is now ready to be used to enhance the model.

Modifying model relationships

In this recipe, we will create the necessary relationships for the new tables. These relationships will be used in the model in order for the SSAS engine to perform correct calculations.

How to do it...

1. Open your model in the Diagram view and you will see the four tables that you imported from the previous recipe.

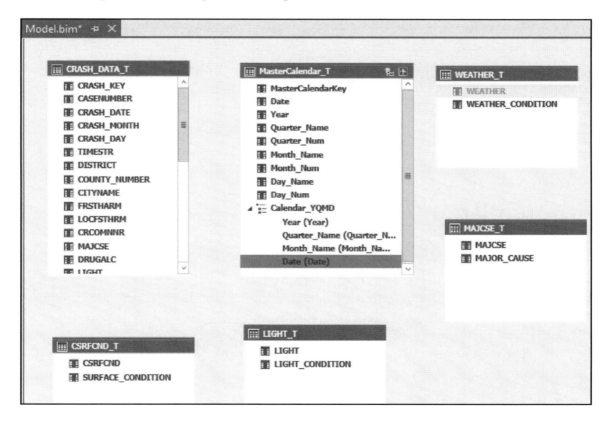

2. Select the **CSRFCND** field in the **CSRFCND_T** table and drag the CSRFCND table in the **Crash_Data** table.

3. Select the **LIGHT** field in the **LIGHT_T** table and drag to the **LIGHT** table in the **Crash_Data** table.

4. Select the **MAJCSE** field in the **MAJCSE_T** table and drag to the **MAJCSE** table in the **Crash_Data** table.

5. Select the **WEATHER** field in the **WEATHER_T** table and drag to the **WEATHER** table in the **Crash_Data** table.

How it works...

Each table in this section has a relationship built between the code columns and the **Crash_Data** table corresponding columns. These relationships allow for DAX calculations to be applied across the data tables.

Modifying model measures

Now that there are more tables in the model, we are going to add an additional measure to perform quick calculations on data. The measure will use a simple DAX calculation since this recipe is focused on how to add or modify the model measures. The future chapters will focus on more advanced DAX calculations.

How to do it...

1. Open the **Chapter 3_Model** project in the **Model.bim** folder and make sure you are in Grid view.

2. Select the cell under **Count_of_Crashes** and in the **fx** bar add the following DAX formula to create **Sum_of_Fatalities**:

```
Sum_of_Fatalities:=SUM(Crash_Data[FATALITIES])
```

3. Then, hit *Enter* to create the calculation:

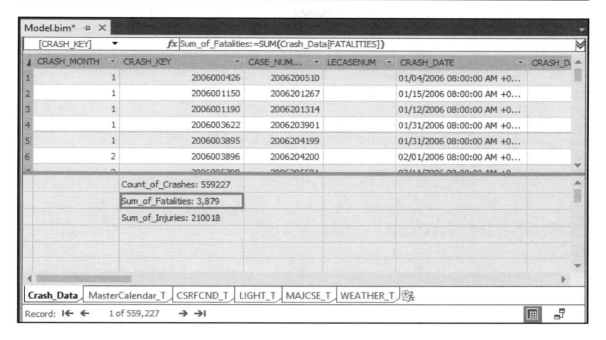

4. In the **Properties** window, enter **Injury_Calculations** in the **Display Folder**. Then, change the **Format** to **Whole Number** and change the **Show Thousand Separator** to **True**. Finally, add it to **Description Total Number of Fatalities Recorded**:

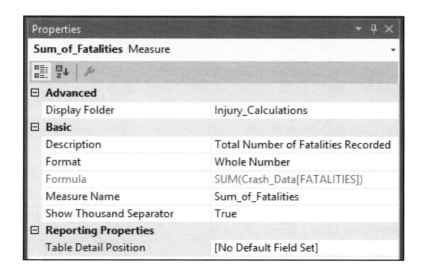

How it works...

In this recipe, we added a new measure to the existing model that calculates the total number of fatalities on the **Crash_Data** table. Then we added a new folder for the users to see the calculation. We also modified the default behavior of the calculation to display as a whole number and show commas to make the numbers easier to interpret. Finally, we added a description to the calculation that users will be able to see in the reporting tools. If we did not make these changes in the model, each user will be required to make the changes each time they accessed the model. By placing the changes in the model, everyone will see the data in the same format.

Modifying model columns

In this recipe, we will modify the properties of the columns on the **WEATHER** table. Modifications to the columns in a table make the information easier for your users to understand in the reporting tools. Some properties determine how the SSAS engine uses the fields when creating the model on the server.

How to do it...

1. In **Model.bim**, make sure you are in the Grid view and change to the **WEATHER_T** tab.
2. Select **WEATHER Column** to view the available **Properties** and make the following changes:

   - Select the **Hidden** property to **True**
   - Select the **Unique** property to **True**

- In the **Sort By Column** select **WEATHER_CONDITION**
- Select **Summarize By** to **Count**

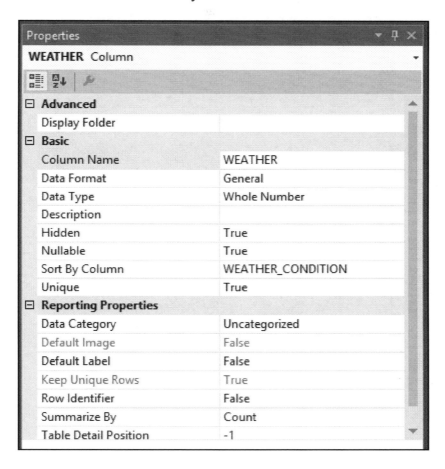

3. Next, select the **WEATHER_CONDITION** column and modify the following properties:
   - In the **Description** add **Weather at time of crash**
   - Set the **Default Label** property to **True**

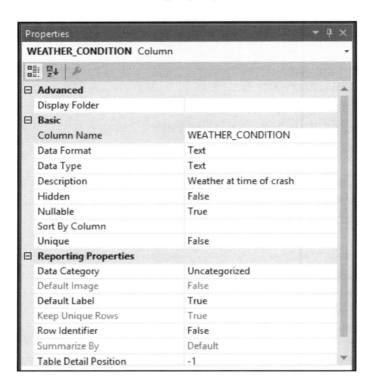

How it works...

This recipe modified the properties of the measure to make it better for your report users to access the data. The **WEATHER** code column was hidden so it will not be visible in the reporting tools and the **WEATHER_CONDITION** was sorted in alphabetical order. You set the default aggregation to **Count** and then added a description for the column. Now, when this dimension is added to a report only the **WEATHER_CONDITION** column will be seen and pre-sorted based on the **WEATHER_CONDITION** field. It will also use count as the aggregation type to provide the number of each type of weather condition. If you were to add another new description to the table, it would automatically be sorted correctly.

Modifying model hierarchies

Once you have created a hierarchy, you may want to remove or modify the hierarchy from your model. In this recipe, we will make modifications to the Calendar_YQMD hierarchy.

How to do it...

1. Open **Model.bim** in the Diagram view and find the **Master_Calendar_T** table.
2. Review the **Calendar_YQMD** hierarchy and included columns.
3. Select the **Quarter_Name** column and right-click on it to bring up the menu.

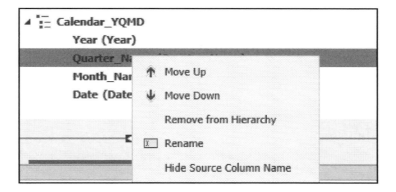

4. Select **Remove from Hierarchy** to delete **Quarter_Name** from the hierarchy and confirm on the next screen by selecting Remove from Hierarchy.

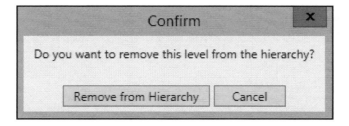

5. Select the **Calendar_YQMD** hierarchy and right-click on it and select **Rename**.

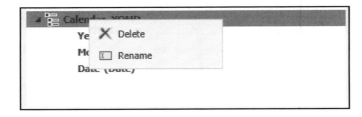

6. Change the name to **Calendar_YMD** and hit on *Enter*.

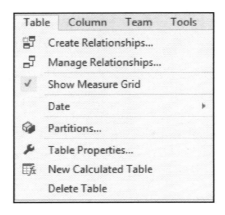

How it works...

In this recipe, we opened the Diagram view and selected the **Master_Calendar_T** table to find the existing hierarchy. After selecting the **Quarter_Name** column in the hierarchy, we used the menus to view the available options for modifications. Then we selected the option to remove the column from the hierarchy. Finally, we updated the name of the hierarchy to let users know that the quarter column is not included.

There's more...

Another option to remove fields from the hierarchy is to select the column and then press the delete key. Likewise, you can double-click on the **Calendar_YQMD** hierarchy to bring up the edit window for the name. Then edit the name and hit **Enter** to save the change in the designer.

Creating a calculated table

Calculated tables are created dynamically using functions or DAX queries. They are very useful if you need to create a new table based on information in another table. For example, you could have a date table with 30 years of data. However, most of your users only look at the last 5 years of information when running most of their analysis. Instead of creating a new table you can dynamically make a new table that only stores the last 5 years of dates. In this recipe, you will use a single DAX query to filter the **Master_Calendar_T** table to the last 5 years of data.

How to do it...

1. Open **Model.bim** in the Grid view and then select the **Table** menu and **New Calculated Table**.

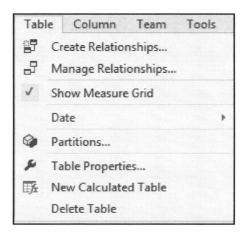

2. A new data tab is created. In the function box, enter this DAX formula to create a date calendar for the last 5 years:

```
FILTER(MasterCalendar_T,
MasterCalendar_T[Date]>=DATEADD(MasterCalendar_T[Date],6,YEAR))
```

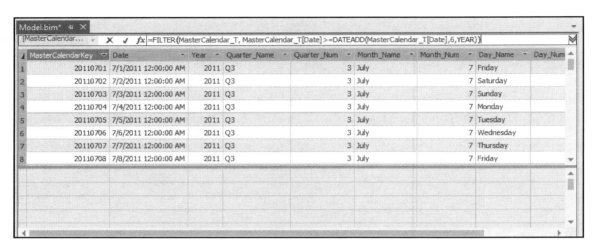

3. Double-click on the **CalculatedTable 1** tab and rename it to Last_5_Years_T.

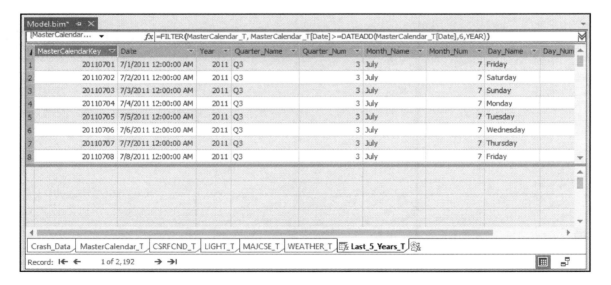

How it works...

This recipe works by creating a new table in the model that is built from a DAX formula. In order to limit the number of years shown, the DAX formula reduces the total number of dates available for the last 5 years of data.

There's more...

After you create a calculated table, you will need to create the necessary relationships and hierarchies just like a regular table:

1. Switch to the Diagram view in the **Model.bim** and you will be able to see the new table.

2. Create a new hierarchy and name it Last_5_Years_YQM and include **Year**, **Quarter_Name**, **Month_Name**, and **Date**

3. Replace the **Master_Calendar_T** relationship with the **Date** column from the **Last_5_Years_T** date column to the **Crash_Date.Crash_Date** column.

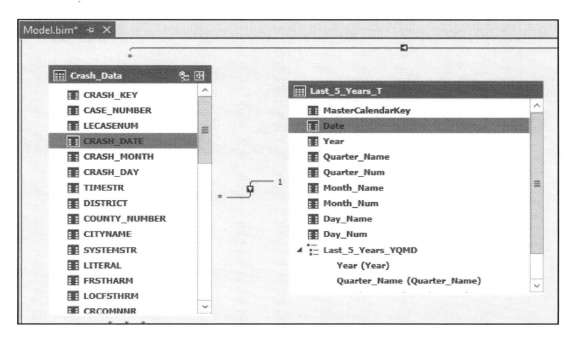

Now, the model will only display the last 5 years of crash data when using the **Last_5_Years_T** table in the reporting tools. The **Crash_Data** table still contains all of the records if you need to view more than 5 years of data.

Creating key performance indicators (KPIs)

Key performance indicators are business metrics that show the effectiveness of a business objective. They are used to track actual performance against budgeted or planned value such as Service Level Agreements or On-Time performance. The advantage of creating a KPI is the ability to quickly see the actual value compared to the target value. To add a KPI, you will need to have a measure to use as the actual value and another measure that returns the target value. In this recipe, we will create a KPI that tracks the number of fatalities and compares them to the prior year with the goal of having fewer fatalities each year.

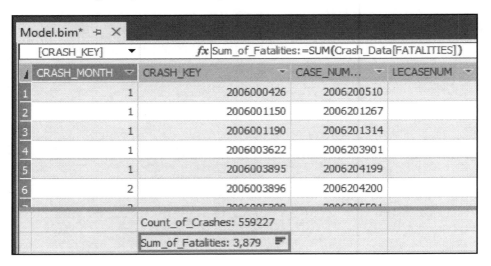

How to do it...

1. Open the **Model.bim** in the Grid view and select an empty cell and create a new measure named
   Last_Year_Fatalities: Last_Year_Fatalities:=CALCULATE(SUM(Crash_Data [FATALITIES]),DATEADD(MasterCalendar_T[Date],-1, YEAR))

2. Select the already existing **Sum_of_measure**, then right-click, and select **Create KPI...**.

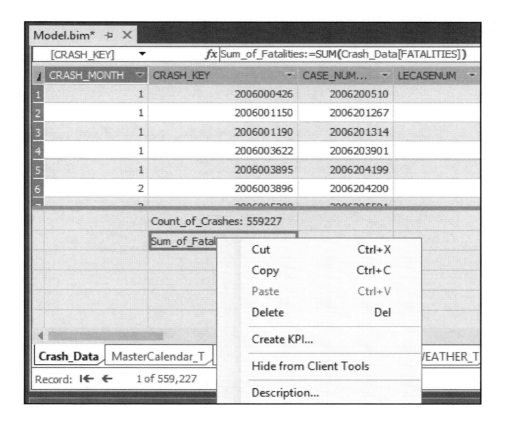

3. On the **Key Performance Indicator (KPI)** window, select **Last_Year_Fatalities** as the **Target Measure**. Then, select the second set of icons that have red, yellow, and green with symbols. Finally, change the KPI color scheme to green, yellow, and red and make the scores 90 and 97, and then click on **OK**.

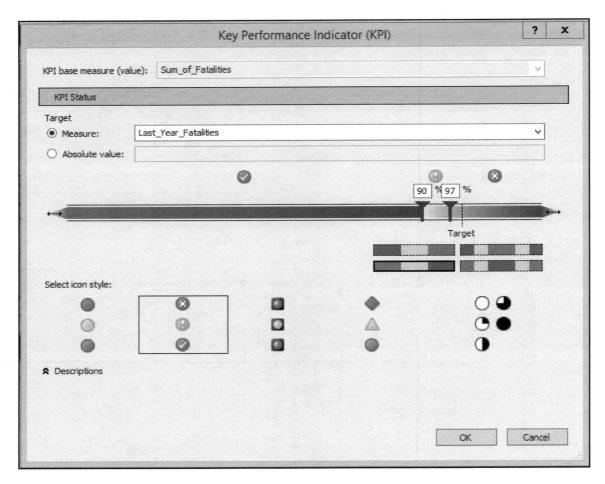

4. The **Sum_of_Fatalites** measure will now have a small graph next to it in the measure grid to show that there is a KPI on that measure.

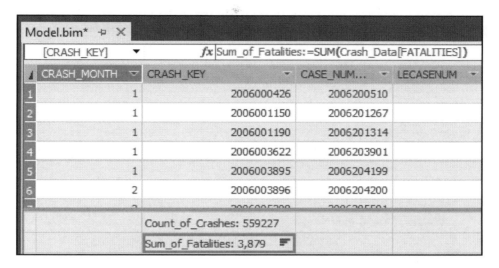

How it works...

You created a new calculation that compared the actual count of fatalities compared to the same number for the prior year. Then you created a new KPI that used the actual and **Last_Year_Fatalities** measure. In the KPI window, you set up thresholds to determine when a KPI is red, yellow, or green. For this example, you want to show that having less fatalities year over year is better. Therefore, when the KPI is 97% or higher, the KPI will show red. For values that are in the range of 90% to 97%, the KPI is yellow and anything below 90% is green. By selecting the icons with both color and symbols, users that are color-blind can still determine the appropriate symbol of the KPI.

Modifying key performance indicators (KPIs)

Once you have created a KPI, you may want to remove or modify the KPI from your model. In this recipe, you will make modifications to the Last_Year_Fatalities hierarchy.

How to do it...

1. Open **Model.bim** in the Grid view, select the **Sum_of_Fatalities** measure, then right-click to bring up **Edit KPI settings...**.

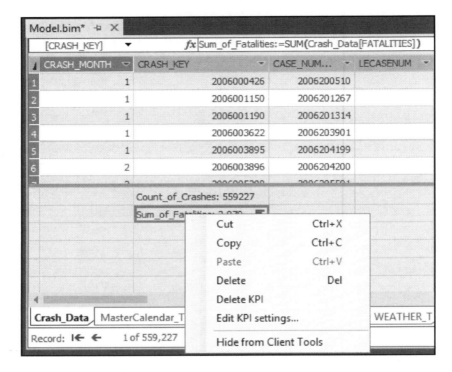

2. Edit the appropriate settings to modify an existing KPI.

How it works...

Just like models, KPIs will need to be modified after being initially designed. The icon next to a measure denotes that a KPI is defined on the measure. Right-clicking on the measure brings up the menu that allows you to enter the **Edit KPI** setting.

Deploying a modified model

Once you have completed the changes to your model, you have two options for deployment. First, you can deploy the model and replace the existing model. Alternatively, you can change the name of your model and deploy it as a new model. This is often useful when you need to test changes and maintain the existing model as is.

How to do it...

1. Open the **Chapter3_Model** project in Visual Studio.
2. Select the **Project** menu and select **Chapter3_Model Properties...** to bring up the **Properties** menu and review the **Server** and **Database** properties. To overwrite an existing model make no changes and click on **OK**.

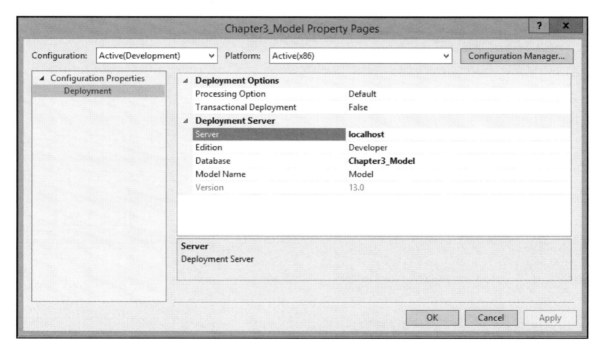

3. Select the **Build** menu from the **Chapter3_Model** project and select the **Deploy Chapter3_Model** option.

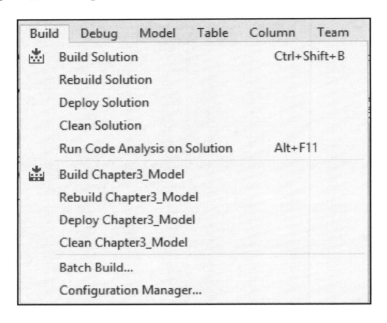

4. In the following screen, enter the impersonation credentials for your data and hit **OK** to deploy the changes that were made using the recipes in this chapter.

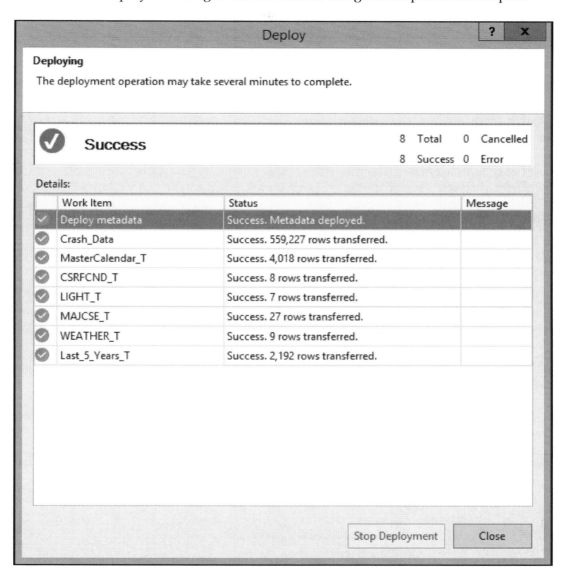

How it works...

This recipe takes the model that is on your local machine and submits the changes to the server. By not making any changes to the existing model properties, a new deployment will overwrite the old model. By completing all of the recipes in this chapter, all of your changes are now published on the server and users can begin to leverage the changes.

There's more...

Sometimes you might want to deploy your model to a different database without overwriting the existing environment. This could be to try out a new model or test different functionality with users that you might want to implement. You can modify the properties of the project to deploy to a different server such as development, UAT, or production. Likewise, you can also change the database name to deploy the model to the same server or different servers for testing.

1. Open the **Project** menu and then select **Chapter3_Model Properties**.
2. Change the name of the **Database** to **Chapter4_Model** and click on **OK**.

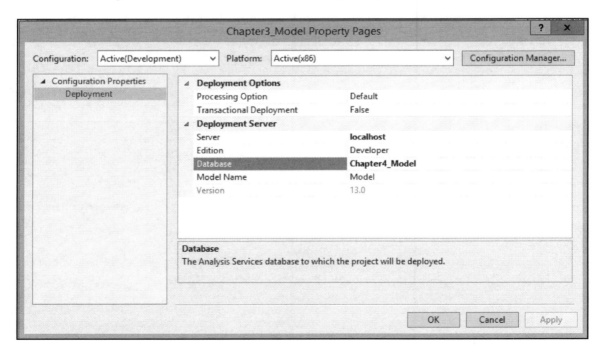

3. Next, on the **Build** menu, select **Deploy Chapter3_Model** to deploy the model to the same server under the new name of **Chapter4_Model**.

4. When you review the Analysis Services databases in SQL Server Management Studio, you will now see a database for **Chapter3_Model** and **Chapter4_Model**.

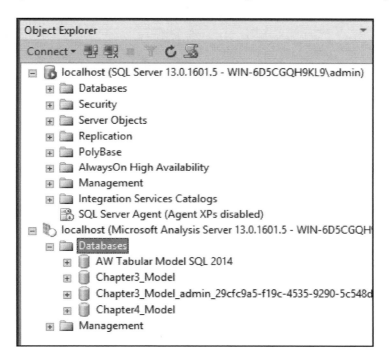

5
Administration of Tabular Models

In this chapter, we will cover the following recipes:

- Managing tabular model properties
- Managing perspectives
- Managing partitions
- Managing roles
- Managing server properties
- Managing Analysis Services memory

Introduction

In the previous chapters, we focused on the recipes that would create a new model focused on the data and how it is organized and displayed. This chapter focuses on recipes that will modify the model properties, how data is stored in partitions, role-based security and server properties. You will learn about the tabular model properties and the most common properties to modify. In addition, there are many ways to change how the model is seen and used by the users. These techniques include adding perspectives, partitions, roles, and server properties.

Managing tabular model properties

Tabular model properties are set inside the project in Visual Studio. These properties affect how the model is built, deployed in the workspace, and the backup method being used. When creating a new model project, there are several properties that are set to default values that include workspace server, workspace retention, and data backup. All model properties are accessed through the Solution Explorer window and by selecting the **Model.bim** file. You will then see the various properties that you can modify to change the default behavior of the model. The following recipes show how to make modifications to the most common properties.

Changing data backup locations

You can change the model to perform a backup to disk and set the location of the backup. This can be helpful if you want to store the backup in a shared folder and let others restore it to their machine. You can also use it to back up the model to a different disk drive if you have more than one in your development machine.

1. Open the **Chapter3_Model** solution and select the **Model.bim** file in the solution explorer to bring up the properties window.

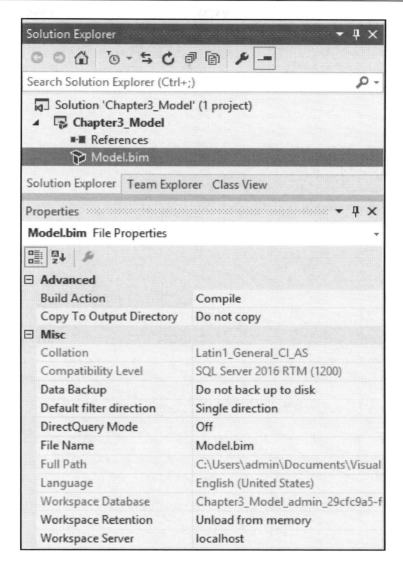

2. Select the **Data Backup** property. It is currently set to **Do not back up to disk**. Change the property to **Back up to disk**.

3. Make a change to the model to force a backup and then click on **Save All** to bring up the **Save File As** window.

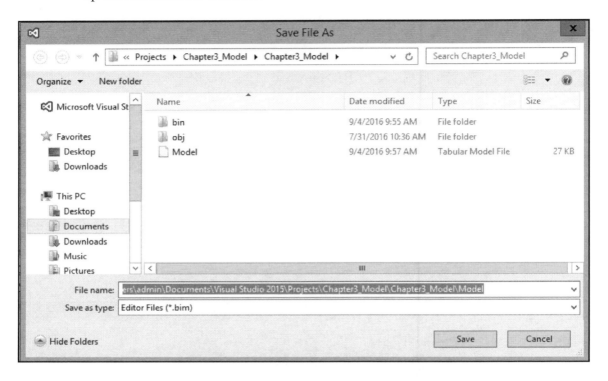

4. Click on **Save** and then click on **Yes** and then on **Confirm Save As**.
5. Save the **Model.bim** file to create an Analysis Services backup file (.abf). While this option is being used, it will take longer to save and load the model.

Changing DirectQuery mode

The default setting for your project is to have DirectQuery Mode turned off. While this setting is off, queries against the data will be directed at the in-memory VertiPaq cache. Data is loaded into the VertiPaq cache when you process the model. One limitation to be mindful of is the amount of data you are loading and how much memory your server has available. The additional details on the benefits and limitations of DirectQuery will be provided in the later recipes.

1. Open the **Chapter3_Model** solution and select the **Model.bim** file in the solution explorer to bring up the properties windows.

2. Select the dropdown for **DirectQuery Mode** and change to **On**.

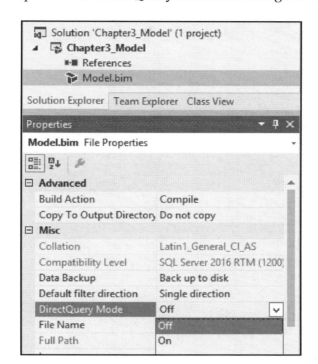

Changing workspace retention

There are three settings available for handling the data when working building a Tabular Model. By default, the model is set to *Unload from memory*. This setting removes the data from memory once the project is closed. One drawback is that opening of large projects will take more time while the project is loaded. Using the **Keep in memory** setting will maintain the database in memory on the server. This reduces the amount of time to open the model in Visual Studio. The final option is to **Delete workspace**. This option deletes the workspace database from memory and does not keep a copy on disk. Using this option consumes the least amount of memory and storage; however, it requires the most time to load the model when it requires changes.

1. Open the **Chapter3_Model** solution and select the **Model.bim** file in the solution explorer to bring up the **Properties** window.

2. Select the dropdown for **Workspace Retention** to choose the new settings.

Changing workspace server

If required, you can change the server used when building models. This is required if you have a new development server that you need to leverage and are opening old models that use a now out of date server.

1. Open the **Chapter3_Model** solution and select the **Model.bim** file in the solution explorer to bring up the properties window.

2. Select **Workspace Server** and type in the appropriate server name.

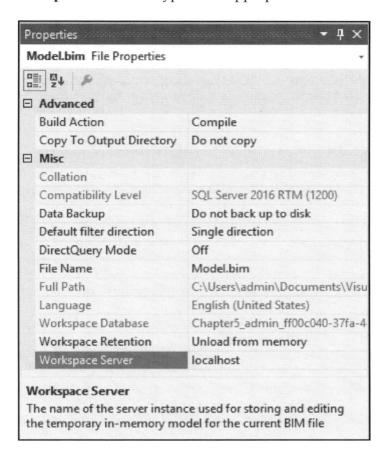

Managing perspectives

As your models grow in size and complexity, it is easy for users to be overwhelmed by the amount of data, dimensions, and measures. Perspectives enable you to create views of the model that are limited in size based on your requirements. Using our example, you could create a perspective that limits the data to being greater than 2010 and weather accidents that occurred under rain and severe winds.

Getting ready

Download the code for the **Crash_Data** database from the Packt website and load into a SQL Server database named **Crash_Data_DB**.

How to do it...

In this recipe, you will create a new perspective to limit the dimensions and measures that are exposed. Users who have access to this partition, will only see the selected data.

Adding a new perspective

1. Open the **Crash_Data_Solution** in Visual Studio.
2. On the **Model** menu, select **Perspectives**, and then select**Create and Manage**.

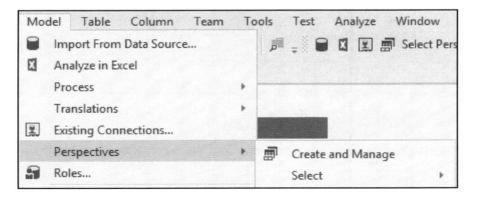

3. On the **Perspectives** windows, click on **New Perspective** to bring up the menu.

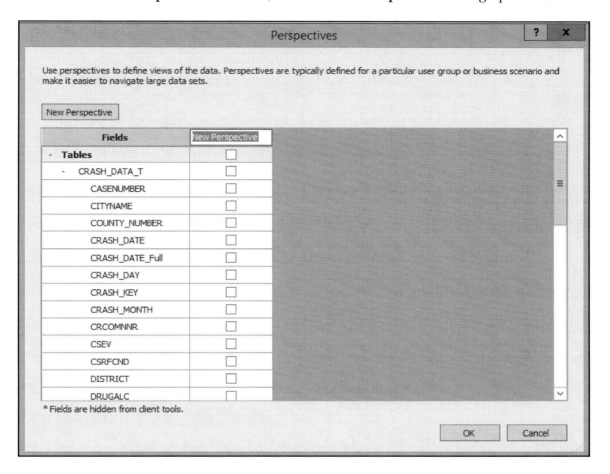

4. Type **Weather** in the **New Perspective** Name. Expand the **Crash_Data_T** table and select **CASENUMBER** and **Count_of_crashes**. Then select the YQMD hierarchy from the**MasterCalendar_T** table, and **WEATHER_CONDITION** and then click on **OK**.

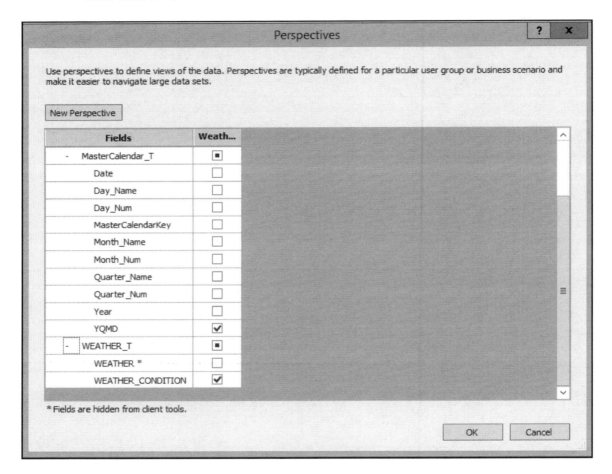

5. To test the change, deploy the model. Then change the **Select Perspective** dropdown to **Weather**.

6. Notice the only tables and fields that are now visible are the ones selected in step 4.

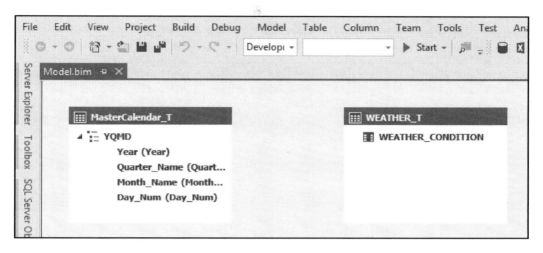

7. To select the perspective in Excel, open a new document and then select the **Data** tab and **Get External Data | SQL Server Analysis Services**. In **Data Connection Wizard**, select the **Crash_Data_SSASTM** model and you will see two cubes.

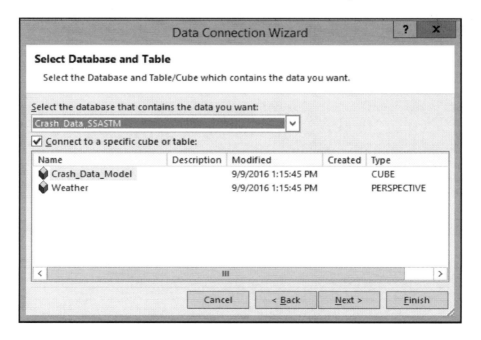

8. Select the **Weather** cube and click on **Finish** and import into a pivot table. You will now only be able to see the items selected in Step 4 as the only selectable items in the Excel pivot table.

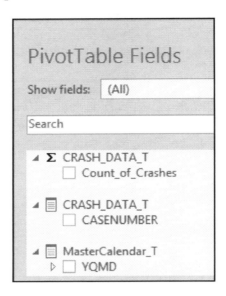

Editing a perspective

Editing a perspective enables you to modify the tables and fields that are included in the perspective.

1. Open the **Model** menu, perspectives, and then create and manage.

2. From the **Perspectives** window, select **SURFACE_CONDITION,
   LIGHT_CONDITION**, and **MAJOR_CAUSE** and then click on **OK**.

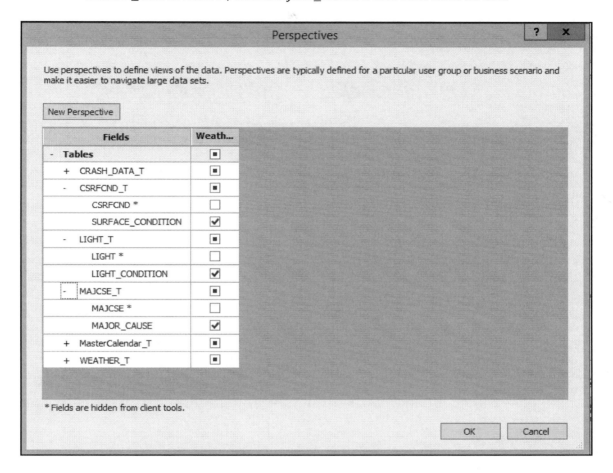

3. Change the **Model.bim** to the Diagram view to see the available tables in the perspective.

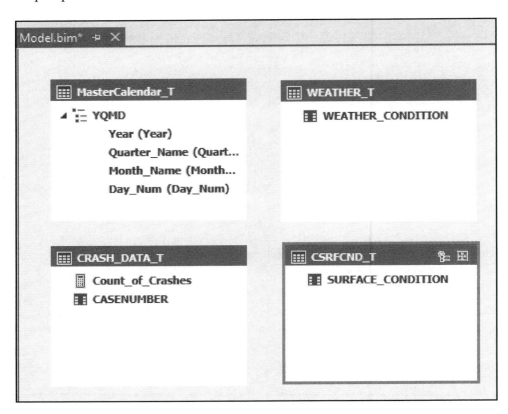

Renaming a perspective

1. Open the **Model** menu, perspectives, and then create and manage.
2. From the **Perspectives** window, place your cursor over the **Weather** name and select the middle box to rename the perspective, **Weather_All**, and click on **OK**.

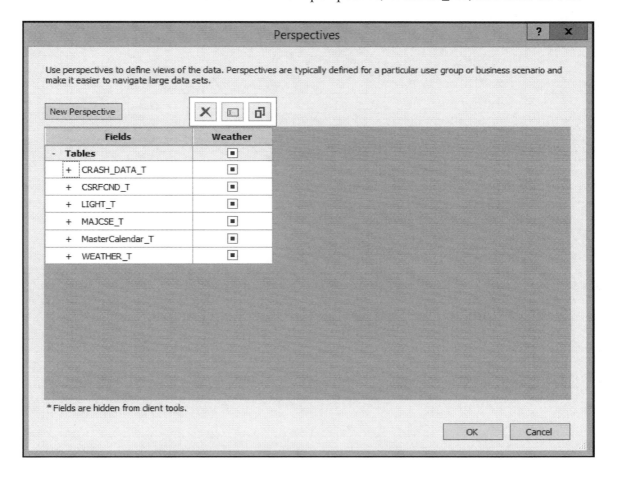

Deleting a perspective

1. Open the **Model** menu, **Perspectives** window, and then create and manage.
2. From the **Perspectives** window, place your cursor over the **Weather** name and select the first box containing the red x to delete the perspective and click on **OK** to remove the perspective.

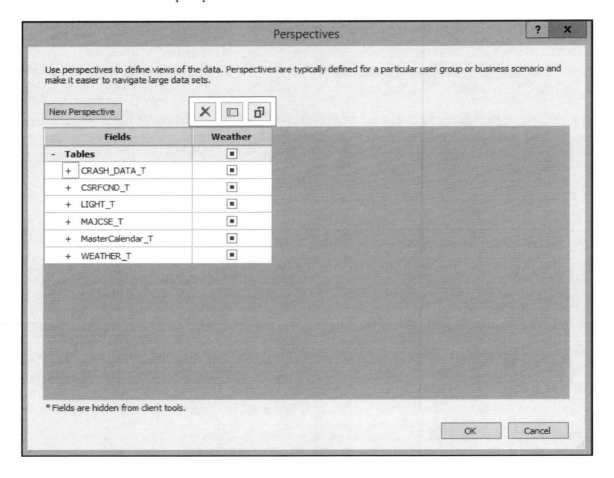

Copying a perspective

1. Open the **Model** menu, **Perspectives** window, and then create and manage.
2. From the **Perspectives** window, place your cursor over the **Weather** name and select the last box containing the two boxes to copy the perspective and click on **OK**.

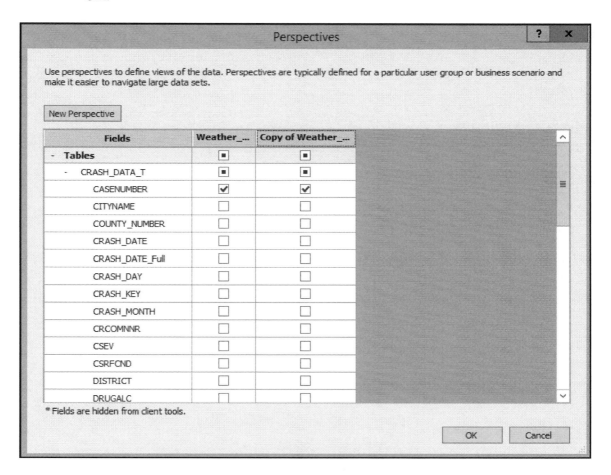

Managing partitions

Partitions in Analysis Services enable you to break up your data into manageable parts. Typically, you use them when you want to limit the amount of data you need to process in the model when the data is updated. Using our crash data table, we will add a new partition to the one that includes only crash data from January 1, 2015 onwards. Partitions are commonly created to break up large datasets based on common properties such as dates, regions, or stores. When you create a partition, only the data that matches the condition in the SQL statement will be inserted into each partition. In this recipe, you will create a new partition to move the crashes that occurred after **1/1/2012** to a new partition. Then you will edit the partition to limit the data to crashes that occurred prior to **1/1/2015**.

How to do it…

Creating a Partition

1. Open **Crash_Data_Solution** in Visual Studio.
2. Select the **Table** menu and then **Partitions…** to bring up the **Partition Manager** window.

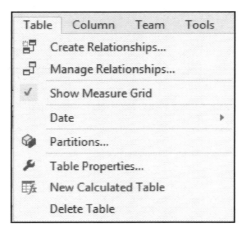

3. Select **New** to create a new partition. Change **Partition Name** to
   CRASH_DATA_GT_2015 and then select the **SQL** icon to change from the Grid
   view and select **OK**.

```
SELECT [dbo].[CRASH_DATA_T].* FROM [dbo].[CRASH_DATA_T]
where crash_date >= '01/01/2012'
```

4. The previous query creates a new partition for all data greater than
   January 1, 2012.

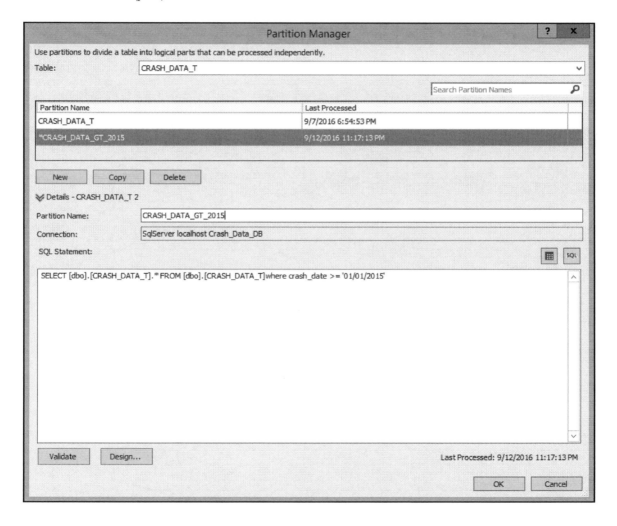

Editing a partition

The process to edit a partition begins the same way as creating a partition, as follows:

1. Open **Crash_Data_Solution** in Visual Studio.
2. Select the **Table** menu and then **Partitions...** to bring up the **Partition Manager** window.
3. Select the first partition **CRASH_DATA_T** and rename to **CRASH_DATA_LT_2015** and select the **SQL** icon.
4. Modify the SQL statement to limit the data to less than January 1, 2015:

```
SELECT [dbo].[CRASH_DATA_T].* FROM [dbo].[CRASH_DATA_T]
where crash_date < '01/01/2015'
```

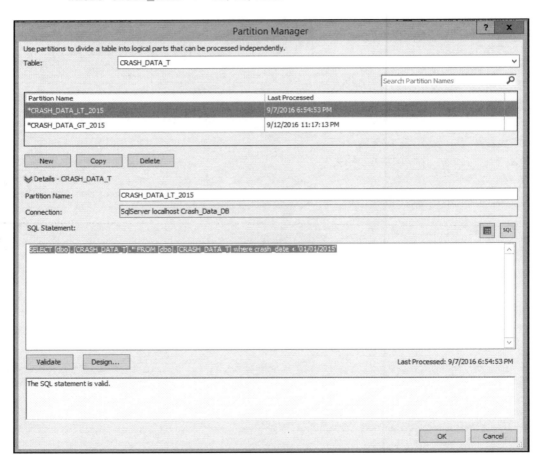

Processing partitions

Once the data has been partitioned in order for Analysis Services to take advantage of the partition, you must process them. In your example, you do not have older data stored in a partition prior to 2015. If no further data is being added or modified to that partition, you can process it once and would only need to process it for modifications to the model. As new data is being added to the newer partition, you would process it to incorporate the new data as required by your load process.

1. Open the **Model** menu and select **Process** to bring up the available options.

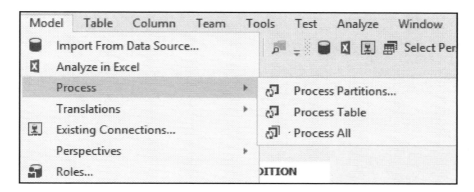

2. From the **Process Partitions** window, change **Mode** to **Process All** and then check the boxes next to **CRASH_DATA_LT_2015** and **CRASH_DATA_GT_2015** and then click on **OK**. This forces the model to reprocess all data, which would otherwise not be required.

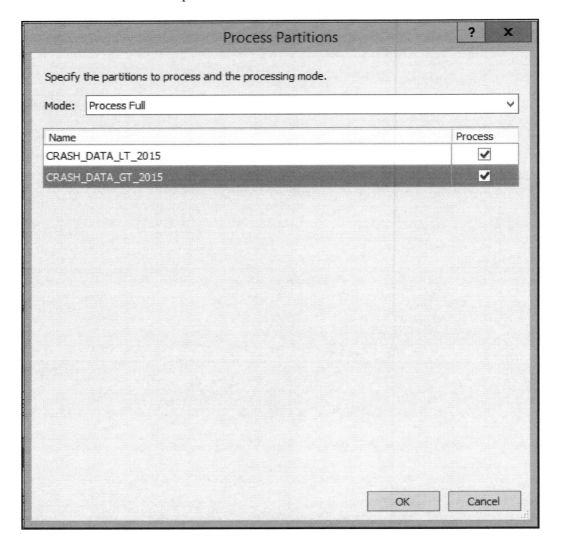

3. The model will then process the data for both partitions.

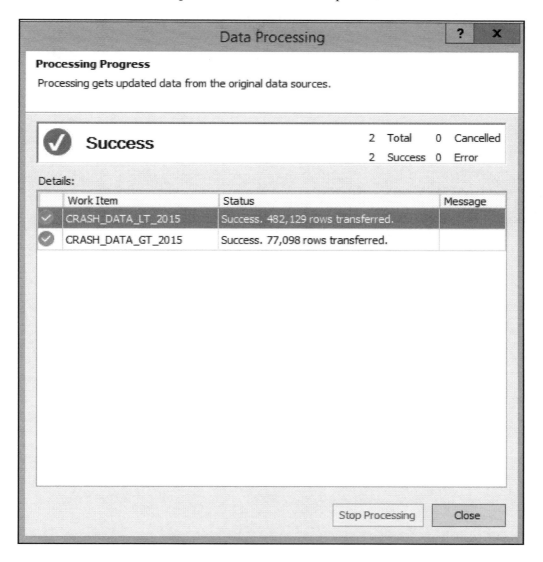

How it works...

In this recipe, you created a new partition for the **Crash_Data_T** table that is split based on the crash date value. The new partition only has records from January 1, 2015 onwards. Then, to get the data into the partitions, you performed a full partition of the model. This processing moved the data into proper partitions.

Managing roles

Each tabular model that you develop in Analysis Services can have unique permissions as required for your use cases. Permissions are assigned by implementing defined roles and associating Windows users or Windows groups to each role. In addition, you are able to limit the data that users can see by adding row-level filters.

In this recipe, you will be able to create a new role for four of the types of permissions that are defined in Analysis Services.

Permission	Abilities	Row Filter
Read	Members assigned to this role can query the data	Yes
Read and process	Members assigned to this role can query the data. In addition, they can execute commands to process the model.	Yes
Process	Members assigned to this role can process the model only	No
Administrator	Members assigned to this role have full control and can query the data	No

There is one additional permission: None, which does not allow anyone to view or process the model. If required, you could configure this permission in the same way as the others.

Getting ready

On your Windows machine, you will need to create four new users that will be assigned to various roles in the following recipes:

- **SSAS_READ**
- **SSAS_READ_PROCESS**
- **SSAS_PROCESS**
- **SSAS_Admin**

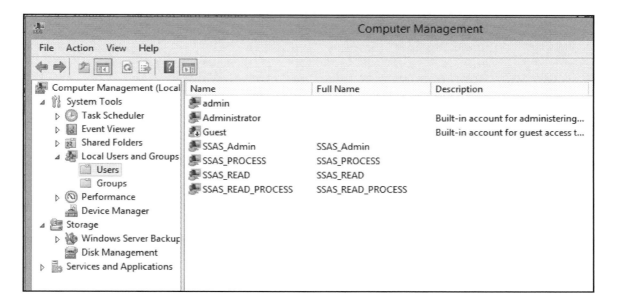

How to do it...

In these recipes, you will assign the users you've created to different roles. Then, test the ability of each role in the model to ensure they work and understand the impact of each.

Creating Admin role

1. Open the **Crash_Data_Solution** in Visual Studio.

2. On the **Model** menu and select **Roles…** to bring up the **Role Manager** window.

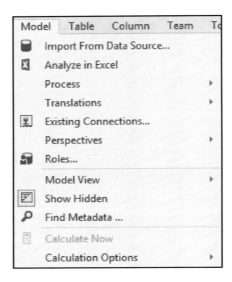

3. In the top box, select **Administrator** from the **Permissions** dropdown to enable this role as an admin. Then, select the **Members** tab and click on **Add…** to bring up the **Select Users** or **Groups** window. Add the **SSAS_Admin** user and click on **OK** to return to the **Role Manager** window.

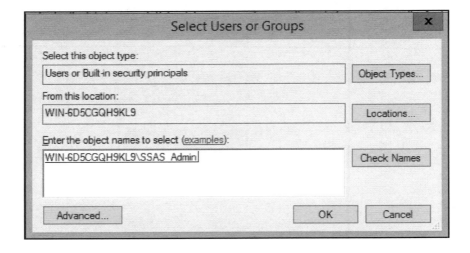

4. Review that you have the proper settings and then click on **OK** to create the new **Admin** role.

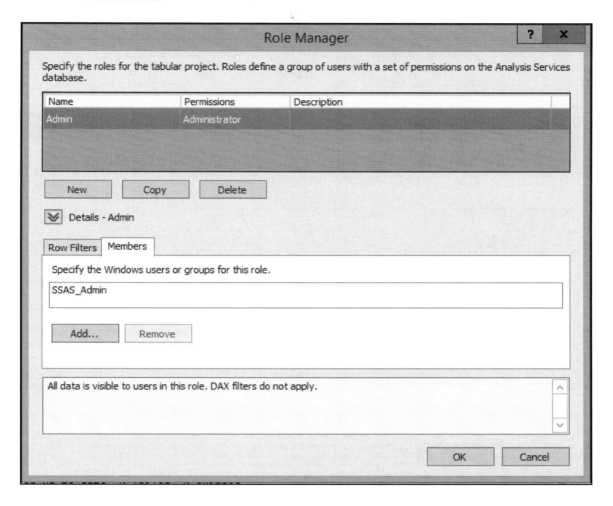

Creating a Read role

In this recipe, you will create a new role that uses the read permission and then limit data to the role by adding a row filter to show only data relating to ice surface conditions.

1. In the **Model** menu, select **Roles…** to bring up the **Role Manager** window.
2. In the row under admin, change the permission to read and name the role **Read_Ice**.
3. Using the DAX filter box, enter:

   ```
   =CSRFCND_T[SURFACE_CONDITION]="Ice"
   ```

4. Then, limit the role for only seeing data pertaining to ice surface conditions.

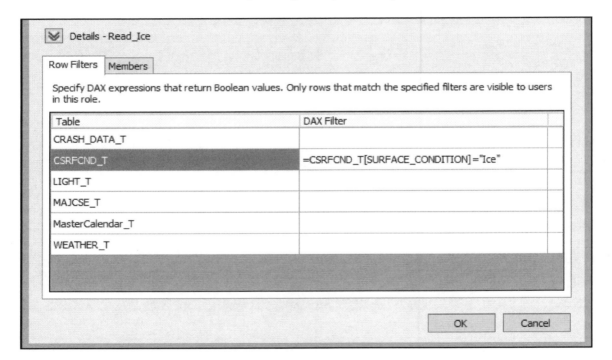

5. Then, select the **Members** tab and click on **Add…** to bring up the **Select Users** or **Groups** window. Add the **SSAS_Read** user and click on **OK** to return to the **Role Manager** window and then click on **OK**.
6. To confirm that the filter is working correctly, deploy the model and then connect to it using SQL Server Management Studio. Change the role to **SSAS_READ**.

7. From SSMS, drag **SURFACE_CONDITION** and **Count_of_Crashes** to the model browser. Because the filter is limiting data to only surface conditions of ice, only data for ice is returned.

Creating a read and process role

In this recipe, you will create a new role that uses the read and process permission.

1. In the **Model** menu, select **Roles...** to bring up the **Role Manager** window

2. In the row under **Admin**, change the permission to read and name the role `Read_and_Process`.

3. Then, select the **Members** tab and click on **Add...** to bring up the **Select Users** or **Groups** window. Add the **SSAS_READ_PROCESS** user and click on **OK** to return to the **Role Manager** window and then click on **OK**.

Creating a process role

In this recipe, you will create a new role that uses the process permission.

1. In the **Model** menu, select **Roles...** to bring up the **Role Manager** window
2. In the row under **Admin**, change the permission to read and name the role `Read_and_Process`.
3. Then, select the **Members** tab and click on **Add...** to bring up the **Select Users or Groups** window. Add the **SSAS__PROCESS** user and click on **OK** to return to the **Role Manager** window and then click on **OK**.

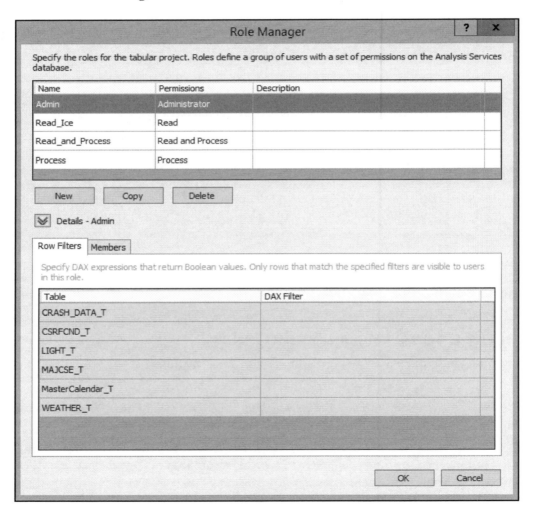

Editing roles

In this recipe, you will see how to go back and edit existing roles:

1. In the **Model** menu, select **Roles...** to bring up the **Role Manager** window.
2. Once the available roles are shown, you can modify filters and memberships to roles.

There's more...

You can also bring up the **Role Manager** window using the icon in Visual Studio.

Managing server properties

You can modify the installed Analysis Server by modifying the properties. Changes to these properties affect all models deployed to the server.

How to do it...

1. Connect to Tabular Services in SQL Server Management Studio.
2. Select the localhost service, right-click and then select properties to bring up the **Analysis Services Properties** windows.

3. Select the **General** page; to bring up **Advanced Properties** click on the **Show Advanced (All) Properties** checkbox.

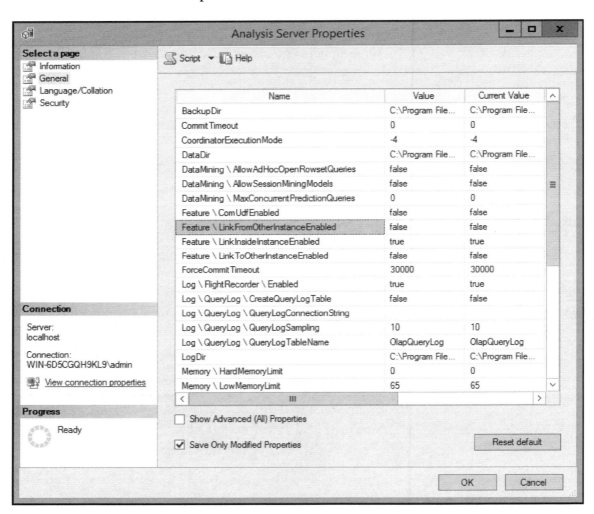

Managing Analysis Services memory

SQL Server Analysis Services running in Tabular mode stores data in memory as the default behavior. In some cases, you can load more data than you have memory, which would result in failed processing. The default setting is to allow the engine to page data to disk when required. By design, the engine will begin paging to disk when the memory consumption goes higher than 60% of the total memory. When running Tabular Models, be sure to monitor the server's total memory consumption. If the system becomes stressed, you will need to reduce the amount of data being processed or add more memory.

How to do it...

1. Connect to Tabular Services in SQL Server Management Studio.
2. Select the localhost service, right-click and then select properties to bring up the **Analysis Services Properties** windows.
3. Select the **General** tab and then scroll down to the **Memory** items.
4. To change VertiPaq memory limit, update the **Value** to **70** and then click on **OK**.

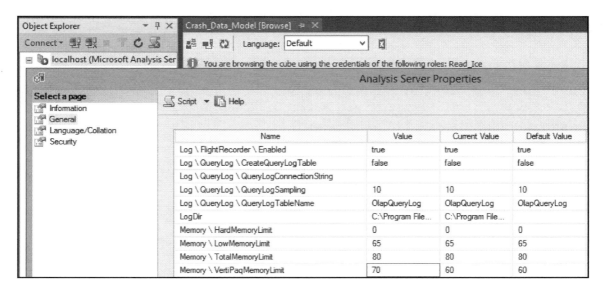

Name	Value	Current Value	Default Value
Log \ FlightRecorder \ Enabled	true	true	true
Log \ QueryLog \ CreateQueryLogTable	false	false	false
Log \ QueryLog \ QueryLogConnectionString			
Log \ QueryLog \ QueryLogSampling	10	10	10
Log \ QueryLog \ QueryLogTableName	OlapQueryLog	OlapQueryLog	OlapQueryLog
LogDir	C:\Program File...	C:\Program File...	
Memory \ HardMemoryLimit	0	0	0
Memory \ LowMemoryLimit	65	65	65
Memory \ TotalMemoryLimit	80	80	80
Memory \ VertiPaqMemoryLimit	70	60	60

How it works...

In this recipe, you updated the amount of memory that must be consumed before paging to disk would occur. In this case, the percentage of memory that can be used is up to 70%. Once more than 70% is consumed, the data will then be paged to disk. This is a serverwide setting and affects all Tabular models that are published to the server.

6
In-Memory Versus DirectQuery Mode

In this chapter, we will cover the following recipes:

- Creating a new DirectQuery project
- Configuring DirectQuery table partitions
- Testing DirectQuery mode

Introduction

When developing a tabular model, you have two primary choices for where and how the data is stored and accessed from end user tools. Tabular models are unlike SQL Server Analysis Services Multidimensional models, which only store all data to disk. Tabular models by default store data in memory with an option for storing data to disk when appropriate. By storing the data in memory there is faster query performance since there is no disk I/O for retrieving data results. Modeling can be accomplished in visual studio and does not require a full data transformation or load process which speeds up the time to develop and deploy the model to production. This chapter focuses on the available storage modes for tabular models, in-memory mode and DirectQuery mode. You will learn how each mode operates and best practices for choosing the appropriate mode for your solution.

Understanding query modes

There are two unique values that you can choose to implement the query mode in your model. Before changing the value of the property you need to review how each mode works when deciding the optimal solution for your project before choosing in-memory and DirectQuery mode.

QueryMode Property	Description
In-memory (Default)	Queries are answered using the data stored in cache.
DirectQuery	Queries are answered by accessing the data directly from the relational database.

Understanding in-memory mode

The default storage for a tabular model is to use the in-memory data cache to store and query data. By storing the data in memory, queries accessing the data perform faster than having to retrieve data from disk. Starting with SQL Server 2012, Microsoft integrated an in-memory technology that they branded as xVelocity in-memory technologies. At the core of this technology is the analytics engine found in Analysis Services, as well as in-memory optimized columnstore indexes added to the SQL Server engine.

All of the recipes that you have performed in Chapters 1-5 leveraged the in-memory functionality. When you are using in-memory mode, the following steps occur when you deploy your model to the Analysis Services server:

1. Developer builds the model in Visual Studio and deploys.
2. Data is sent to the Analysis Services Server.
3. Model is processed to load into memory on the server.
4. When a user accesses the model from any tool, the query is executed against the in-memory data.

5. Results from the query are returned to the user's tool.

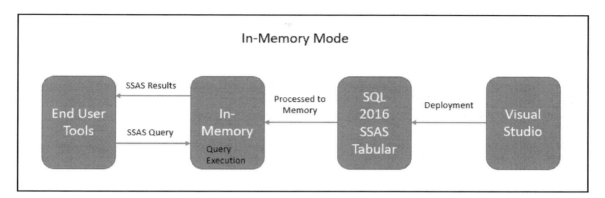

Typically, this configuration will have the best performance due to the data being cached to memory and eliminating the need to access physical disks.

Advantages of in-memory

Using in-memory caching allows for the most available performance and options in tabular mode. You have full access to all the available DAX functions to build out your solution. In addition, you can leverage the ability to create calculated tables. These tables are created and stored in-memory to optimize query performance. This is also the most flexible mode since it allows you to connect data from a variety of data source systems and join them in model creation. This speeds up the creation of your BI solution by eliminating the need to create a separate ETL process to load and stage the data.

Limitations of in-memory

While in-memory mode is highly effective for creating BI solutions, there are limitations. First, since all data is cached in-memory, you have to ensure your server has adequate memory, not only for the dataset. Be sure to include the operating system, Analysis Services, and any other third-party software your company may require. If loading very large datasets into memory, you can exceed available memory and the deployment and processing will fail. If you are using the same Analysis Services server for multiple models, you will need to monitor the total size of data being loaded into memory. You could have a small model fail to deploy because other models have used most of the available free memory.

Another limitation of in-memory mode is having to keep the data refreshed. If your data needs to be kept near real time, it can be difficult to reprocess the data in the memory cache.

Understanding DirectQuery mode

The alternate storage for a tabular model is to use the DirectQuery mode to store and query data. Using this mode, data is stored in the SQL server relational database engine and queries to the model are passed to the SQL engine.

When you are using DirectQuery mode, the following steps occur when you deploy your model to the Analysis Services server:

1. Developer builds the model in Visual Studio and deploys tabular model.
2. The model is processed with location of data.
3. When a user accesses the model from any tool, the query is sent to SSAS and then sent to the SQL Engine.
4. Results from the SQL Engine are sent to SSAS.
5. SSAS translates the data and returns the results to the end user:

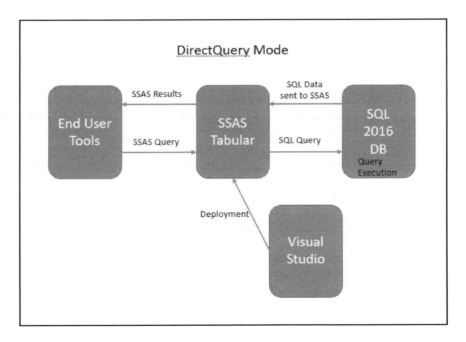

Advantages of DirectQuery

There are many benefits to using DirectQuery mode for your model instead of in-memory mode.

As discussed earlier, in-memory mode requires an extra step of processing the data to ensure the data in the memory cache is refreshed. DirectQuery mode overcomes this limitation by reading directly from the source tables. For instance, if you have a model built against a table that is being updated in real time and a user queries data from the model, the query goes directly to the source table not the in-memory data to get the data with no need to refresh the model.

Since in-memory mode is limited by the amount of available memory on the server, DirectQuery mode can overcome that limitation by allowing you to access datasets larger than the available memory of the Analysis Services server. This is done by leveraging the data being stored in the relational database engine.

The performance of DirectQuery mode can be further enhanced by leveraging the ability of the model to access column store indexes in the SQL Server database.

Limitations of DirectQuery mode

While DirectQuery mode does have many advantages, there are limitations to the functionality compared with in-memory mode.

If you are pulling data from multiple sources, then you cannot use DirectQuery mode. Due to the nature of how DirectQuery mode works, it can only access a single relational database. Allowed databases for DirectQuery mode include:

- Microsoft SQL Server 2008 and up
- Microsoft Azure SQL Database and Data Warehouse
- Microsoft Analytics Platform System (APS)
- Oracle 9i and up
- Teradata relational database V2R6 and up

Query sources are limited in DirectQuery mode. If you have leveraged stored procedures, then you will not be able to use DirectQuery mode. Data pulled from stored procedures would have to be rewritten to a query that is used when building the model. Also you cannot leverage calculated tables. If possible, you would need to recreate the calculated table as a physical table or view it on the relational database engine to enable DirectQuery mode.

When queries are run against DirectQuery mode, the DAX or MDX queries are transformed into T-SQL and sent to the SQL database. Therefore, if you are using any DAX or MDX formulas that cannot be converted and processed successfully, you will receive an error. It is better to decide early in model development whether you will be using DirectQuery mode. You can then test your formulas and performance as you develop the model.

DirectQuery restrictions summary:

Feature	Restriction
Data source	Can only pull from a single relational database
Calculated tables	Calculated Tables are not supported in DirectQuery models
Query limit	By default DirectQuery is limited to 1 million rows
Stored procedures	Tables cannot be defined from stored procedures
DAX formulas	DAX formulas that cannot be converted to SQL syntax will return an error

Creating a new DirectQuery project

In this recipe you will create a new tabular model project that will be configured to use DirectQuery mode.

How to do it...

1. Create a new tabular model solution in Visual Studio named **DirectQuery_CrashData**.
2. Change the model to use DirectQuery mode by selecting the **Model.bim** to bring up the properties and change **DirectQuery Mode** to **On** from **Off**:

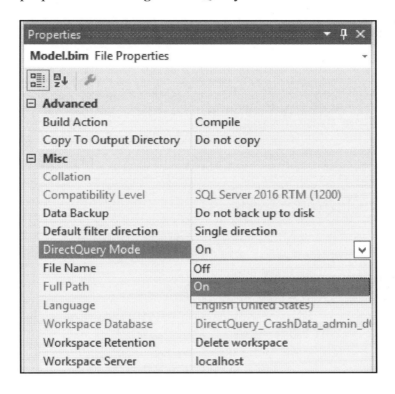

3. Select **Microsoft SQL Server** and then click **Next**:

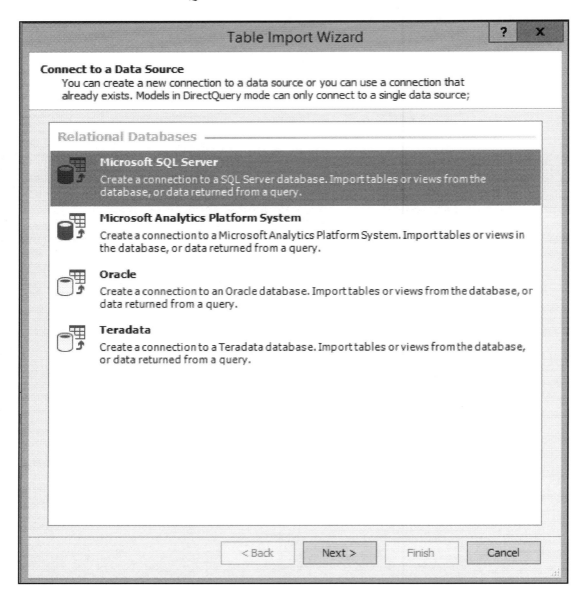

4. On the **Table Import Wizard**, select your server and the **Crash_Data_DB** and click **Next**. Then enter a username and password that has access to your data and click **Next**.

5. Select the table in the **Crash_Data_DB** and select **Finish**:

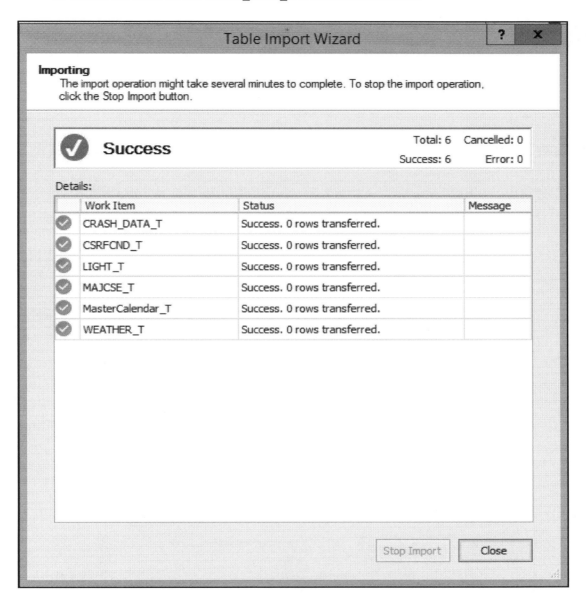

How it works...

By enabling DirectQuery prior to building anything in the model, the options for importing data are limited to those data sources that are compatible with this mode. You will notice that unlike in-memory mode, upon completion of the table import step no data is loaded into SQL Server Analysis Services. The connections have been established so queries can pass through to the underlying data.

Configuring DirectQuery table partitions

Before you can deploy and use the model, you must configure the sample partitions for each table that is being used in the model. When you first try to deploy the model, you will receive an error on each table. These errors occur because there is no data loaded into the sample partition:

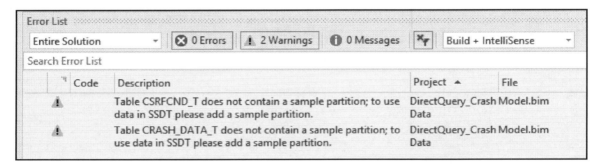

This recipe walks you through the steps to create a sample partition on a table to clear the error.

How to do it...

1. In the data Grid view select the **CRASH_DATA_T** table and then select the **Table** menu and **Partitions** to bring up the **Partition Manager**.

2. On the **Partition Manager,** click **Copy** to make a copy of the data. Select the **SQL** icon and filter the results to data greater than January 1st 2015 and click **Validate** to ensure that the SQL statement is correct and click **OK** to finish:

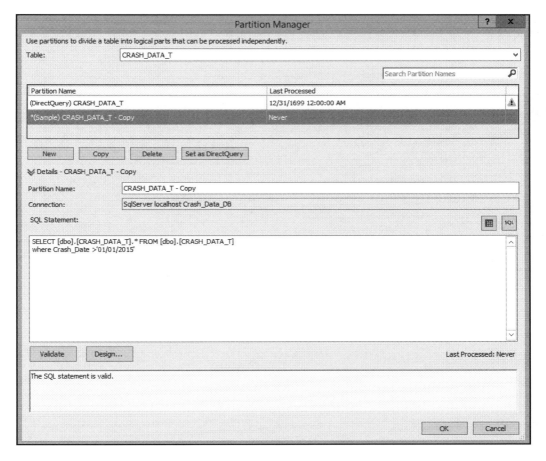

3. Now repeat the process for the remaining tables in the project to create sample data and clear the errors. You will not need to add a filter on the other tables.

4. Select the **Build** menu and then **Deploy** to deploy your model to the server.

How it works...

This process prepares the Visual Studio project to have sample data by making a copy of the data from the underlying relational database source. Until this step is done, you will not have any data in Visual Studio to view. By creating a copy of the data, Visual Studio has sample data that you can see to build your model and calculations. Once completed, you will be able to deploy the model to the server.

Testing DirectQuery mode

By running an SQL Server profiler trace, you can see exactly what is happening when a DirectQuery mode query is executed. In this recipe, you will use SQL Server Management Studio to execute a query and trace the results:

1. Connect to your model using SQL Server Management Studio.
2. Drag **SURFACE_CONDITION**, **MAJOR_CAUSE**, and **Count_of_Crashes** to the query window:

SURFACE_CONDIT...	MAJOR_CAUSE	Count_of_Crashes
(null)	(null)	46918
(null)	Animal	17
(null)	Collision culvert	26
(null)	Collision Guard...	7
(null)	Collision with b...	30
(null)	Collision with b...	45
(null)	Collision with c...	282
(null)	Collision with d...	25
(null)	Collision with T...	4
(null)	Collision with u...	2
(null)	Fire	254
(null)	Immersion	1092
(null)	impact with At...	1
(null)	Jackknife	70
(null)	Non-motorist	6
(null)	Overall/rollover	556
(null)	Parked motor ...	3
(null)	Railway vehicle	4
(null)	Unknown	2
Dry	(null)	249651

How it works...

Since the QueryMode property is set to DirectQuery, the tabular engine is accessing the data from the SQL Server Engine tables. The actual query can be seen when you use SQL Server Profiler to trace the query on the SQL Server Database. In this instance, the query results are sent back to SSAS tabular mode and then presented to the end user tool:

```
SELECT
TOP (1000001) [t1].[SURFACE_CONDITION],[t3].[MAJOR_CAUSE],
COUNT_BIG([t0].[CASENUMBER])
 AS [a0]
FROM
(
((SELECT [dbo].[CRASH_DATA_T].* FROM [dbo].[CRASH_DATA_T]) AS [t0]

 left outer join

( SELECT [dbo].[CSRFCND_T].* FROM [dbo].[CSRFCND_T] ) AS [t1] on
(
[t0].[CSRFCND] = [t1].[CSRFCND]
)
)

 left outer join

( SELECT [dbo].[MAJCSE_T].* FROM [dbo].[MAJCSE_T] ) AS [t3] on
(
[t0].[MAJCSE] = [t3].[MAJCSE]
)
)

GROUP BY [t1].[SURFACE_CONDITION],[t3].[MAJOR_CAUSE]
```

As you can see, the tables being queried are the base tables, and they are being accessed using T-SQL syntax not DAX or MDX.

7
Securing Tabular Models

In this chapter, we will cover the following recipes:

- Configuring static row-level security
- Configuring dynamic filter security

Introduction

Tabular models leverage the use of Windows users and groups. Recall that in `Chapter 5`, *Administration of Tabular Models*, you added row-level security to a user to filter for one role to only see **Ice** conditions in the crash data. When the query is run, the security is checked to ensure that the user's role has the ability to retrieve the rows of data associated with the permission of the role, unlike multidimensional security, which uses cells and dimensions to determine what data can be accessed. In addition, tabular models do not have the ability to deny permissions such as does the multidimensional model. Tabular models rely on row-level security only. If a user is assigned to multiple roles, they obtain the rights from all the associated roles; for example, if the **Read_Ice** user is added to the **Admin** role, they would have all rights as an administrator as well. Pay close attention when setting up and deploying security. Tabular model security can be configured to use row filters or dynamic filters. When preparing to implement security on your model, you need to understand how each filter type works and choose the most appropriate method for your requirements.

Configuring static row-level security

Static row-level security applies the filter to all members of the role. Roles can have filters on multiple tables. This recipe demonstrates this by adding a new filter on the **Read_Ice** role already created on the model.

Getting ready

Open the **Crash_Data_Model** in Visual Studio to bring up **Model.bim**. Then, change your view to the Diagram view to see the table relationships. In this recipe, you will review how row-level security is added and how it works. You will add a filter on the **LIGHT_T** table and then add a filter on the **CRASH_DATA_T** table.

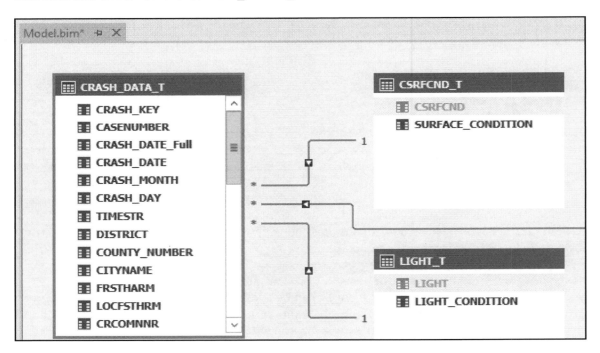

In SQL Server Management Studio, the current security is only limiting rows to **Ice** conditions.

Dimension	Hierarchy	Operator	Filter Expression
<Select dimension>			

SURFACE_CONDIT...	LIGHT_CONDITION	Count_of_Crashes
Ice	Dark, roadway lighted	4687
Ice	Dark, roadway not lighted	7091
Ice	Dark, unknown lighting	222
Ice	Dawn	1492
Ice	Daylight	21119
Ice	Dusk	937
Ice	Unknown	116
Ice	(null)	24

How to do it...

1. Select the **Model** menu and then **Roles** to bring up the **Role Manager** window.
2. Select **Read_Ice** to see the row filter already applied.

3. In the DAX Filter area for the **LIGHT_T** table enter:

```
=LIGHT[LIGHT_CONDITION]="Dawn"
```

Role Manager ? X

Specify the roles for the tabular project. Roles define a group of users with a set of permissions on the Analysis Services database.

Name	Permissions	Description
Admin	Administrator	
Read_Ice	Read	
Read_and_Process	Read and Process	

[New] [Copy] [Delete]

⊻ Details - Read_Ice

Row Filters | Members

Specify DAX expressions that return Boolean values. Only rows that match the specified filters are visible to users in this role.

Table	DAX Filter
CRASH_DATA_T	
CSRFCND_T	=CSRFCND_T[SURFACE_CONDITION]="Ice"
LIGHT_T	=LIGHT_T[LIGHT_CONDITION]="Dawn"
MAJCSE_T	
MasterCalendar_T	
WEATHER_T	

[OK] [Cancel]

4. Deploy the model and review the results in SQL Server Management Studio.

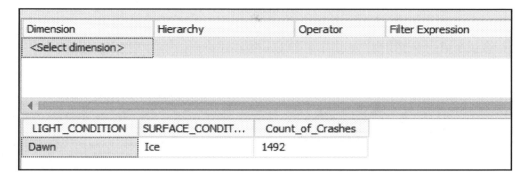

How it works...

In this recipe, you added an additional filter to the **Read_Ice** role since there is a defined relationship. In this case, a many to one relationship is defined from the **LIGHT_T** table to the **CRASH_DATA_T** table. The **Read_Ice** role has been filtered to only see **Dawn** conditions in addition to the **Ice** conditions previously defined. When the query is executed, the DAX formula is evaluated in-memory and the filtered result set is returned.

This type of filtering does not work if you apply the filter on the **CRASH_DATA_T** table. You must apply the filter to the correct table of the relationship to enable the row-based filtering to work.

Configuring dynamic filter security

Dynamic security uses additional information to filter the data to allow more flexibility than row-level security. In this recipe, you will create a security table that has two users, Bob and John. Then, by implementing dynamic security, the data that each is able to see will be shown.

Getting ready

Open the **Crash_Data_Model** in Visual Studio to bring up **Model.bim**. Then change your view to the Diagram view to see the table relationships. In this recipe, you will create a new security table and then implement dynamic security for these users by using the **USERNAME()** function. The **USERNAME()** function will return the DOMAIN\User from the account accessing the model.

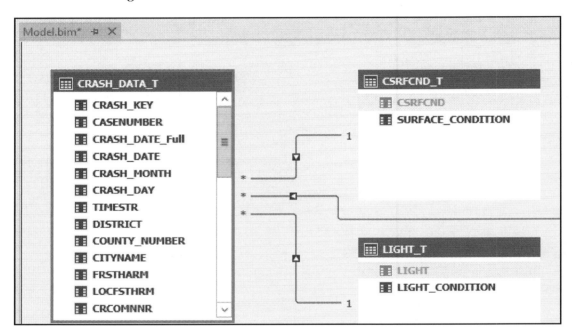

How to do it...

1. Select the **Model** menu and the **Existing Connections...**:

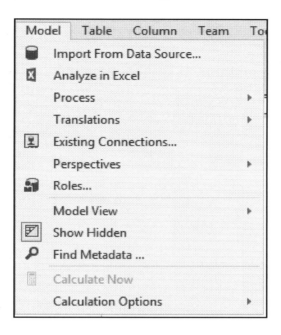

2. Then select **Open** to bring up the existing connection information:

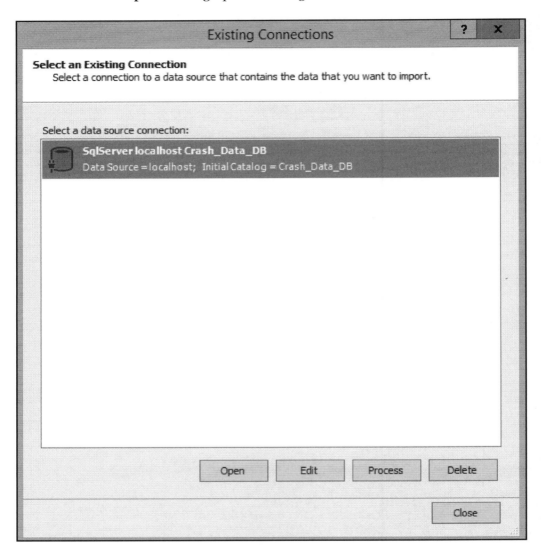

3. The default import wizard is set to **Select from a list of tables and views to choose the data to import.** Click on **Next**:

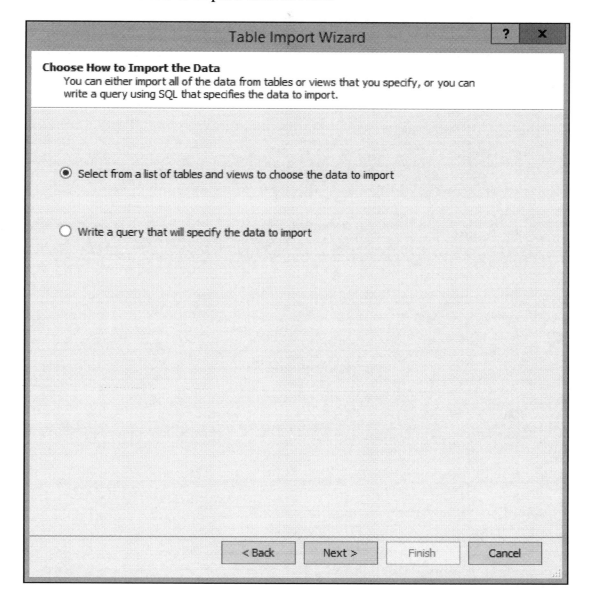

4. Select the **DynamicSecurity_T** table and then click on **Finish** to import the data:

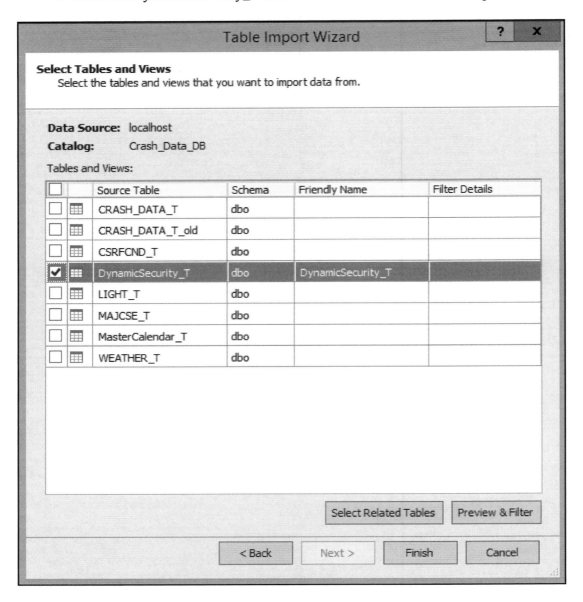

5. The **DynamicSecurity_T** is now added to your model using the same connection information:

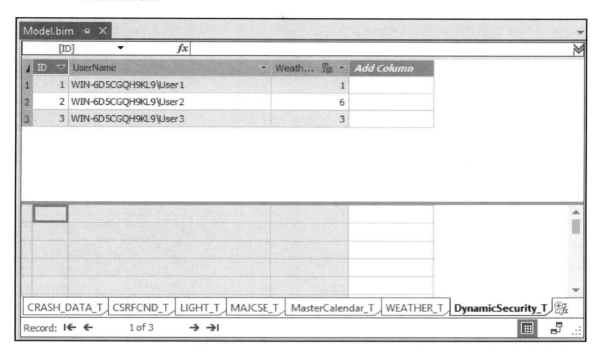

6. In the Diagram view, create a relationship between the **DynamicSecurity_T** table and the **Weather_T** table:

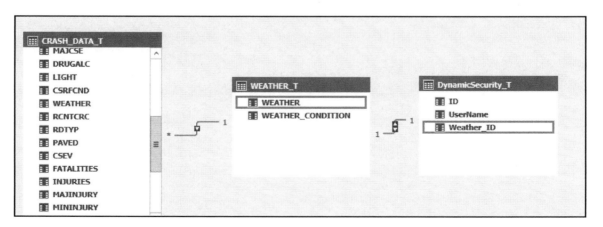

7. Then, in the **Model** menu, select **Roles** to bring up the **Role Manager** window. Create a new role name, **DynamicSecurity**, and grant it read permissions. Then add **User1** to the **Members** tab:

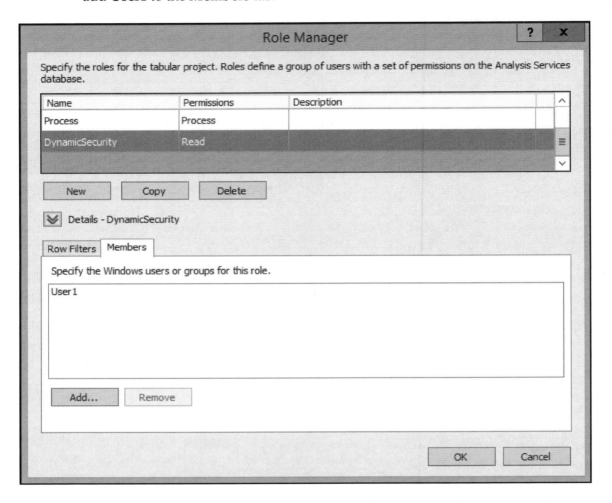

8. Now we add the DAX expression to leverage the USERNAME() function. In the **DynamicSecurity** table, enter = FALSE(). In the **Weather_T** table, enter:

```
=WEATHER_T[WEATHER]=LOOKUPVALUE(DynamicSecurity_T[Weather_ID]
,DynamicSecurity_T[UserName]
,USERNAME()
,DynamicSecurity_T[Weather_ID]
,WEATHER_T[WEATHER])
```

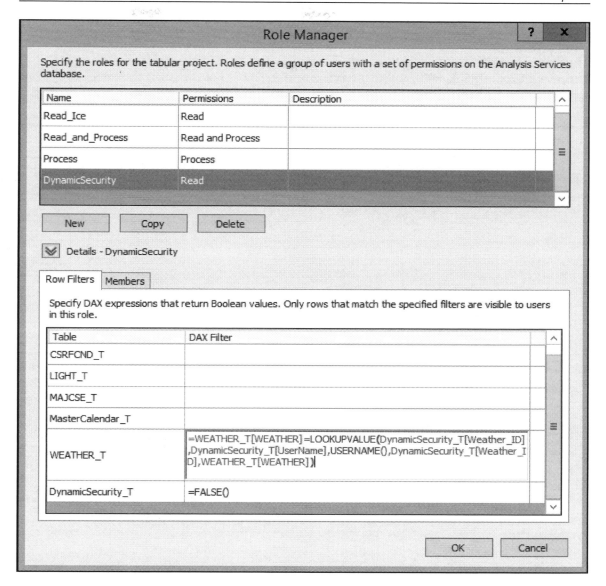

9. Then deploy the model. When a user logs in, the security permission will limit
   the rows they can see to what is defined in the **DynamicSecurity** table.

How it works...

The **DynamicSecurity_T** table stores the domain names and key to the data a user is permitted to access. Once this table is loaded into the model and a relationship is established between it and the **WEATHER_T** table, filters can be applied. Then you created a new role to leverage the **DynamicSecurity_T** table. To this, you add the users to the members in the role. Then you added the = FALSE() statement to prevent users from being able to query the **DynamicSecurity_T** table. The other DAX statement leverages the LOOKUPVALUE function to return the rows that meet the condition of the Windows user.

8
Combining Tabular Models with Excel

In this chapter, we will cover the following recipes:

- Using Analyze in Excel from SSMS
- Connecting to Excel from SQL Server Data Tools
- Using PivotTables with tabular data
- Using the timeline filter with pivot tables
- Analyzing data with Power View
- Importing data with Power Pivot
- Modeling data with Power Pivot
- Adding data to Power Pivot
- Moving Power Pivot to SSAS via Management Studio
- Moving Power Pivot to SSAS via SQL Server Data Tools

Introduction

Excel is the most popular tool for people to use when reporting on data. It is widely adopted, very flexible, and loaded with features. Most users turn to Excel as their data analytic tool of choice to help them make better decisions. It is easy to get data from a variety of sources into Excel such as text files, relational databases, other Excel files, or Analysis Services. Once data is loaded in Excel, you can easily manipulate the data using the standard filtering, sorting, and data deduplication. From there you can enhance how the data is shown by creating different types of charts and visualizations. With the additions of Power View and Power Pivot, users can now go even further with their analysis by making interactive reports in Power View. Or they can create their own analytic models in Power Pivot by combining data from various sources into a single view. The recipes in this chapter provide an overview of connecting Excel to your Tabular model. You will then create a Power View report to understand the basics of leveraging Power View. Finally, you will enhance the Crash Data model with two new sets of codes by connecting Power Pivot to the SQL Server and loading up the new data from Excel.

Using Analyze in Excel from SSMS

Often you will have users that use SQL Server Management Studio (SSMS) to write queries or browse data. When you are using SQL Server Management Studio to browse the cube, there is an easy way to quickly connect to Excel to interact with your model. Built into the browser in SSMS is a feature called Analyze in Excel. Once clicked the data and connection that you are viewing is lifted into Excel for further exploration.

How to do it...

1. Open SQL Server Management Studio and connect to your Tabular Service. Right-click on the database model, **Crash_Data_SSASTM**, to analyze and select **Browse....**

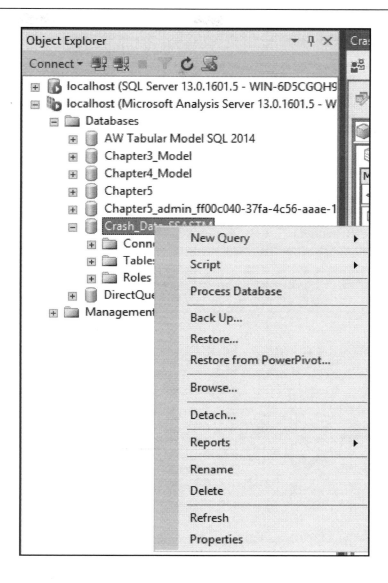

2. Once the browser opens, select the columns to review the data in the browser, select **Year** from the **MasterCalendar_T**, **LIGHT_CONDITION** from the **LIGHT_T**, and **Count_of_Crashes** from the measures **CRASH_DATA_T**.

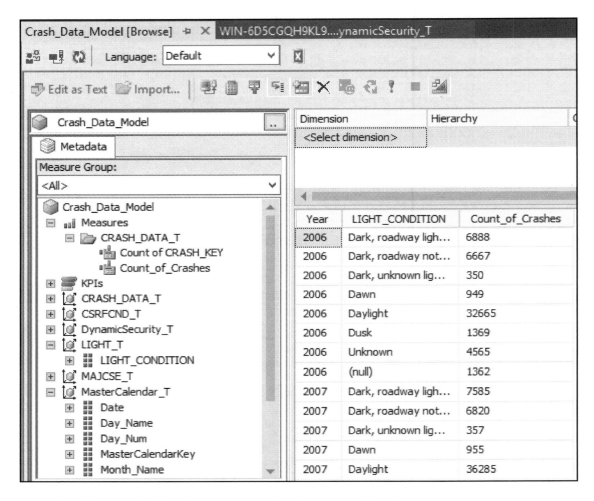

3. Click on the **Excel** icon to start the **Analyze in Excel** window.

4. Select the **Perspective** you would like to use, if multiple perspectives are displayed.

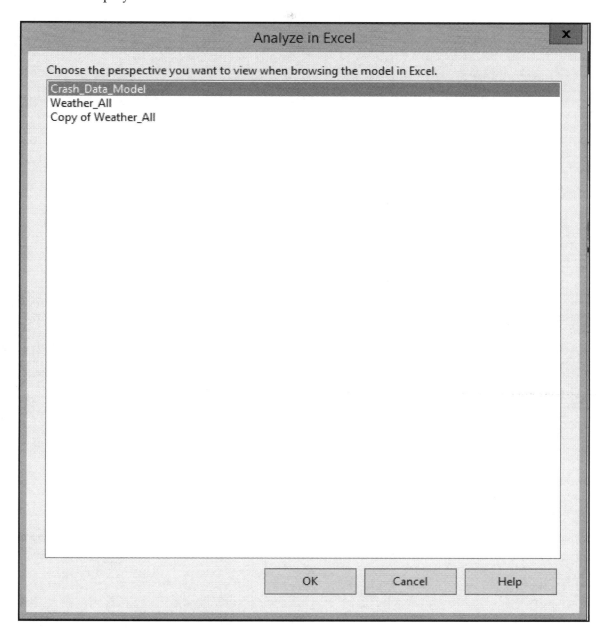

5. Select the **Crash_Data_Model** and then click **OK**.

6. The next screen displays the **Microsoft Excel Security Notice**; choose **Enable** to let Excel read data from the tabular model.

7. Once completed, you will have a connection established to the cube and a new PivotTable created in an Excel workbook.

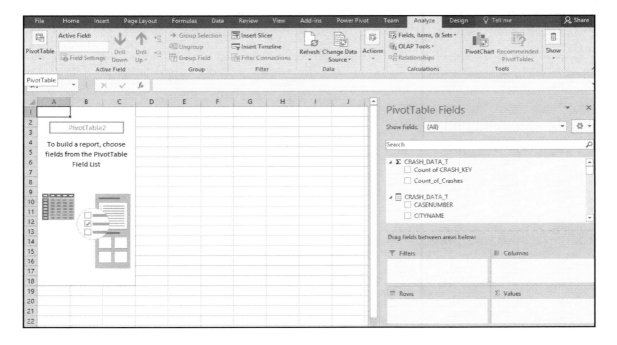

8. Select **MAJOR_CAUSE** as rows and **YQMD** as columns, and finally add
   Count_of_Crashes as values to ensure you have successfully connected to the
   model.

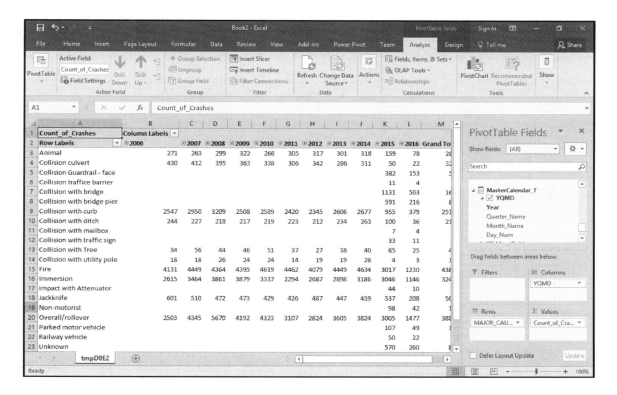

How it works...

From within SQL Server Management Studio you can quickly change to Excel and explore
how the model you designed and built as end users would interact. In this recipe, you
created an initial view of your data in the data browser and then selected the Analyze in
Excel icon to auto create the connection and launch Excel. Once approving the connection,
Excel started with a pivot table. Finally, you created a simple pivot table to ensure that all
the connections and access to your model were successful.

Connecting to Excel from SQL Server Data Tools

SQL Server Data Tools also has the built-in feature to Analyze in Excel. When prompted you must select the role or user that you want to connect to the model. Users would not typically leverage SQL Server Data Tools. Therefore, this feature allows you to test the perspectives and security to ensure it is working as designed.

How to do it...

1. Open Visual Studio and the **Crash_Data_Solution**.
2. Click on the **Analyze in Excel** icon.

3. On the **Analyze in Excel** Window, select the role that you want to use. In this case, keep **Current Windows User** and click **OK**.

4. Excel opens using the permissions of the account you selected by creating a new workbook and pivot table.

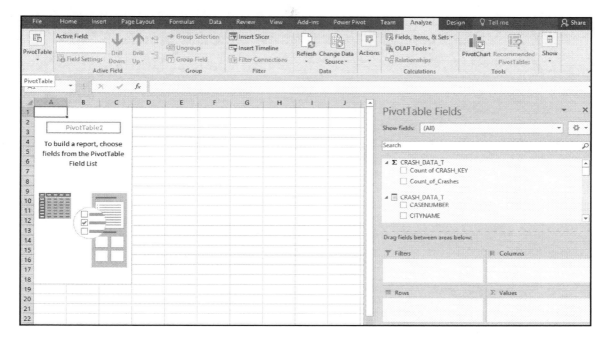

5. Select **MAJOR_CAUSE** as rows and **YQMD** as columns, and finally add **Count_of_Crashes** as values to ensure you have successfully connected to the model.

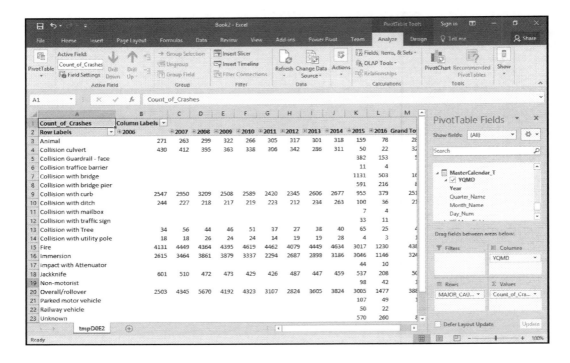

How it works...

This recipe allows you to connect to Excel and explore the data the same way your users see the model. While using SQL Server Data Tools, you selected the **Analyze in Excel** icon to launch the program. In order to test out the model, you selected the security role that you wanted to use. Then Excel is launched using the security access of the role. Finally, you built a simple pivot table report to check that the security and data are accessible as required.

Using PivotTables with tabular data

These recipes explain how to do fundamental operations with PivotTables against a tabular model. You will create slicers in Excel. You will then see how to sort and filter the data within Excel that is connected to your model.

Using Slice, Sort, and Filter

In this recipe, you will learn how to insert a slicer, filter your data, and sort the data in an Excel PivotTable.

How to do it...

1. Connect to the model as described in the *Connecting to Excel from SQL Server Data Tools* recipe.
2. On the **Analyze** menu, click on **Insert Slicers** to bring up the **Insert Slicers** window:

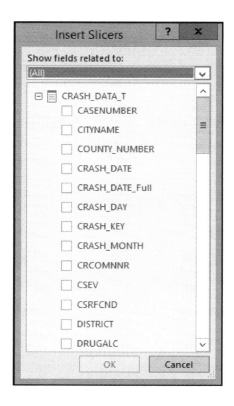

3. Scroll down and select the **LIGHT_CONDITION** checkbox and click **OK**:

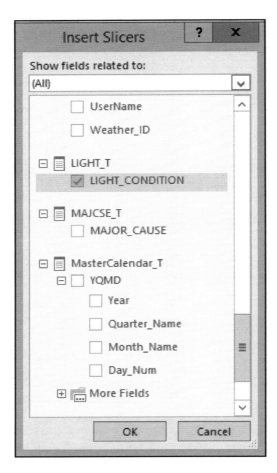

4. A new Slicer menu is created and added to the worksheet:

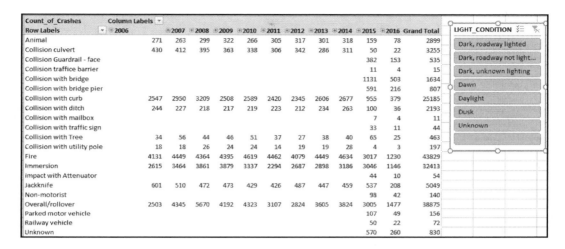

Count_of_Crashes	Column Labels											
Row Labels	2006	2007	2008	2009	2010	2011	2012	2013	2014	2015	2016	Grand Total
Animal	271	263	299	322	266	305	317	301	318	159	78	2899
Collision culvert	430	412	395	363	338	306	342	286	311	50	22	3255
Collision Guardrail - face										382	153	535
Collision traffice barrier										11	4	15
Collision with bridge										1131	503	1634
Collision with bridge pier										591	216	807
Collision with curb	2547	2950	3209	2508	2589	2420	2345	2606	2677	955	379	25185
Collision with ditch	244	227	218	217	219	223	212	234	263	100	36	2193
Collision with mailbox										7	4	11
Collision with traffic sign										33	11	44
Collision with Tree	34	56	44	46	51	37	27	38	40	65	25	463
Collision with utility pole	18	18	26	24	24	14	19	19	28	4	3	197
Fire	4131	4449	4364	4395	4619	4462	4079	4449	4634	3017	1230	43829
Immersion	2615	3464	3861	3879	3337	2294	2687	2898	3186	3046	1146	32413
impact with Attenuator										44	10	54
Jackknife	601	510	472	473	429	426	487	447	459	537	208	5049
Non-motorist										98	42	140
Overall/rollover	2503	4345	5670	4192	4323	3107	2824	3605	3824	3005	1477	38875
Parked motor vehicle										107	49	156
Railway vehicle										50	22	72
Unknown										570	260	830

LIGHT_CONDITION
- Dark, roadway lighted
- Dark, roadway not light...
- Dark, unknown lighting
- Dawn
- Daylight
- Dusk
- Unknown

5. To use the slicer to filter the data, select the **Dawn** condition:

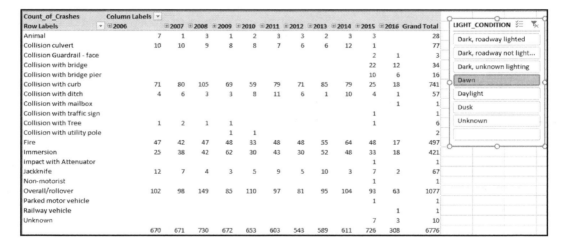

Count_of_Crashes	Column Labels											
Row Labels	2006	2007	2008	2009	2010	2011	2012	2013	2014	2015	2016	Grand Total
Animal	7	1	3	1	2	3	3	2	3	3		28
Collision culvert	10	10	9	8	8	7	6	6	12	1		77
Collision Guardrail - face										2	1	3
Collision with bridge										22	12	34
Collision with bridge pier										10	6	16
Collision with curb	71	80	105	69	59	79	71	85	79	25	18	741
Collision with ditch	4	6	3	3	8	11	6	1	10	4	1	57
Collision with mailbox											1	1
Collision with traffic sign										1		1
Collision with Tree	1	2	1	1						1		6
Collision with utility pole				1	1							2
Fire	47	42	47	48	33	48	48	55	64	48	17	497
Immersion	25	38	42	62	30	43	30	52	48	33	18	421
impact with Attenuator										1		1
Jackknife	12	7	4	3	5	9	5	10	3	7	2	67
Non-motorist										1		1
Overall/rollover	102	98	149	85	110	97	81	95	104	93	63	1077
Parked motor vehicle										1		1
Railway vehicle											1	1
Unknown										7	3	10
	670	671	730	672	653	603	543	589	611	726	308	6776

LIGHT_CONDITION
- Dark, roadway lighted
- Dark, roadway not light...
- Dark, unknown lighting
- Dawn
- Daylight
- Dusk
- Unknown

6. To select multiple filters, click on the icon to enable the selection of more than one filter:

7. Select **Dawn**, **Daylight**, and **Dusk** to filter for those three conditions:

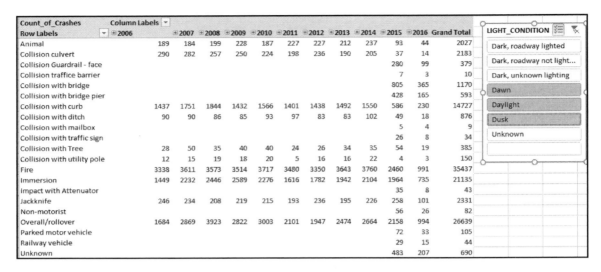

Count_of_Crashes	Column Labels												
Row Labels	2006	2007	2008	2009	2010	2011	2012	2013	2014	2015	2016	Grand Total	
Animal	189	184	199	228	187	227	227	212	237	93	44	2027	
Collision culvert	290	282	257	250	224	198	236	190	205	37	14	2183	
Collision Guardrail - face										280	99	379	
Collision traffice barrier										7	3	10	
Collision with bridge										805	365	1170	
Collision with bridge pier										428	165	593	
Collision with curb	1437	1751	1844	1432	1566	1401	1438	1492	1550	586	230	14727	
Collision with ditch	90	90	86	85	93	97	83	83	102	49	18	876	
Collision with mailbox										5	4	9	
Collision with traffic sign										26	8	34	
Collision with Tree	28	50	35	40	40	24	26	34	35	54	19	385	
Collision with utility pole	12	15	19	18	20	5	16	16	22	4	3	150	
Fire	3338	3611	3573	3514	3717	3480	3350	3643	3760	2460	991	35437	
Immersion	1449	2232	2446	2589	2276	1616	1782	1942	2104	1964	735	21135	
impact with Attenuator										35	8	43	
Jackknife	246	234	208	219	215	193	236	195	226	258	101	2331	
Non-motorist										56	26	82	
Overall/rollover	1684	2869	3923	2822	3003	2101	1947	2474	2664	2158	994	26639	
Parked motor vehicle										72	33	105	
Railway vehicle										29	15	44	
Unknown										483	207	690	

LIGHT_CONDITION
- Dark, roadway lighted
- Dark, roadway not light...
- Dark, unknown lighting
- Dawn
- Daylight
- Dusk
- Unknown

8. To clear the selection, click on the icon to reset all filters in the slicer:

9. To sort the rows by number of crashes, right-click on a cell to bring up the **Sort** menu and then select the sort order you want. Click on the first column under 2015 and **Sort Largest to Smallest**:

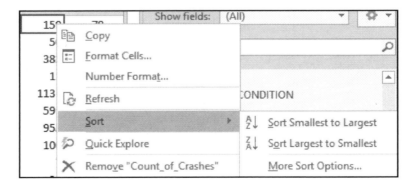

10. To add a filter, right-click and select **Filter** and then the filter option you would like to use. Click on the column header for 2015 and then **Keep Only Selected Items**:

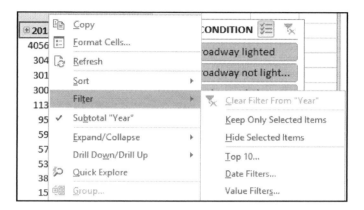

11. You will now have a PivotTable that has a slicer, sort order, and filtering all applied:

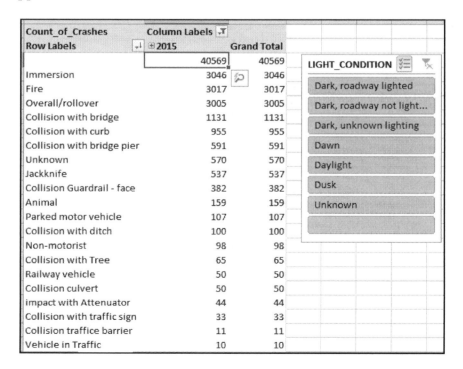

How it works...

Slicers are graphical ways for you to interact with the PivotTable. You selected the field that you wanted to expose as a clickable button. This created the Slicer menu that you can now leverage to filter your dataset in an easier format. Then you sorted the data from largest to smallest by selecting the cell value. Finally, you filtered the data by selecting only the row that you wanted to explore.

Using the timeline filter with pivot tables

In this recipe, you will create a new timeline filter that enables users to quickly choose the time frame that they want to analyze. The timeline filter is easier to use than having to select rows from the pivot table fields.

How to do it...

1. Open Excel and connect to the **Crash_Data_SSASTM** model and create a new pivot table report.
2. Add **WEATHER_CONDITION** to columns, from the **MasterCalendar_T** select **YQMD**, and finally add **Count_of_Crashes** to the values.

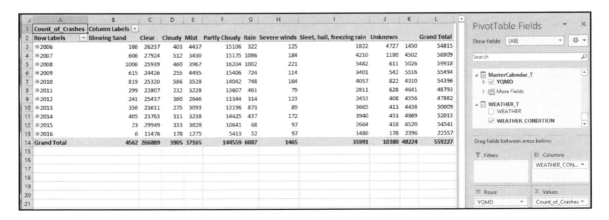

3. Select the **Insert** menu and then in the filter area select **Timeline**.
4. On the **Insert Timelines** windows, select the **MasterCalendar_T** table and click **OK**.

5. A new filter window will be added to your worksheet. Change the dropdown on the right to Years from Months to see all available years. You change your filter criteria by selecting the different hierarchy of the YQMD to change what the slicer shows.

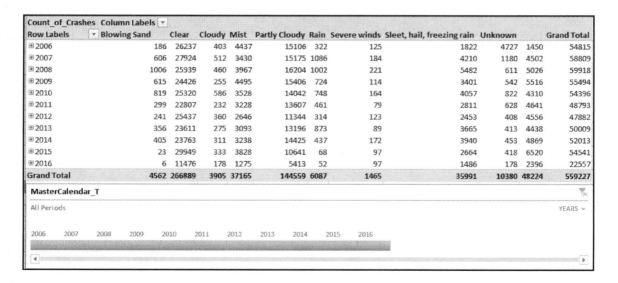

Count_of_Crashes	Column Labels											
Row Labels	Blowing Sand	Clear	Cloudy	Mist	Partly Cloudy	Rain	Severe winds	Sleet, hail, freezing rain	Unknown			Grand Total
2006	186	26237	403	4437	15106	322	125	1822	4727	1450		54815
2007	606	27924	512	3430	15175	1086	184	4210	1180	4502		58809
2008	1006	25939	460	3967	16204	1002	221	5482	611	5026		59918
2009	615	24426	255	4495	15406	724	114	3401	542	5516		55494
2010	819	25320	586	3528	14042	748	164	4057	822	4310		54396
2011	299	22807	232	3228	13607	461	79	2811	628	4641		48793
2012	241	25437	360	2646	11344	314	123	2453	408	4556		47882
2013	356	23611	275	3093	13196	873	89	3665	413	4438		50009
2014	405	23763	311	3238	14425	437	172	3940	453	4869		52013
2015	23	29949	333	3828	10641	68	97	2664	418	6520		54541
2016	6	11476	178	1275	5413	52	97	1486	178	2396		22557
Grand Total	4562	266889	3905	37165	144559	6087	1465	35991	10380	48224		559227

MasterCalendar_T

All Periods

2006   2007   2008   2009   2010   2011   2012   2013   2014   2015   2016

YEARS ▾

6. To interact with the data, select the years that you want to focus your analysis on. Select **2010** to see only that year's data.

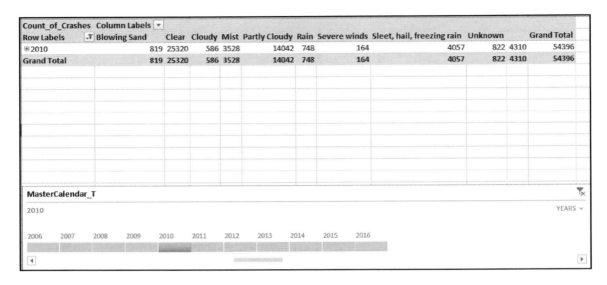

Count_of_Crashes	Column Labels ▾											
Row Labels ▾	Blowing Sand	Clear	Cloudy	Mist	Partly Cloudy	Rain	Severe winds	Sleet, hail, freezing rain	Unknown			Grand Total
⊞ 2010	819	25320	586	3528	14042	748	164	4057	822	4310		54396
Grand Total	819	25320	586	3528	14042	748	164	4057	822	4310		54396

MasterCalendar_T

2010   YEARS ▾

2006   2007   2008   2009   2010   2011   2012   2013   2014   2015   2016

7. Then select the right side of the **2010** year to get the slider bar and then select **2010** to **2013**.

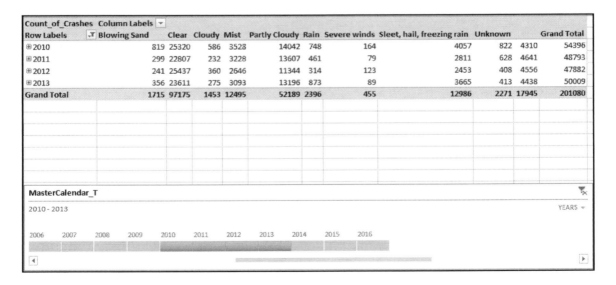

Count_of_Crashes	Column Labels ▾											
Row Labels ▾	Blowing Sand	Clear	Cloudy	Mist	Partly Cloudy	Rain	Severe winds	Sleet, hail, freezing rain	Unknown			Grand Total
⊞ 2010	819	25320	586	3528	14042	748	164	4057	822	4310		54396
⊞ 2011	299	22807	232	3228	13607	461	79	2811	628	4641		48793
⊞ 2012	241	25437	360	2646	11344	314	123	2453	408	4556		47882
⊞ 2013	356	23611	275	3093	13196	873	89	3665	413	4438		50009
Grand Total	1715	97175	1453	12495	52189	2396	455	12986	2271	17945		201080

MasterCalendar_T

2010 - 2013   YEARS ▾

2006   2007   2008   2009   2010   2011   2012   2013   2014   2015   2016

How it works...

In this recipe, you connected Excel to the tabular model. Then you created a timeline filter that uses the **MasterCalendar_T** table's YQMD hierarchy. You are using the predefined hierarchy in the model for the date control with the relationship between each hierarchy level established. The timeline filter leverages the relationships and allows for easy viewing of the data in the Excel sheet. For the first example, you selected the year 2010 and reviewed how the filter worked. Then you changed the filter selection to use 2010 to 2013 and viewed the results.

Analyzing data with Power View

Power View enables highly flexible analytical views view from within Excel. Users can leverage Power View to create interactive data exploration, visualizations, and presentations. Users who are familiar with pivot tables will quickly be able to leverage Power View. The Power View interface enables faster exploration of data over traditional pivot tables. This recipe will show you how to connect to your model from Excel. You will then see how to build and interact with Power View against the data.

How to do it...

1. Open a new worksheet in Excel and select the **Data** menu. Then **Get External Data**, **From Other Sources**, and select **From Analysis Services**.

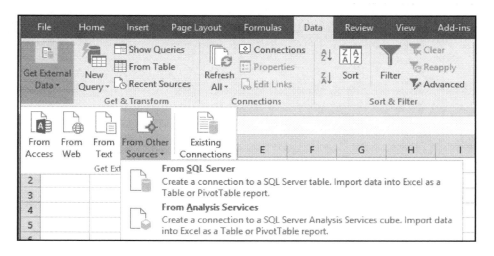

2. On the **Data Connection Wizard**, enter your server name (this example uses WIN-6D5CGQH9KL9) and your **Log on Credentials**, then click **Next**.

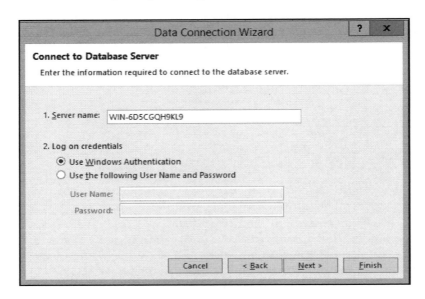

3. Select the**Crash_Data_SSASTM** database, then the**Crash_Data_Model**, and then click **Next**.

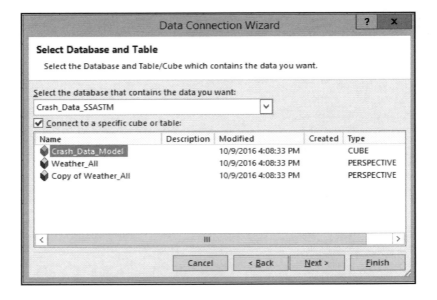

4. Review your connection information and then click **Finish**.

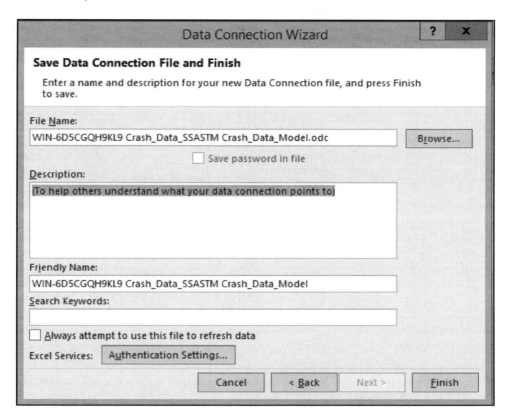

5. On the **Import Data** window, choose **Power View Report** and **New Worksheet** and then**OK** to have your data ready to view.

6. A new Power View1 worksheet is opened in Excel with connections to the data in the tabular model.

7. Then select the **LIGHT_CONDITION** and **Count_of_Crashes** from the Power View fields to create a simple data grid.

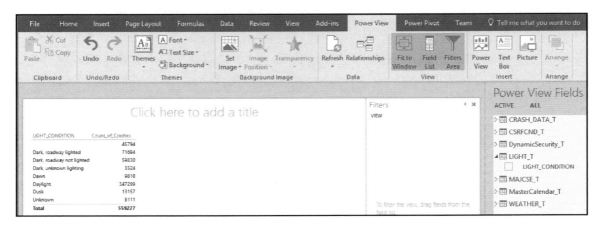

8. To change the data grid to a chart click on the field on the grid to bring up the **DESIGN** menu. Then choose **Bar Chart** and **Stacked Bar**.

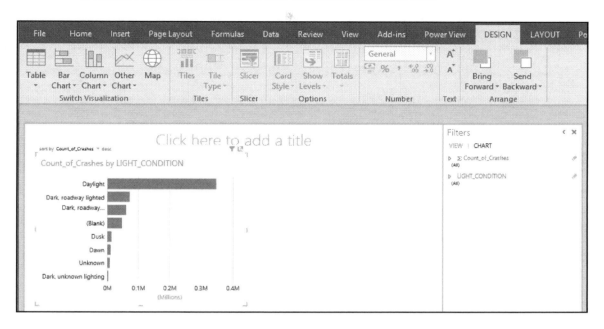

9. Now add another data grid by dragging the **MAJOR_CAUSE** and **Count_of_Crashes** from the **Power View Fields** to a blank area on the **Power View1** sheet.

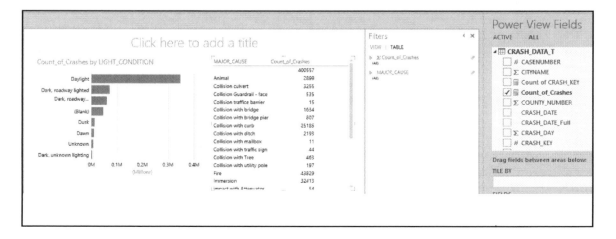

10. To see how the filtering works, click on the **Dark, roadway lighted** graph and you will see the major cause data grid be filtered at the same time.

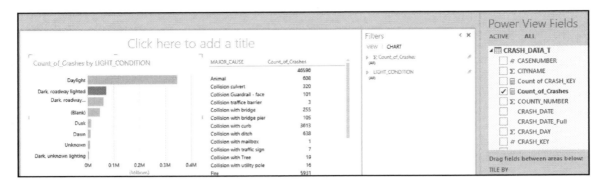

How it works...

You connected Excel directly to the tabular model and launched the Power View interface. Then you explored the data and created a data grid report that showed the number of crashes by light conditions. Then you changed the data grid to a bar graph. To show how the interactivity works, you added a new data grid that shows the number of crashes by major cause. Then by selecting a light condition on the bar graph, you filtered the major cause data grid to only those crashes related to the light condition of **Dark, Roadway lighted**.

There's more...

Power View has many more functions and features that allow users to easily interact with data. There are options to create maps, different types of graphs, and sorting features. To get the most from this feature in Excel, take the time to explore and see how you can leverage it to perform better data analysis.

Importing data with Power Pivot

Power Pivot is an add-in for Excel that enables business users to create models using disparate data sources. Once the data is gathered, you can build PivotTables, PivotCharts, or Power View reports. For example, a user could import internal business data and mash it up with external data to create an analytical model to share with others in the company. Instead of requiring IT to be involved in building the solution, PowerPivot empowers users to go beyond requirements and actually build a solution. If the solution is required for the enterprise, the PowerPivot model can be used as the basis for the tabular model deployed to the server.

Getting ready

Before you can use PowerPivot for the first time, you will need to enable it in Microsoft Excel:

1. Open Excel and go to **File** | **Options** and then **Add-Ins**.
2. In the **Manage** dropdown, select **COM Add-ins**, and then click **Go....**

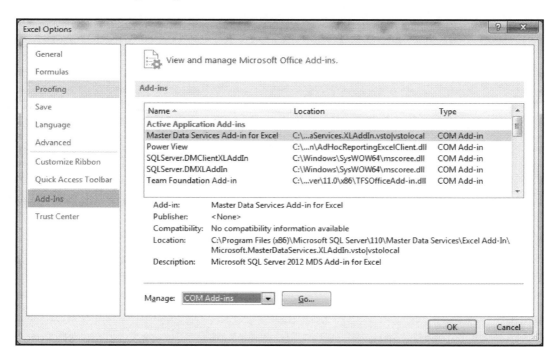

3. Select **Microsoft Power Pivot for Excel** and click **OK**.

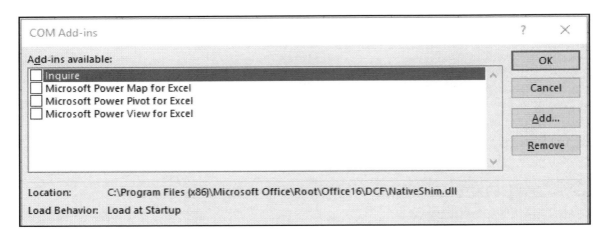

4. You will now have a new menu option in Excel – **Power Pivot**.

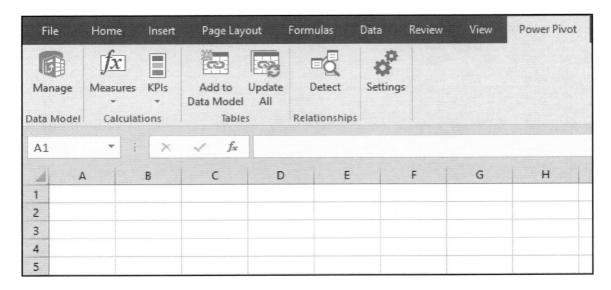

5. You have now enabled Power Pivot. Click on **Manage** to begin working with **Power Pivot**. This will bring up the model window where you add data to your model.

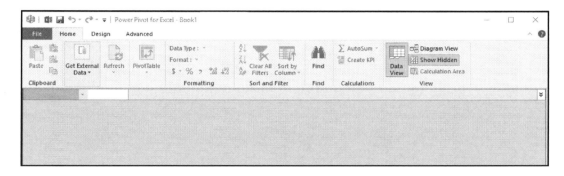

6. Click on **Manage and Get External Data**, select **SQL Server**, and then connect to your **Crash_Data_DB** database.

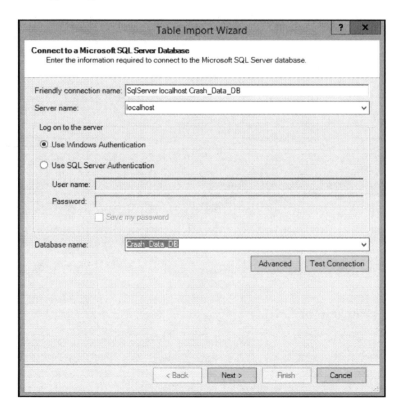

7. Accept the default setting and then click **Next**.

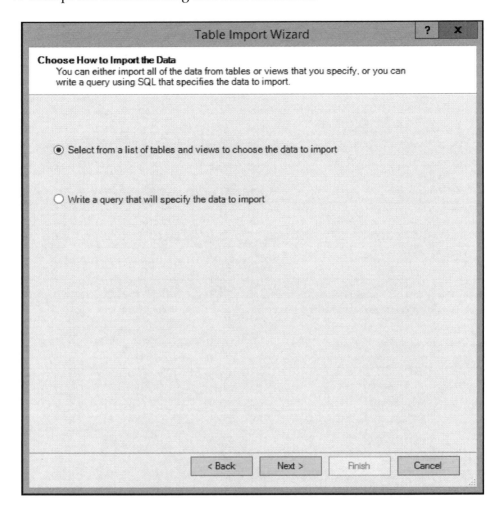

8. Then select **CRASH_DATA_T, LIGHT_T,** and **WEATHER_T,** and then click **Finish**.

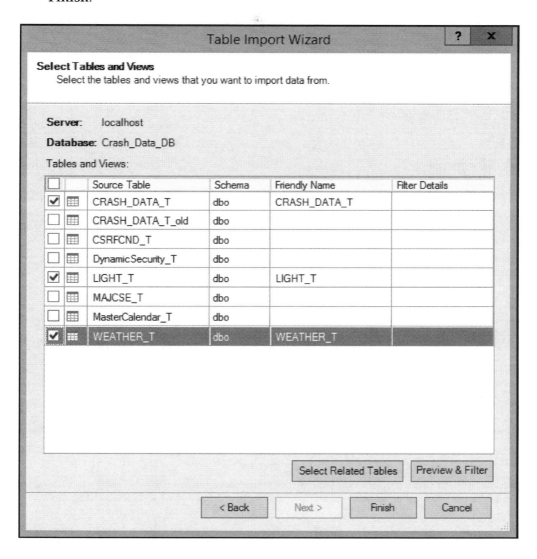

9. Upon completion, the data is imported into your Power Pivot model locally.

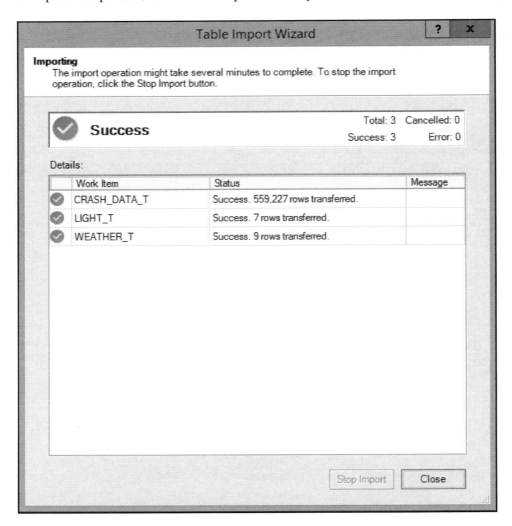

How it works...

In this recipe, you set up Excel to add the PowerPivot add-in. By selecting the COM Add-ins, you reviewed the available options and then selected PowerPivot. Then once enabled you connected to an SQL Server database and imported data from three tables into your PowerPivot model. The PowerPivot model is now ready for use within Excel.

Modeling data with Power Pivot

Getting ready

Follow the steps in the Importing data with Power Pivot recipe to get your Excel environment ready.

How to do it...

1. Click on the **Manage** icon from the Power Pivot menu button to bring up the data you just loaded.

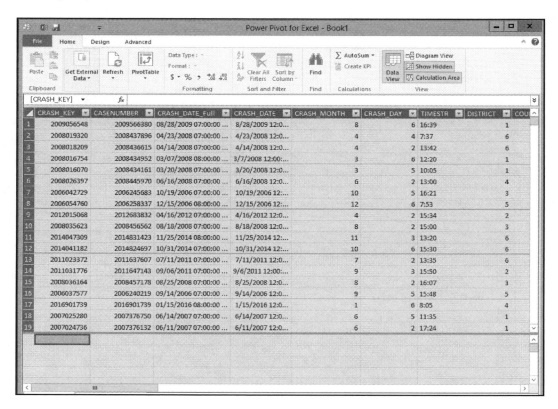

2. Click on a blank cell to create a new measure
   called Count_of_Crashes, Count_of_Crashs:=COUNT([CASENUMBER]), and
   then press **Enter**.

3. You will now have a new measure added to your model.

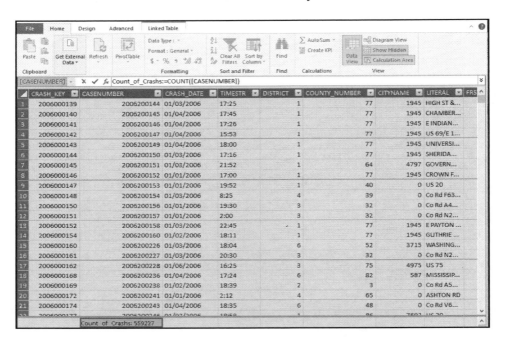

4. Next switch to the Diagram View in the upper right corner to show the tables
   loaded in the model.

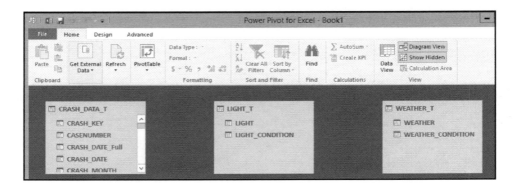

5. Now you need to create relationships between the tables to enable DAX calculations to work properly. Drag the **LIGHT** column from **LIGHT_T** to the **LIGHT** column in **CRASH_DATA_T**. Then do the same for **WEATHER**, from **WEATHER_T** to **WEATHER** in the **CRASH_DATA_T** table to create the relationships.

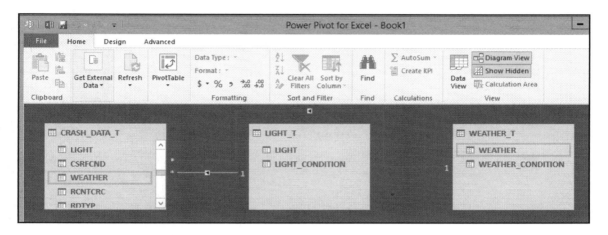

6. Next create a Pivot Table chart to show the data. Select **PivotTable**, then **Two Charts (Horizontal)**, and then select **New Worksheet** on the next window.
7. Finally, you are ready to create charts in your worksheet.

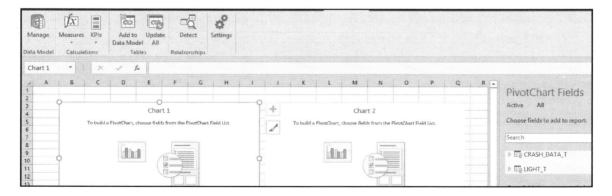

8. Select **Chart 1** and then move **WEATHER_CONDITION** to the **Axis** and then **Count_of_Crashes** to the **Values**. Then select **Chart 2** and move **LIGHT_CONDITION** to the axis and **Count_of_Crashes** to values to create two charts.

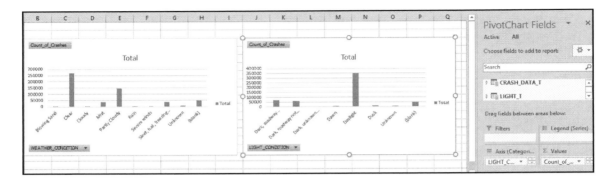

How it works...

After importing data from an SQL database into Power Pivot you created a calculation to find the number of crashes in the data. Then you modeled the relationship between the tables by adding a new relationship between the **WEATHER_CONDITION** and the **Crash_Data_T** table. You then created another relationship between the **LIGHT_CONDITION** and the **Crash_Data_T** table. Finally, you created graphs on the data that show how the relationships interact with each other by displaying the **Count_of_Crashes** for both light and weather conditions.

Adding data to Power Pivot

Now that you have a working model in PowerPivot, you will enhance your SQL Server data that was imported with new external data that is stored in Excel. You will add new data from an Excel sheet that contains codes for two other columns. This is an example of how users can continue to enhance corporate data and make the model more useful for all people that need to leverage the data.

Getting ready

This recipe requires the `Crash_Data_PowerPivot_new_tables.xlsx` Excel data that is available from the Packt Publishing site.

How to do it...

1. Open your model by clicking the **Manage** icon in PowerPivot to bring up the model window.
2. Select **Get External Data** and **From Other Sources,** scroll to the bottom and select **Excel file,** and then click **Next.**

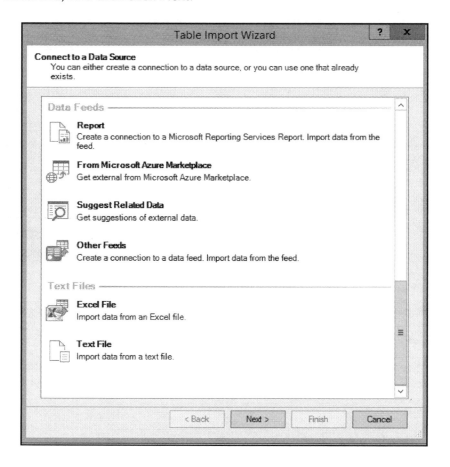

3. Select the **Use first row as column headers** and then **Next>**. Then select
CRASH_SEVERITY and **MANNER_of_CRASH** to add those tables to your
model and select **Finish**.

4. Now switch to the Diagram View and build a relationship from the new tables
you just imported. Drag **Severity_ID** from **CRASH_SEVERITY** to CSEV in
CRASH_DATA_T. Then drag **Manner_of_Crash_ID** to CRCOMNNR
in **CRASH_DATA_T**.

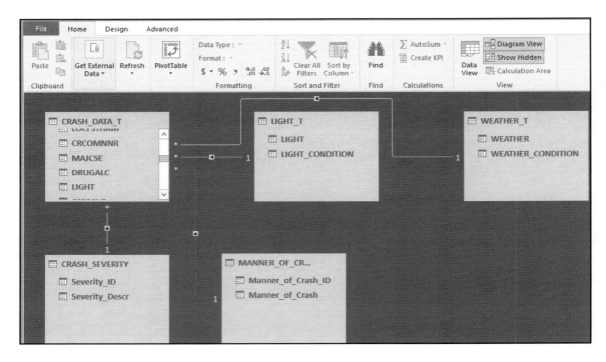

5. To test the new tables, select PivotTable and then **Two charts (Vertical)** and **New
Worksheet**, and then **OK**.

6. Drag **Severity_Description** to **Axis** and **Count_of_Crashes** to **Values** on the top chart. Then select the bottom chart and drag **Manner_of_Crash** and **Count_of_Crashes** to **Values** to produce graphs based on the old and new data.

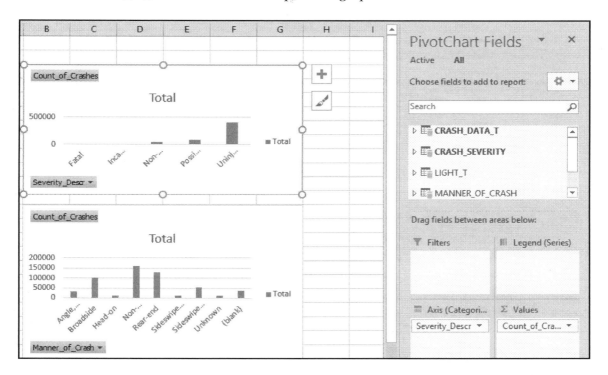

How it works...

This recipe extends the base data by adding new data sources from an Excel file and mashing them together with the existing SQL database tables that were originally imported. You imported the **CRASH_SEVERITY** and **MANNER_OF_CRASH** data and then created the required relationships in the model. Finally, you created new Pivot Charts that leverage the data to show how the model responds. You now have a working model that combines data from two sources. If additional data was required, importing the data is the method to continue to extend your model.

Moving Power Pivot models to the enterprise

Having your business users create Power Pivot models enables quicker collaboration between IT and business needs. Users are able to source data, model the relations, create calculations, and then analyze the results. IT developers can then take the Excel book and start a project with many pieces already in place, and move the model to production using the organizations **software development lifecycle** (**SDLC**) process.

There are several reasons why you will need to move your user-created model to an SSAS solution. First, Excel is currently limited to workbook sizes of 2 GB. When users are accessing the data from the SSAS model, there is no limitation on the size of the data. The SSAS model could hold terabytes of data and users can access over the 2 GB limit of Excel. In addition, once the model is moved to SSAS, you can implement security at the server level. Then users across the enterprise that have access can leverage the model.

Moving Power Pivot to SSAS via Management Studio

Once you have a developed Power Pivot solution that you would like to move to SSAS, you can save a copy of your Excel workbook and place it in the SSAS backup folder location. Then use the Excel file as the basis for the SSAS model.

How to do it...

1. Open the Chapter 8 Power Pivot Excel workbook.

2. Save a copy of the file as the `Crash_Data_PowerPivot_SSAS` workbook, and then copy or move the file to the backup location of your SSAS server. In this example, the folder is `c:\Program Files\Microsoft SQL Server\MSAS13.MSSQLSERVER\OLAP\Backup`.

3. Open SQL Server Management Studio and connect to your tabular instance. Expand the Server menu to see the folders.

4. Right-click on **Databases** to bring up the menu window, and then select **Restore from PowerPivot...**.

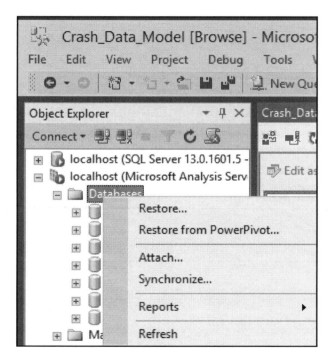

5. In the **Restore from PowerPivot...** window, update the options to create the
   database from the Excel file. In the **Restore Source** section, to restore the file you
   just saved in step 2, select the folder with the **OLAP\Backup** and then select the
   `Crash_Data_PowerPivot_SSAS.xlsx` file and select **OK**.

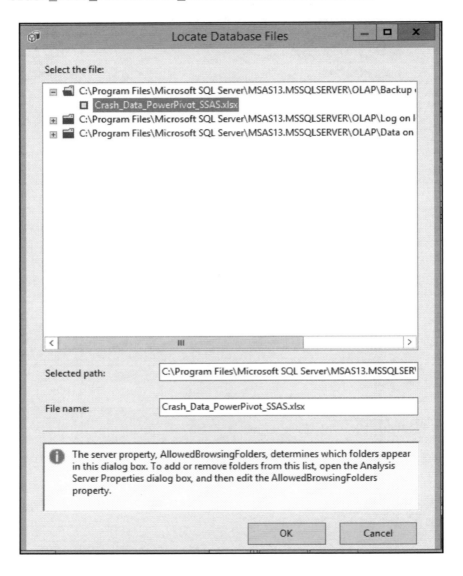

6. Then in the **Restore Target** section, type `SSAS_from_PowerPivot` in the **Restore database** field to create a new database from the file. If you had an existing database that you wanted to restore the PowerPivot file to, you would select it from the drop-down list. Next, in the storage location field, select the browse button and then select the location to use for the data file.

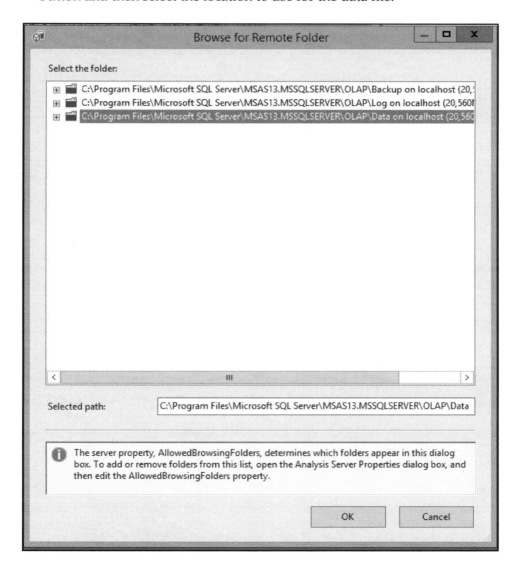

7. Now that the source and restoration fields are completed, on the main window select **OK** to start the import process.

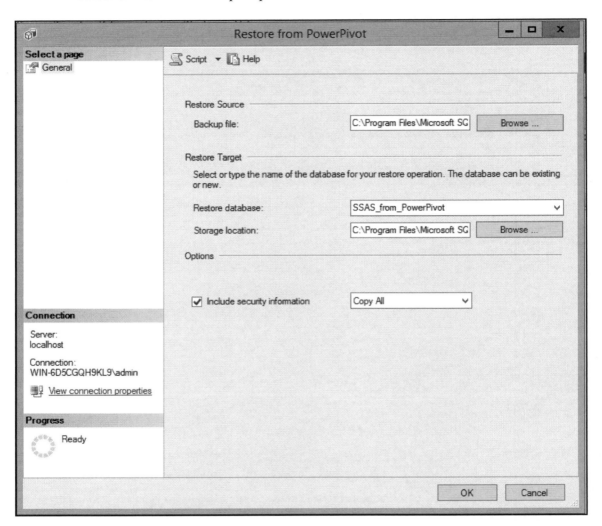

8. Once completed, right-click on the **Databases** folder in SSMS, and then you will see your new model – **SSAS_from_PowerPivot**.

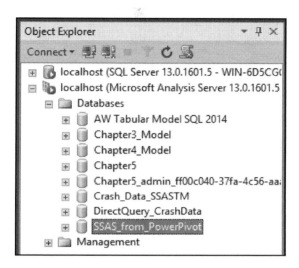

9. To test the model, right-click on **SSAS_from_PowerPivot**, and then select **Browse**. In the **Browse** window, drag over the **Count_of_Crashes** and the **Manner_of_Crash** to see the data that you added in Excel now being used in SSAS.

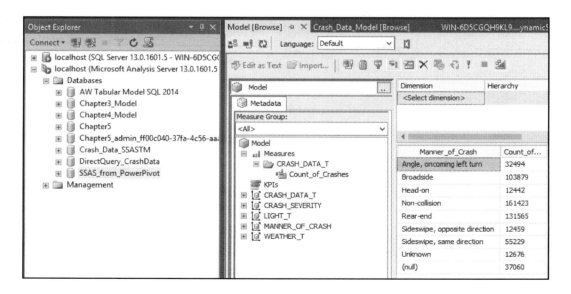

How it works...

In this recipe, you used the SQL Server Management Studio option to restore a tabular model from an Excel database. First you opened an Excel workbook that contained a Power Pivot model and saved it to the SSAS backup folder. Then you switched to SQL Server Management Studio and used the **Restore from PowerPivot...** option to bring up the **option** window. Next you chose the location to use as the source and typed in the new SSAS tabular model to restore the Excel file along with the location to store the data. Finally, you completed the import and then refreshed SQL Server Management Studio. By viewing the data, you were able to ensure that the new model was created and the data you added was present in the model.

Moving Power Pivot to SSAS via SQL Server Data Tools

The other option to migrate Power Pivot models to SSAS is through the SQL Server Data Tools in Visual Studio. This option uses the import from the PowerPivot template to take the model from the Excel file and load it into a new Visual Studio project. Developers would use this mode to create a solution in Visual Studio and then be able to follow the normal SDLC process and version control that they do for other projects.

How to do it...

1. Open Visual Studio and create a new project and then select the **Business Intelligence** installed templates to find **Import from PowerPivot**. Change the name to **SSAS_PP_from_SSDT** and select **OK**.

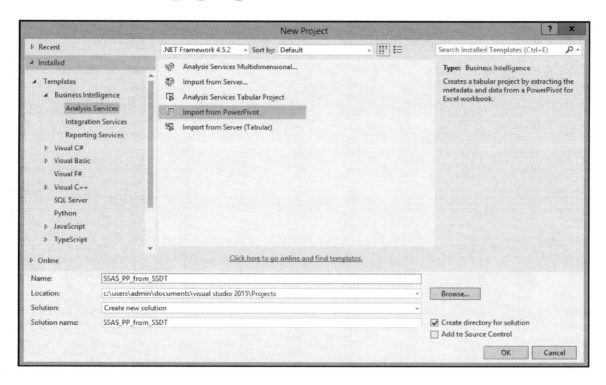

2. On the next screen, select the **Workspace server** if asked and click **OK**.

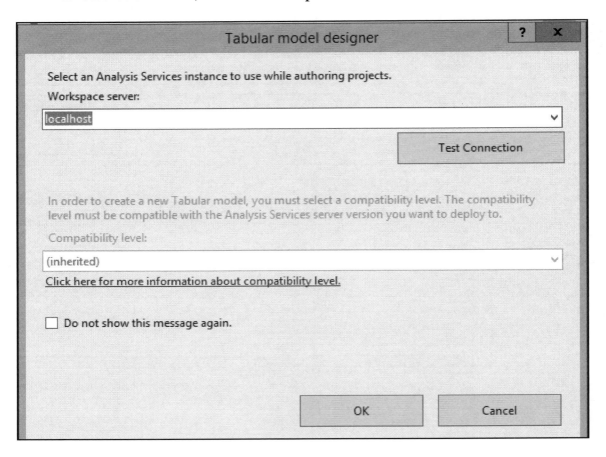

3. Now select the location and file for your Excel workbook that has a Power Pivot model and select **Open**. In this recipe, the workbook is on the desktop labeled **Chapter 8 PowerPivot**. Once this is selected click **OK**.

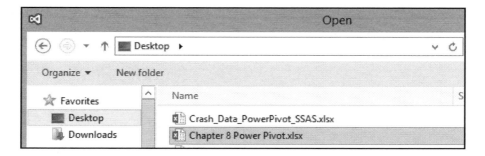

4. The data will be imported into a new project in Visual Studio. To see that the model imports the data and relationships, change to the Diagram View and you will see the tables with the relationships that you built in Excel Power Pivot.

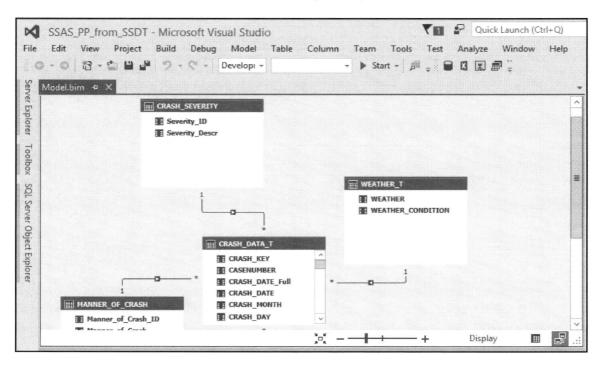

How it works...

In this recipe, you opened Visual Studio and then created a new project using the installed import from the PowerPivot template. You then selected the Excel file that has a Power Pivot model. Visual studio then imported the model and created a project with the data and all features that were built in Power Pivot. Finally, you switched to the Diagram View and ensured that the relationships were imported correctly.

9
DAX Syntax and Calculations

In this chapter, we will cover the following recipes:

- Understanding DAX formulas
- Using the AutoSum measure in Visual Studio
- Creating calculated measures
- Creating calculated columns
- Using the IF function
- Using the AND function
- Using the SWITCH function
- Using the CONCATENATE function
- Using the LEFT function
- Using the RELATED function
- Using the RELATEDTABLE function
- Using EVALUATE in DAX queries
- Filtering based on a value
- Filtering a related table
- Using ALL to remove filters
- Using ALL to calculate a percentage
- Using the SUMMARIZE function
- Adding columns to the SUMMARIZE function
- Using ROLLUP with the SUMMARIZE function

Introduction

This chapter will explore how to leverage **Data Analysis Expressions (DAX)** in Power Pivot, tabular models, and SQL Server Management Studio. DAX is a formula-based language similar to functions in Excel that allows you to create calculations and queries. When designing models, you will leverage these formulas to enhance the model to make it easier for users to leverage. There are two ways to add DAX into your model, either as a calculated column or a calculate measure. When you create a calculated column you apply a function that evaluates each row independently and returns the result. Calculated measures are applied to the table and column by using functions to determine the result based on the context. In addition, you can use DAX to query your model much like using T-SQL to query a relational database.

 There are several categories of DAX functions designed to perform a variety of calculations. These include logical, aggregation, text, mathematical, statistical, date and time, and time intelligence functions.

When a DAX formula is calculated, it is evaluated in its context. There are two types of context that apply in DAX: row and filter context. Row context applies to cells in a row, such as creating a calculated column. The DAX expression is calculated on each row separately. The concept of filter context refers to any filtering that has been applied that affects the results returned from the model. In previous recipes, you have created basic DAX calculations to count the number of crashes in the Iowa crash data using the COUNT function. For example, the **Count_of_Crashes** measure when originally applied gives the total of **559,227**. As you apply other filters, the DAX expression is recalculated based on the new filter context. For instance, when you query the data through a tool such as Power View and use different columns, the formula is recalculated based on the new rows. In this example, the formula is filtered by the **LIGHT_T** table using the same calculation. The evaluation context applies the expression to each row in the **LIGHT_T** table to calculate the count of crashes by **LIGHT_CONDITION**.

LIGHT_CONDITION	Count_of_Crashes
	45794
Dark, roadway lighted	71694
Dark, roadway not lighted	59830
Dark, unknown lighting	3524
Dawn	9818
Daylight	347299
Dusk	13157
Unknown	8111
Total	**559227**

In this chapter, you will explore more capabilities of the DAX language to continue to enhance the Iowa crash data model developed in `Chapter 8`, *Combining Tabular Models with Excel*.

Understanding DAX formulas

There are two basic types of DAX formulas. The most common one that you will use performs a function on the data to return a value. The other returns data as a table most commonly used to create a new dataset or is used as input for another function. To create any DAX formula, you need to understand the basic syntax. This recipe explains how the **Count_of_Crashes** formula works and creates the formula using Power Pivot in Excel.

Getting ready

This recipe will use the **Chapter 9 Power Pivot.xlsx** workbook available from the Packt Publishing website.

How to do it...

1. Open the **Chapter 9 Power Pivot.xlsx** workbook and click on the Power Pivot menu.
2. Then select the **Measures** tab and **New Measure**.

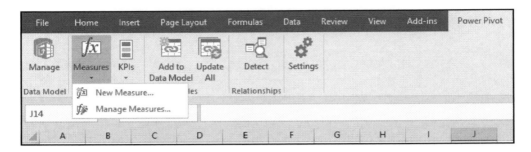

3. The **Measure** window will open.

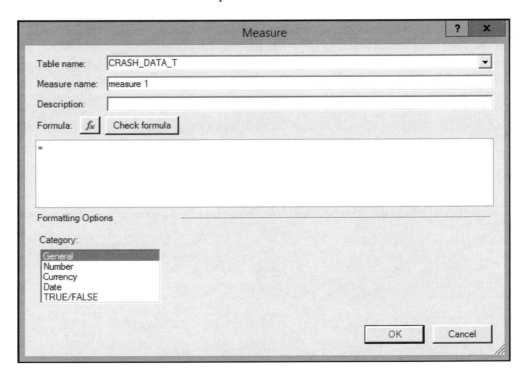

4. Enter **Count_of_Crashes** in the **Measure Name**, and in the **Formula** area enter

   ```
   =COUNT([CASENUMBER])
   ```

5. Finally, change the **Category** to **Number**, **Format** to **Whole Number**, and check the **Use 1000 seperator (,)**, and hit **OK** to close the window.

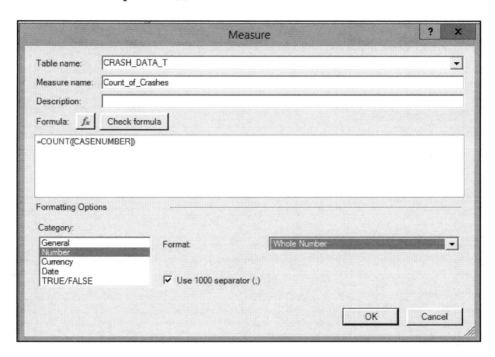

How it works...

In this recipe, you opened the Excel workbook and switched to Power Pivot. Then you opened the **Measures** menu, created a new measure, and then updated the formatting. The formatting was changed to always display this measure in whole numbers using the 1000 separator. Since this is done in the model, whenever someone uses this field in Excel, it will be automatically shown using the applied formatting. The basic syntax of DAX is shown in this formula =COUNT(<column>). Every function begins with an equal sign and the function name followed by the argument to pass to the function. In this recipe, you passed the COUNT function the column of CASENUMBER as the argument. The function then counts the number of rows that have a CASENUMBER and returns the result.

There's more...

To edit an existing calculation in Power Pivot, go back to the Power Pivot tab and then select the **Measures** menu. Select **Manage Measures** and a list of existing measures is shown. Select the measure you want to edit and then select **Edit** on the top window. To delete a measure, select the measure and then select **Delete**.

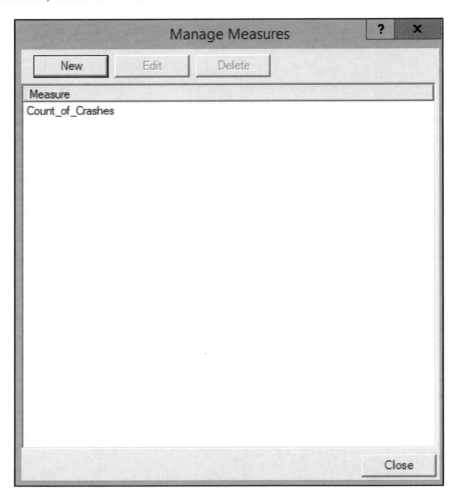

Using the AutoSum measure in Visual Studio

It is common when building a new model or enhancing an existing model that you will need to apply formatting onto various columns. Updating the formats in the model prevents users from needing to modify the format each time to access the model. For example, to determine the number of records in a table using a record ID column that is numerical would need to be aggregated with a COUNT function and not a SUM function. This behavior when set at the model level affects how everyone using the model sees the data. When designing your model in Visual Studio, there is an option to quickly apply one of six predefined common functions to numerical columns:

- Sum
- Average
- Count
- DistinctCount
- Max
- Min

This option is very helpful when you need to add calculations on several columns quickly that are numerical data types.

How to do it...

1. Open the Visual Studio solution for your crash data tabular model.
2. Select the **CRASH_DATA_T** table in the Grid View and then scroll to the right to find the **FATALITIES, INJURIES, MAJINJURY, MININJURY, POSSINJURY,** and **UNKINJURY** columns.

3. Hold down *Shift* and then select the five columns.

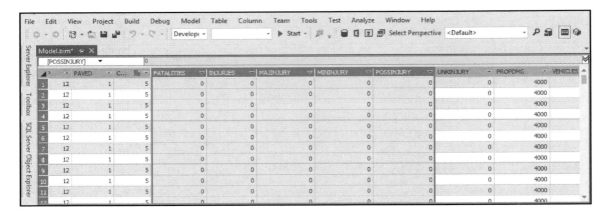

4. Each of these columns are whole numbers and are currently being summarized by the default function on the model. To change them to be summarized by the SUM function, select the **AutoSum** icon and then **Sum**.

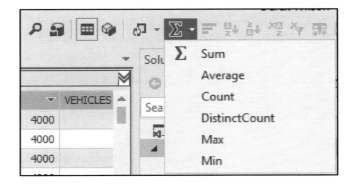

5. Five new measures will be added to the model, one beneath each column chosen in step 3. Each column will be named *Sum of* with the column name.

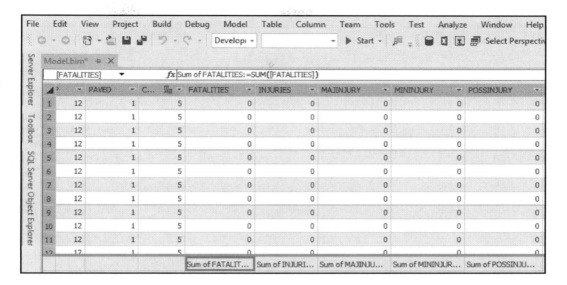

6. To update the format to show thousand separators and display as a whole number, while all of the columns are selected, update the **Properties** window and change the **Data Format** to **Whole Number** and then the **Show Thousand Separator** to **True**. The numbers are now set to use this format in all client tools.

7. To change the name of the new measures, change the text on the left side of := in the formula bar. For example, change Sum of FATALITIES:=SUM([FATALITIES]) to Total Fatalities:=SUM([FATALITIES]). The measure will now show the new name and totals.

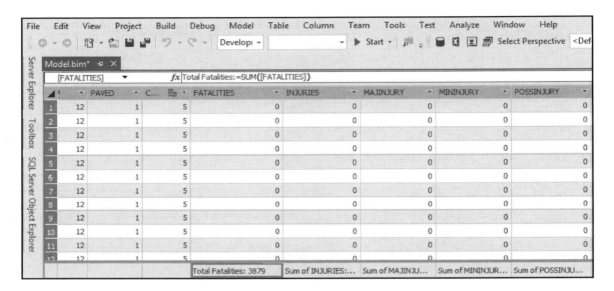

How it works...

In this recipe, you created five new measures in your model. You selected the **CRASH_DATA_T** table and then five columns that are numerical. Next, you used the AutoSum feature to quickly create five new summary measures. Finally, you renamed a column to make the name more meaningful for your users.

Creating calculated measures

Calculated measures are formulas that do more than simple aggregations of values. These formulas add additional information to the tabular model by creating business calculations. In addition, calculated measures are calculated based on the filter context applied to the data. For example, using a row or column filter in Excel PivotTables or Power View. Depending upon the filters selected, the DAX expression is calculated using the information of the filter in real time. In this recipe, you will use a measure that has the total number of fatal crashes. You will then create a new measure that calculates the total number of crashes minus the number of fatalities.

Getting ready

Follow the steps in the *Using Autosum measures in Visual Studio* recipe to create the **Total Fatalities** measure.

How to do it...

1. On the **CRASH_DATA_T** table in the Grid view, select an empty cell under the **Count_of_Crashes** measure.
2. Enter the calculation in the formula bar:

```
Total_NonFatal_Crashes:=([Count_of_Crashes] - [Total
Fatalities])
```

3. Once you have entered the calculation, hit **Enter**.

	CRASH_KEY	CASENUMBER	CRASH_DATE_Full	CRASH_DATE
1	2009056548	2009566380	08/28/2009 07:00:00 AM ...	8/28/2009 12:00:0...
2	2008019320	2008437896	04/23/2008 07:00:00 AM ...	4/23/2008 12:00:0...
3	2008018209	2008436615	04/14/2008 07:00:00 AM ...	4/14/2008 12:00:0...
4	2008016754	2008434952	03/07/2008 08:00:00 AM ...	3/7/2008 12:00:00 ...
5	2008016070	2008434161	03/20/2008 07:00:00 AM ...	3/20/2008 12:00:0...
6	2008026397	2008445970	06/16/2008 07:00:00 AM ...	6/16/2008 12:00:0...
7	2006042729	2006245683	10/19/2006 07:00:00 AM ...	10/19/2006 12:00:...
8	2006054760	2006258337	12/15/2006 08:00:00 AM ...	12/15/2006 12:00:...
9	2012015068	2012683832	04/16/2012 07:00:00 AM ...	4/16/2012 12:00:0...
10	2008035623	2008456562	08/18/2008 07:00:00 AM ...	8/18/2008 12:00:0...
11	2014047309	2014831423	11/25/2014 08:00:00 AM ...	11/25/2014 12:00:...
12	2014041182	2014824697	10/31/2014 07:00:00 AM	10/31/2014 12:00:

Model.bim*

[CRASH_KEY] ▼   *fx* Total_NonFatal_Crashes:=([Count_of_Crashes]-[Total Fatalities])

Count_of_Crashes: 559227

Total_NonFatal_Crashes: 555348

4. To correct the formatting to make it better for users, select the **Total_NonFatal_Crashes** in the **Measures** window and change the following fields in the **Properties** window. Change the **Format** to **Whole Number** and the **Show Thousand Separator** to **True**.

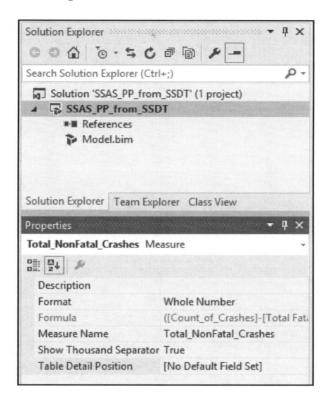

How it works...

In this recipe, you created a calculated measure that uses two other measures. To determine the number of non-fatal crashes in the data, you subtracted the number of fatalities from the total number of records. Your users now have the option of looking at the total number of crashes, total fatalities, and total crashes less fatalities. In the **Properties** window, you updated the formatting to only show whole numbers and include the thousand separator, making it easier for your client tools and users to better use the data.

Creating calculated columns

When creating DAX formulas, there are two ways to apply them to the model. The first is to create a calculated column. When you add a calculated column to the model, it applies the function on a row-by-row basis. For example, if you want to parse the datetime format of a table to only show the current year, adding a new calculated column would evaluate the formula on the date column and add it to a new column on the table evaluated once for each row in the table. When the data is refreshed, the formula is evaluated on the table and no user interaction is required for the formula to be applied to its context.

How to do it...

1. Open Visual Studio and the tabular model project.
2. On the **CRASH_DATA_T** table, review the **CRASH_DATE** column. It is a Date column that includes a timestamp.

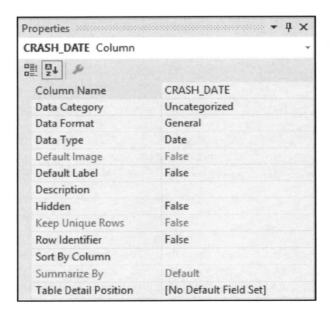

3. Scroll to the end of the CRASH_DATA_T table and enter the DAX expression to parse the year from the **Crash_date** column:

```
=YEAR(CRASH_DATA_T[CRASH_DATE])
```

4. The tabular engine will now immediately parse the expression and add it to the column. Change the name by updating the **Column Name** in the **Properties** window to **Crash_Year**.

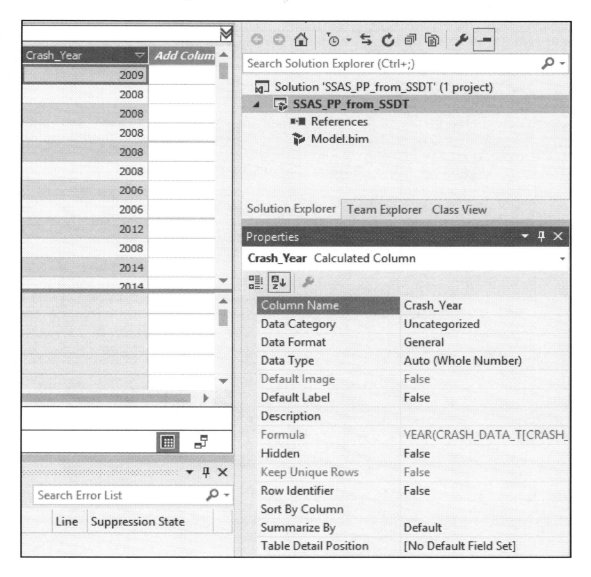

How it works...

In this recipe, you added a new calculated column. The DAX expression uses the YEAR function and applies it to the **Crash_Date** column, the required argument. This parses the column to return only the four-digit year to the column. You then updated the column name to **Crash_Year** to make it easier for reports to leverage.

There's more...

As an additional step, you can concatenate text with the YEAR function to add context to the values in the table. You can leverage the & symbol to join the data together. To add a label before the **Crash_Year**, you modify the formula to include the following: `="Year of Crash: " & YEAR(CRASH_DATA_T[CRASH_DATE])`.

Once completed, your column will be updated to include the text with the date.

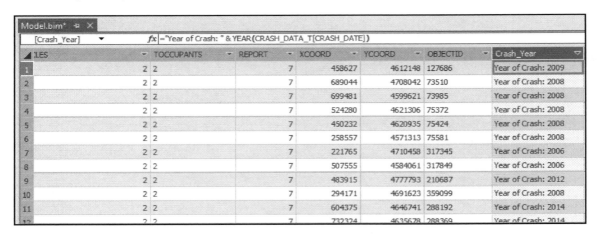

The addition of more detailed information to the columns can make the reports easier to leverage. The more descriptive a field will help enable a self-service BI environment. When building a report in Power View, the data is clearly displayed in the **Crash_Year** column with the content.

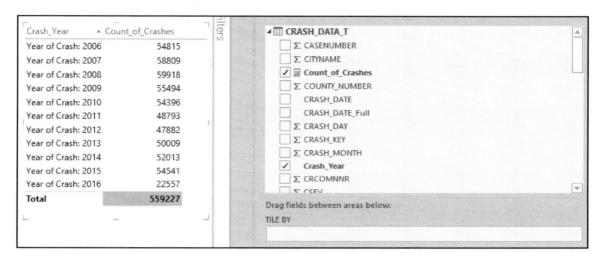

Using the IF function

DAX includes several functions that are classified as logical functions. These functions let you apply conditions to your calculations and measures when required. Some of the more common functions that you will use include IF, AND, and SWITCH. Recipes for each of these functions will be provided in this section.

The IF function performs a logical test to return either true or false when the condition is met. In this recipe, you will add a formula that creates a label on each row. This label will let your users know which rows had fatalities or were non-fatal. The IF function has a required syntax of IF(<logical_test>,<value_if_true>,<value_if_false>).

Getting ready

All of these recipes will use the **Chapter_9_DAX** tabular model to add calculations. The sample model is available to download.

How to do it...

1. Open the **Chapter_9_DAX** solution, and select the **CRASH_DATA_T** table and make sure you are in the data Grid view.
2. Scroll to the right until you find **Add Column**. Then in the expression box, add the formula to determine fatality type and press Enter to create the calculation. You will then see a label added to each row:

   ```
   =IF( [FATALITIES]>=1, "Was Fatal", "Non Fatal")
   ```

3. On the **Properties** window, change the **Column Name** from **Add Column** to **Fatality Flag**.

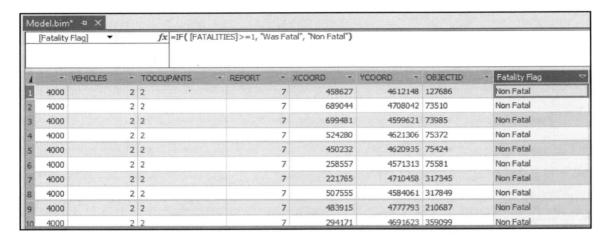

How it works...

In this recipe, the IF function is checking for the condition on each row of the number of fatalities being greater than or equal to 1. On each row that matches this condition, the label of **Was Fatal** is added to the row. On all other rows, the label of **Non Fatal** is added.

Using the AND function

The AND function is similar to the IF function. When you use this function, it is checking two arguments at the same time to determine if the condition is true or false. When both arguments are true, then the function returns true. In this recipe, you will add a function on a new column to determine if the record is a single or multiple vehicle fatality. The AND function has a required syntax of AND(<logical1>, <logical2>).

How to do it...

1. Open the **Chapter_9_DAX** solution, select the **CRASH_DATA_T** table, and make sure you are in the data Grid view.

2. Scroll to the right until you find the **Add Column**. Then in the expression box, add the formula to determine the number of vehicles and number of fatalities involved and press **Enter** to create the calculation. You will then see a label added to each row:

   ```
   =IF( And ( [FATALITIES]>=1, [VEHICLES]=1), "Single Vehicle
   Fatality", "Multiple Vehicle Fatality" )
   ```

3. On the **Properties** window, change the **Column Name** from **Add Column** to **Fatality Group**.

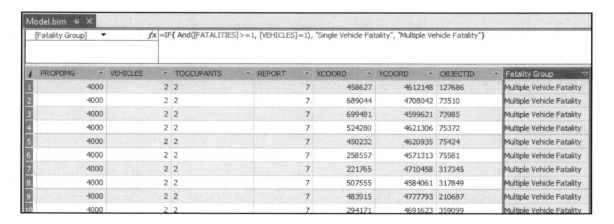

Using the SWITCH function

The SWITCH function is very useful when you need to evaluate an expression and return a result from a list of possible values. In this recipe, you will create a column that can be used to determine if the road was paved or unpaved. This will allow your users to filter the results easily by choosing a label versus a value. The SWITCH function has a required syntax of SWITCH(<expression>,<value>,<result>[, <value>,<result>]).

How to do it...

1. Open the **Chapter_9_DAX** solution, select the **CRASH_DATA_T** table, and make sure you are in the data Grid view.

2. Scroll to the right until you find the **Add Column**. Then in the expression box, add the formula to evaluate each value and return the corresponding label. Then press **Enter** to create the calculation. You will then see a label added to each row:

   ```
   =SWITCH([PAVED], 1, "Paved", 2, "Unpaved", 99, "Unknown")
   ```

3. On the **Properties** window, change the **Column Name** from **Add Column** to **Fatality Group**.

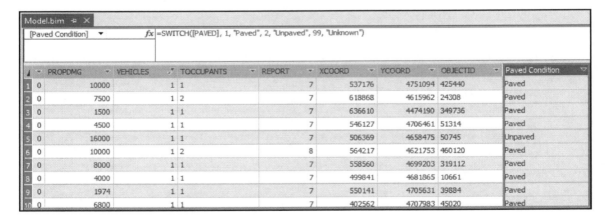

How it works...

In this recipe, you added a formula that creates a label on each row. The SWITCH function you entered has three available values to evaluate in the formula. It works by looking for one of the values (1, 2, 99) and then returning the label that corresponds to each value (Paved, Unpaved, Unknown). The label is then added to the column and can be used in other measures or as a filter.

There's more...

By using the SWITCH function in this recipe, you created a column with unique labels. This could also be accomplished by creating a table that has the same values, and then adding this table to the model as a lookup table with a defined relationship. However, in cases where there are not a lot of values, using the SWITCH function lets you quickly add a value to the model without needing to link additional tables.

Using the CONCATENATE function

DAX includes several functions that are classified as text functions. These functions let you apply and manipulate strings in a variety of ways. Some of the more common functions that you will use include CONCATENATE and LEFT. Recipes for these functions will be provided in this section.

The CONCATENATE function is very useful when you need to join two strings together into a single string. You can join either two columns together or you can join columns to text strings. When using a text string, the value must be enclosed in quotes. In this recipe, you will create a column to join two columns together. This will allow your users to filter the results easily by choosing a label versus a value. The CONCATENATE function has a required syntax of CONCATENATE (<text1>, <text2>).

How to do it…

1. Open the **Chapter_9_DAX** solution, select the **CRASH_DATA_T** table, and make sure you are in the data Grid view.

2. Scroll to the right until you find the **Add Column**. Then in the expression box, add the formula to join the text **Total Property Damage** to the value in the **PROPDMG** column. Then press *Enter* to create the calculation. You will then see a label added to each row:

```
=CONCATENATE("Total Property Damage  $" ,[PROPDMG])
```

3. On the **Properties** window, change the **Column Name** from **Add Column** to **Property Damage**.

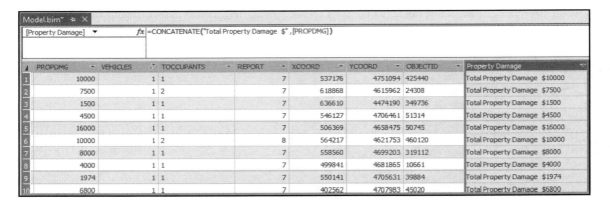

How it works…

This recipe uses the CONCATENATE function to create a new column. This column is created by passing in two arguments, the text "Total Property Damage $" with the value stored in the [PROPDMG].

There's more…

You can also use CONCATENATE in a calculated measure. This can be helpful if you want to add more information to the model or have variations on measures that you want users to understand.

To create a calculated measure that shows all fatalities along with a label, in the measures area, add the following formula:

```
Fatalities_Label:=CONCATENATE("Total Fatalities= ",
CRASH_DATA_T[Nof_Fatalities])
```

Model.bim* ⊣ ×

[CRASH_KEY] ▼   *fx* Fatalities_Label:=CONCATENATE("Total Fatalities= ", CRASH_DATA_T[Nof_Fatalities])

⏀ CRASH_KEY	▼	CASENUMBER	▼	CRASH_DATE_Full	▼	CRASH_DATE	▼	CRASH_MONTH
1	2009056548	2009566380	08/28/2009 07:00:00 AM …	8/28/2009 12:00:0…	
2	2008019320	2008437896	04/23/2008 07:00:00 AM …	4/23/2008 12:00:0…	
3	2008018209	2008436615	04/14/2008 07:00:00 AM …	4/14/2008 12:00:0…	
4	2008016754	2008434952	03/07/2008 08:00:00 AM …	3/7/2008 12:00:00 …	
5	2008016070	2008434161	03/20/2008 07:00:00 AM …	3/20/2008 12:00:0…	
6	2008026397	2008445970	06/16/2008 07:00:00 AM …	6/16/2008 12:00:0…	
7	2006042729	2006245683	10/19/2006 07:00:00 AM …	10/19/2006 12:00:…	
8	2006054760	2006258337	12/15/2006 08:00:00 AM …	12/15/2006 12:00:…	
	2012015068	2012582822	04/16/2012 07:00:00 AM	4/16/2012 12:00:0	

Count_of_Crashes: 559227
Nof_Fatalities: 3879
Fatalities_Label: Total Fatalities= 3879

Using the LEFT Function

The LEFT function is very useful when you need to parse a string to get a subset of the data. This is often used to make the data more meaningful for your users. In this recipe, you will create a column on the **Manner_of_Crash** table to return the first nine letters of each description. Then you will make the LEFT function use a dynamic argument to determine the number of characters to find a comma. On this table, you can now create a hierarchy that would group the two sideswipe rows into a single group. The LEFT function has a required syntax of LEFT(<text>,<num_chars>).

How to do it...

1. Open the **Chapter_9_DAX** solution, select the **CRASH_DATA_T** table, and make sure you are in the data Grid view.

2. Scroll to the right until you find the **Add Column**. Then in the expression box, add the formula to return the first nine characters of the field. Then press **Enter** to create the calculation. You will then see a label added to each row:
   =LEFT([Manner_of_Crash]).

3. On the **Properties** window, change the **Column Name** from **Add Column** to **Manner_Group**.

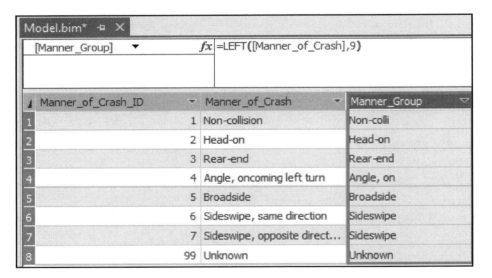

4. Now you only see the first nine characters. The term sideswipe is now consistent on rows 6 and 7; however, rows 1 and 4 are now only showing partial data. To fix the strings to show the full text or the word before the comma, you need to add the FIND function to locate the comma:

```
=LEFT(
  [Manner_of_Crash],
  IFERROR(FIND(",",[Manner_of_Crash],1,20)-1,0)
  )
```

5. Once you have done this, press *Enter*.

[Manner_Group] ▼	*fx* =LEFT([Manner_of_Crash],
	IFERROR(FIND(",",[Manner_of_Crash],1,20)-1,0)
	)

Manner_of_Crash_ID ▾	Manner_of_Crash ▾	Manner_Group ▾
1	1 Non-collision	Non-collision
2	2 Head-on	Head-on
3	3 Rear-end	Rear-end
4	4 Angle, oncoming left turn	Angle
5	5 Broadside	Broadside
6	6 Sideswipe, same direction	Sideswipe
7	7 Sideswipe, opposite direct...	Sideswipe
8	99 Unknown	Unknown

How it works...

This recipe first creates a new column that parses the string and returns the first nine characters of the **Manner_of_Crash**. Once completed, you were able to see that the new column is not parsing all fields to return the full description in cases that have a comma. To correct this, you leveraged the FIND function to locate the position of the comma. The code in part 4 works by making the length of each row dynamic by determining the number of characters to the comma and then subtracting one place. If it does not find a comma, it uses the default length of 20 to pass as the parameter to the LEFT function.

There's more...

If you need to get the data from the end of the column, there is also a RIGHT function that returns the number of characters from the end of a column. The RIGHT function has a required syntax of RIGHT(<text>, <num_chars>).

Using the RELATED function

The RELATED function leverages the relationships built in the model Diagram view. In this model, there is a one to many relationship between the **LIGHT_T** table and the **CRASH_DATA_T** table. The RELATED function is applied on the many table (**CRASH_DATA_T**) and performs a lookup on the one table (**LIGHT_T**).

This recipe uses the RELATED function to create a new calculated column. This column will add the label from the **LIGHT_T** table to the **CRASH_DATA_T** table. This can be helpful when you have a frequently used column and your users do not need to select from the associated table each time they access the data. The RELATED function has a required syntax of RELATED(<column>).

How to do it...

1. Open the **Chapter_9_DAX** solution and select the **CRASH_DATA_T** table and make sure you are in the data Grid view.
2. Scroll to the right until you find the **Add Column**. Then in the expression box, add the formula to return the label from the **LIGHT_T** table. You will then see the corresponding label on each row:

   ```
   =RELATED(LIGHT_T[LIGHT_CONDITION])
   ```

3. On the **Properties** window, change the **Column Name** from **Add Column** to **Light_Condition**.

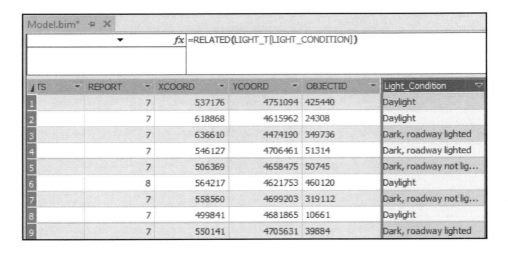

How it works...

In this recipe, you created a new column to add the label from the **LIGHT_T** table to the **CRASH_DATA_T** table. The DAX formula uses the RELATED function to add the text in the light condition column to the table.

There's more...

By viewing the data in a reporting tool such as Power View, users can now quickly select the **Light_Condition** by expanding the **CRASH_DATA_T** folder. Otherwise, they would need to add data from the **CRASH_DATA_T** folder and then expand the **LIGHT_T** folder to add the **Light_Condition** column. By enhancing the model to add commonly used fields to the main table, users can more easily leverage the data for analysis.

Light_Condition	Count_of_Crashes
	45794
Dark, roadway lighted	71694
Dark, roadway not lighted	59830
Dark, unknown lighting	3524
Dawn	9818
Daylight	347299
Dusk	13157
Unknown	8111
Total	**559227**

Using the RELATEDTABLE function

The RELATEDTABLE function changes the context in which the data is filtered, and evaluates the expression in the new context that you specify.

This function is a shortcut for the CALCULATETABLE function with no logical expression.

The RELATEDTABLE function leverages the relationships built in the model Diagram view. In this model, there is a one to many relationship between the **Manner_of_Crash** table and the **CRASH_DATA_T** table. The RELATEDTABLE function is applied on the many table (**Manner_of_Crash**) and performs a lookup on the one table (**CRASH_DATA_T**).

In this recipe, you will create a new column to the **Manner_of_Crash** table. This recipe uses the RELATEDTABLE function to count the number of rows in the **CRASH_DATA_T** table that occur by the **Manner_of_Crash**. This will provide a summary by row. The REALTEDTABLE function has a required syntax of RELATEDTABLE(<tableName>).

How to do it...

1. Open the **Chapter_9_DAX** solution, select the Manner_of_Crash table, and make sure you are in the data Grid view.
2. Scroll to the right until you find **Add Column**. Then in the expression box, add the formula to summarize the number of events related to each type of crash. Then press **Enter** to create the calculation. You will then see the total records added to each row:

   ```
   =COUNTROWS ( RELATEDTABLE (CRASH_DATA_T) )
   ```

3. On the **Properties** window, change the **Column Name** from **Add Column** to **Nof_Events**.

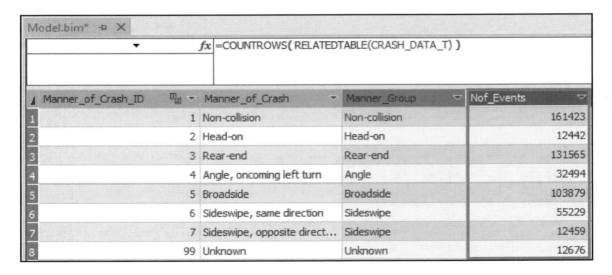

Manner_of_Crash_ID	Manner_of_Crash	Manner_Group	Nof_Events
1	Non-collision	Non-collision	161423
2	Head-on	Head-on	12442
3	Rear-end	Rear-end	131565
4	Angle, oncoming left turn	Angle	32494
5	Broadside	Broadside	103879
6	Sideswipe, same direction	Sideswipe	55229
7	Sideswipe, opposite direct...	Sideswipe	12459
99	Unknown	Unknown	12676

How it works...

The RELATEDTABLE function leverages the relationships built in the model. In this example, it uses the relationship between the **CRASH_DATA_T** table and the **Manner_of_Crash** table. The COUNTROWS functions use the RELATEDTABLE as an argument to count the total number of rows that has a related ID. The totals are then returned in the calculated column.

Using EVALUATE in DAX queries

If you need to query the data in a tabular model, then you can use the EVALUATE function. The Evaluate function is used on a table to return the result set as a table. It is similar to using Select * in T-SQL to return all columns and rows from a table. The EVALUATE function has a required syntax of EVALUATE 'tablename'.

How to do it...

1. Connect to the **CHAPTER_9_DAX** database in SQL Server Management Studio.
2. Right-click on **Databases** and select **New Query** | **MDX** to create a new MDX query window.

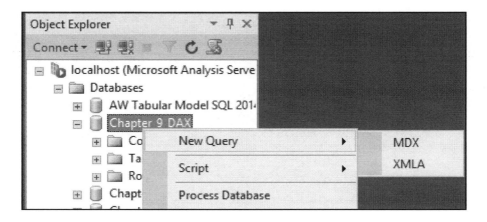

3. In the new window, use the EVALUATE function to return the data in a table. Type in the expression and then press *F5* to run the command:

```
EVALUATE
    'WEATHER_T'
```

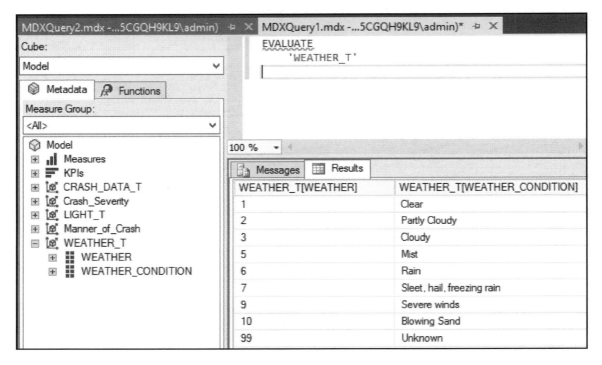

4. To extend this formula a bit more, you can add an order by clause to change the sort order returned in the query. Add an order by clause on the next line to sort the data on the first column in descending order:

```
ORDER BY 'WEATHER'.[WEATHER] DESC
```

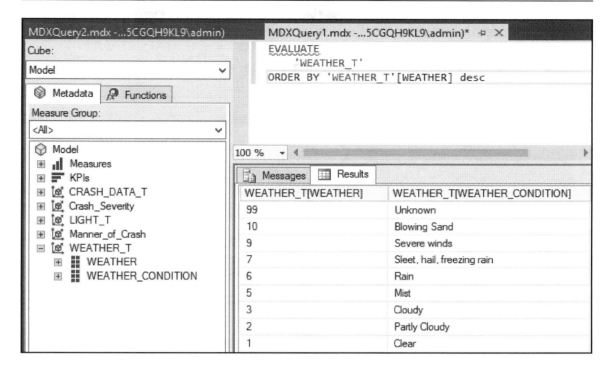

Filtering based on a value

You can also filter your model to return the data you need for your analysis using the `FILTER` function. Using this function, you can limit the results on a table by applying an expression that is evaluated on each row of the table. For example, if you wanted to know the total number of crashes that had more than two major injuries, the `FILTER` function has a required syntax of `FILTER(<table>,<filter>)`.

Getting ready

In this recipe, you will create a filter to sum the total fatalities on crashes that have more than two major injuries.

How to do it...

1. On the **CRASH_DATA_T** table in the Grid view, select an empty cell under the **Count_of_Crashes** measure.
2. Enter the calculation in the formula bar:

```
Total_Fatalities_GT2_MajorInjuries := SUMX(
FILTER(CRASH_DATA_T, CRASH_DATA_T[MAJINJURY]>2),
CRASH_DATA_T[FATALITIES]
  )
```

3. Hit *Enter*.

Model.bim*				
[CRASH_KEY] ▼		*fx*	Total_Fatalities_GT2_MajorInjuries:=SUMX(filter(CRASH_DATA_T, CRASH_DATA_T[MAJINJURY]>2),CRASH_DATA_T[FATALITIES])	
CRASH_KEY	CASENUMBER	CRASH_DATE_Full	CRASH_DATE	
1	2009056548	2009566380	08/28/2009 07:00:00 AM ...	8/28/2009 12:00:0...
2	2008019320	2008437896	04/23/2008 07:00:00 AM ...	4/23/2008 12:00:0...
3	2008018209	2008436615	04/14/2008 07:00:00 AM ...	4/14/2008 12:00:0...
4	2008016754	2008434952	03/07/2008 08:00:00 AM ...	3/7/2008 12:00:00 ...
5	2008016070	2008434161	03/20/2008 07:00:00 AM ...	3/20/2008 12:00:0...
6	2008026397	2008445970	06/16/2008 07:00:00 AM ...	6/16/2008 12:00:0...
7	2006042729	2006245683	10/19/2006 07:00:00 AM ...	10/19/2006 12:00:...
8	2006054760	2006258337	12/15/2006 08:00:00 AM ...	12/15/2006 12:00:...
9	2012015068	2012683832	04/16/2012 07:00:00 AM ...	4/16/2012 12:00:0...

Count_of_Crashes: 559227

Nof_Fatalities: 3879

Total_Fatalities_GT2_MajorInjuries: 88

4. In this recipe, there are 88 total fatalities that meet the condition of `CRASH_DATA_T[MAJINJURY]>2`.

How it works...

In this recipe, you are using the SUMX and the FILTER functions to calculate the total number of fatalities that also had more than two major injuries. The SUMX function applies the sum calculation to the FATALITIES column, only on the records from the **CRASH_DATA_T** table that have MAJINURY with more than the value of 2. The filter expression requires two arguments, the table and the expression. In this recipe, the table is **CRASH_DATA_T** and the expression is CRASH_DATA_T[MAJINJURY]>2.

Filtering a related table

You can also pass to the FILTER function the RELATED function as the condition to limit the rows. In this recipe, you will filter your results to look at the **Crash_Severity** table and only use rows that are labeled as *fatal*.

How to do it...

1. On the **CRASH_DATA_T** table in the Grid view, select an empty cell under the **CASENUMBER** measure.

2. Enter the calculation in the formula bar:

```
Fatal_Crashes:=SUMX(
   FILTER(CRASH_DATA_T,
RELATED(Crash_Severity[Severity_Descr])="fatal"),
CRASH_DATA_T[INJURIES])
```

3. Once you have done this, hit *Enter*.

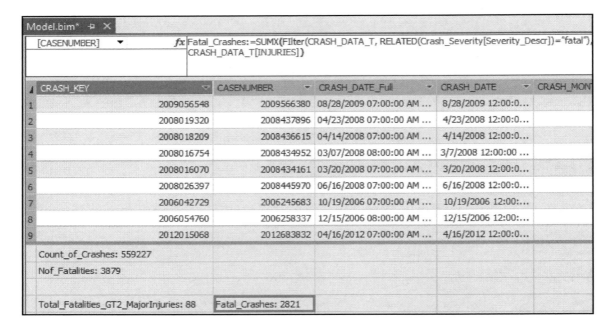

4. In this recipe, there are **2821** total fatalities that meet the condition.

How it works...

In this recipe, you are using the SUMX and the FILTER functions to calculate the total number of fatalities by summing the total INJURIES related to the **Crash_Severity** table. The SUMX function applies the sum calculation to the INJURIES column, only on the records from the **CRASH_DATA_T** table that are related to the **Crash_severity** table with a **Severity_Descr** of *Fatal*.

Using ALL to remove filters

The ALL function works with FILTER to remove any conditions that are on your data. This is helpful when you are creating calculations that need to use the entire dataset as the denominator. Using the ALL function ignores any filters or slices that are applied in a query or end user tool. The ALL function has a required syntax of: ALL(<table>|<column>).

In this recipe, you will create a new measure to show the number of crashes reported using the CALCULATE function and the ALL function to ensure all filtering is removed.

How to do it...

1. On the **CRASH_DATA_T** table in the Grid view, select an empty cell under the **CASENUMBER** measure.
2. Enter the calculation in the formula bar:

```
Crashes_Reported:=
CALCULATE (
COUNT(CRASH_DATA_T[CASENUMBER]),
ALL(CRASH_DATA_T) )
```

3. Once you have done this, hit *Enter*.

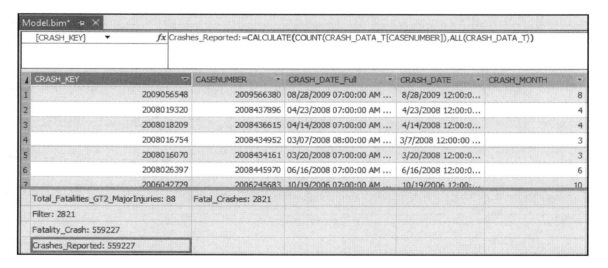

4. The measure now shows the total number of cases on the **CRASH_DATA_T** table. The total will be calculated regardless of any filtering or slicing that is done on the model.

5. Deploy the model to the server by selecting the **Build** menu and the **Deploy Chapter_9_DAX**.

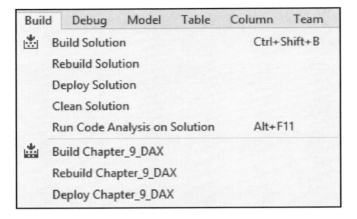

6. Switch to SQL Server Management Studio and connect to the model.
7. Expand the **Measures | CRASH_DATA_T** folder and drag **Count_of_Crashes** and **Crashes_Reported** to the query window.
8. Then select **Severity_Descr** and place it before **Count_of_Crashes** to see how the different formulas work.

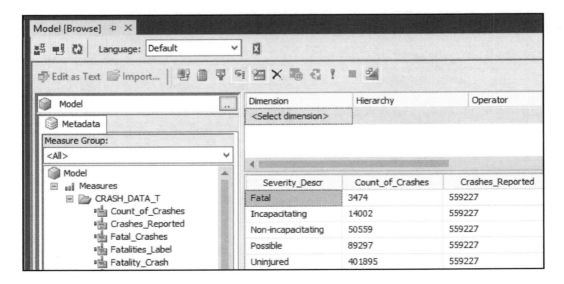

9. Notice how the **Count_of_Crashes** is calculating the number of crashes by the severity description. However, since **Crashes_Reported** uses the ALL function, it ignores the slicer of the severity description and displays the total number of cases.

How it works...

In this recipe, you created a DAX calculation that returns the number of records on the **CRASH_DATA_T** table regardless of any filters. To accomplish this, the ALL function is used to eliminate any filter context and is passed into the CALCULATE function. After adding in the measure, you deployed the changes to the cube to the server. Then you reviewed the results and added it to the cube browser to see how this measure is different than the **Count_of_Crashes** function by slicing the data using the crash severity description.

Using ALL to calculate a percentage

In this recipe, you will use the ALL function in the denominator of a percentage calculation. This ensures that you see all records in the calculation you are performing.

Getting ready

Complete the steps in the *Using ALL to remove filters* recipe to create the initial calculation and understand how ALL ignores any filters.

How to do it...

1. On the **CRASH_DATA_T** table in the Grid view, select an empty cell under the **CASENUMBER** measure.
2. Enter the calculation in the formula bar:

```
Pct_of_Crashes:=
  COUNT(CRASH_DATA_T[CASENUMBER])/
CALCULATE (
COUNT(CRASH_DATA_T[CASENUMBER]),
ALL(CRASH_DATA_T) )
```

3. Once you have done this, hit *Enter*.

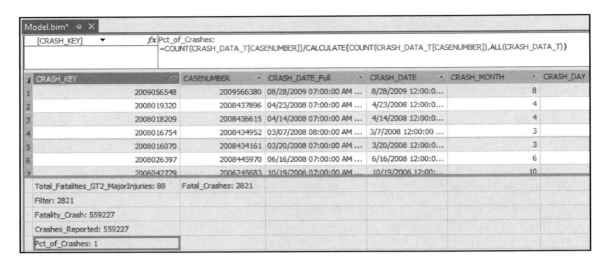

4. The result returns a 1. To change the format to a percentage, edit the **Format** in the **Properties** window to **Percentage**.

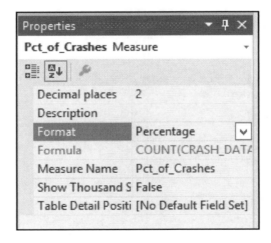

5. The result will now show 100.00 %.
6. Deploy the model to the server by selecting the **Build** menu and the **Deploy Chapter_9_DAX**.

7. Switch to SQL Server Management Studio and connect to the model.
8. Expand the **Measures | CRASH_DATA_T** folder and drag **Count_of_Crashes** and **Pct_of_Crashes** to the query window.
9. Then select **Severity_Descr** and place it before **Count_of_Crashes** to see how the different formulas work.

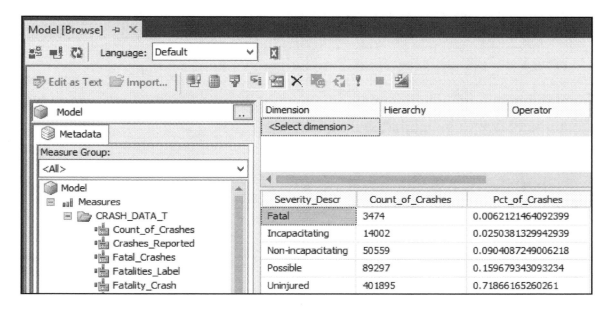

How it works...

In this recipe, you leveraged a DAX calculation that returns the percentage of crashes based on the current context. To accomplish this, you needed to create a function that always returns the number of records using the ALL function as the denominator. You then count the number of cases in the **CRASH_DATA_T** table to determine the numerator. After adding in the measure, you deployed the changes to the cube to the server. Then you reviewed the results and added it to the cube browser to see how this measure is creating the percentage based on the context that you are slicing the data on. In this example, the severity description breakout is shown along with the number of cases and then the percentage of cases is shown as well.

Using the SUMMARIZE function

When you want to get the totals for the data in your model, you can leverage the SUMMARIZE function to create a DAX expression to return the data back as a table.

This recipe uses the SUMMARIZE function on a single column. You will summarize the number of fatalities on the **CRASH_DATA_T** table by the numbers that are related to a weather condition. After building on this foundation, you will add additional columns and other options to round out the features available using this function.

How to do it...

1. Connect to the **CHAPTER_9_DAX** database in SQL Server Management Studio.
2. Right-click on the database, and select **New Query** | **MDX** to create a new MDX query window.
3. To determine the number of fatalities by weather condition you will use the SUMMARIZE function along with the EVALUATE function to return a tableset:

```
EVALUATE
SUMMARIZE (
    CRASH_DATA_T
    ,WEATHER_T[WEATHER_CONDITION]
,"Total Fatalities", SUM('CRASH_DATA_T'.[FATALITIES])
    )
```

4. Then press *F5* to run the query.

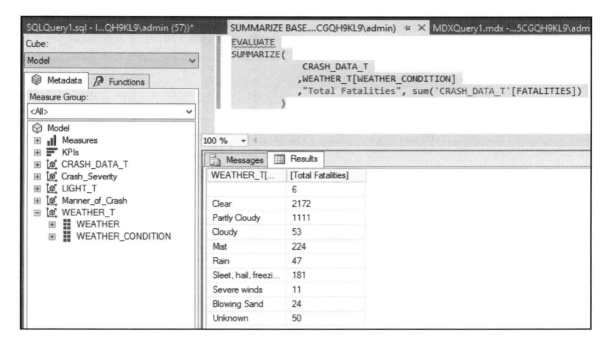

How it works...

In this recipe, you created a query to output the results in SQL Server Management Studio. The query totals the number of fatalities in the **CRASH_DATA_T[FATALITIES]** column. It then uses the weather condition to total the number of fatalities by the type of weather. The results of this data show that most fatalities happened on clear days with 2,172 deaths.

Adding columns to the SUMMARIZE function

In this recipe, you will extend the last calculation to add an additional column to the output. You can summarize the data by including more columns in the SUMMARIZE function to achieve your desired output.

Getting ready

Complete the calculation in the *Using the SUMMARIZE function* recipe.

How to do it...

1. Connect to the **CHAPTER_9_DAX** database in SQL Server Management Studio.
2. Right-click on the database, and select **New Query** | **MDX** to create a new MDX query window.
3. To determine the number of fatalities by the manner of the crash combined with the weather condition, you will use the SUMMARIZE function along with the EVALUATE function to return a table:

```
EVALUATE
SUMMARIZE (
    CRASH_DATA_T
,Manner_of_Crash[Manner_Group]
    ,WEATHER_T[WEATHER_CONDITION]
      ,"Total Fatalities"
, SUM('CRASH_DATA_T'.[FATALITIES])
    )
```

4. Then press *F5* to run the query.

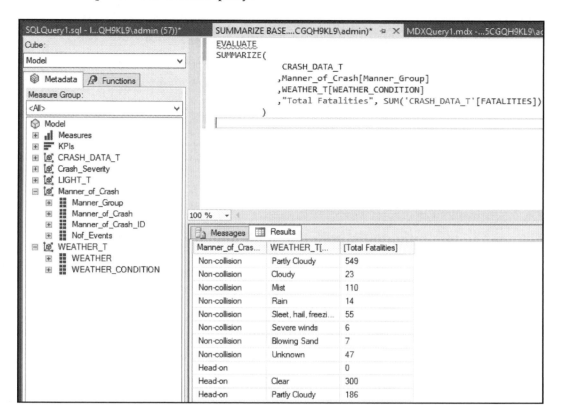

How it works...

In this recipe, you added a new column to show the manner of the crash along with the weather condition and number of records for each group. This recipe totals the number of fatalities associated to both manner of crash and weather condition.

Using ROLLUP with the SUMMARIZE function

In this recipe, you will use the ROLLUP function within an argument for SUMMARIZE to show all totals and subtotals in the query. This will be similar to using group by with rollup in T-SQL. You will determine the number of crashes based on weather and manner of crash to get the grouping and the totals by group. The SUMMARIZE function has a required syntax of SUMMARIZE(<table>,<groupby_columnname>).

How to do it...

1. Connect to the **CHAPTER_9_DAX** database in SQL Server Management Studio.
2. Right-click on the database, and select **New Query | MDX** to create a new MDX query window.
3. To determine the number of fatalities by the manner of the crash combined with the weather condition, you will use the SUMMARIZE function along with the EVALUATE function to return a table. To return all records that are related to these conditions, you need to use the ROLLUP function:

```
EVALUATE
SUMMARIZE (
    CRASH_DATA_T,
    ROLLUP (Manner_of_Crash[Manner_Group]
      ,WEATHER_T[WEATHER_CONDITION])
,"Total Fatalities"
, SUM('CRASH_DATA_T'.[FATALITIES])
    )
```

4. Then press *F5* to run the query.

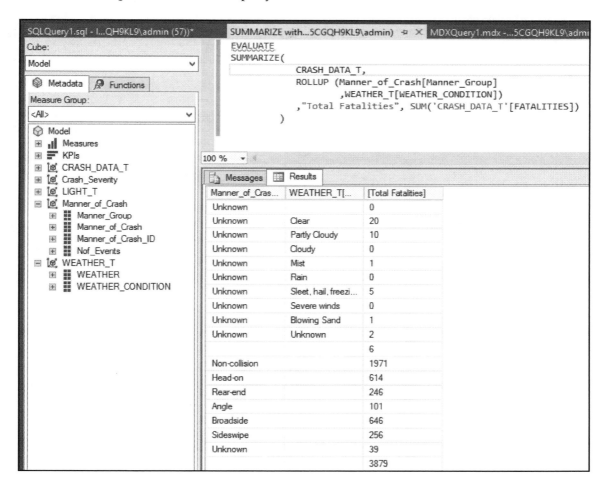

How it works...

In this recipe, you used a combination of functions to create subtotals and totals to determine the number of crashes by manner of crash and weather conditions. The DAX query uses ROLLUP in the group by argument on the **Manner_Group** and then the**WEATHER_CONDITION** to get the sum of fatalities. It then uses the SUMMARIZE function to return the result set.

10
Working with Dates and Time Intelligence

In this chapter, we will cover the following recipes:

- Creating a date table in Visual Studio
- Using the CALENDAR function
- Modifying the date table with the YEAR function
- Modifying the date table to include month data
- Using the NOW and TODAY functions
- Using the DATEDIFF function
- Using the WEEKDAY function
- Understanding time intelligence
- Using the FIRSTDATE function
- Using the PARALLELPERIOD function
- Calculating Year over Year Growth
- Using the OPENINGBALANCEMONTH function
- Using the OPENINGBALANCEYEAR function
- Using the CLOSINGBALANCEMONTH function
- Using the CLOSINGBALANCEYEAR function
- Using the TOTALYTD function

Introduction

DAX includes many functions that enable you to aggregate and compare data over time periods. To use the time intelligence functions, you must ensure that a table has been chosen as the date table in your model. In addition, the date table must have one row for each day in the year. In the following recipes, you will use the **Calc_Date_T** table created in Chapter 9, *DAX Syntax and Calculations*. The **Crash_Date** will be used as the date column. The time functions will use this date table as the basis for all of the calculations.

Date calculations can be either additive or semi-additive. Additive measures can be summed across the date dimension in relation to the fact tables. For instance, total records created by month or year. Semi-additive measures can only be summed across certain dimensions but not all, for example, the opening balance of crashes recorded in a month. If you total the opening balance of crashes for each month in the year 2015, it would not total the total number of records created in the year 2015. When creating measures, be sure to test the outcome to ensure the aggregations are properly summarizing as required for your model.

Creating a date table in Visual Studio

Most models you will create need to have a date table to use for calculating and summarizing data over time. Using DAX functions, you can create a customized date table to add to your model. By leveraging many of the date functions included in DAX, you can extend the columns to make the model easier for end users to leverage. The DAX time and date functions leverage the date table to perform the calculations, without it your time and date functions will not work properly.

Getting ready

To complete the recipes in this section, create a new Visual Studio project and import the **CRASH_DATA_T** table from the **Crash_Data_DB** database. This table has the **CRASH_DATE** column, which contains the date for each record crash. You will use this table as the reference to create a new date table in the model.

In this recipe you will create a date table that is built by using a DAX formula and the calculated table functionality of tabular models.

How to do it...

1. In Visual Studio, open the **Table** menu and then select**New Calculated Table**:

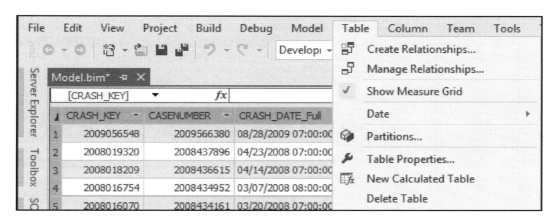

2. This creates a new table in the project that requires a DAX expression to populate the table:

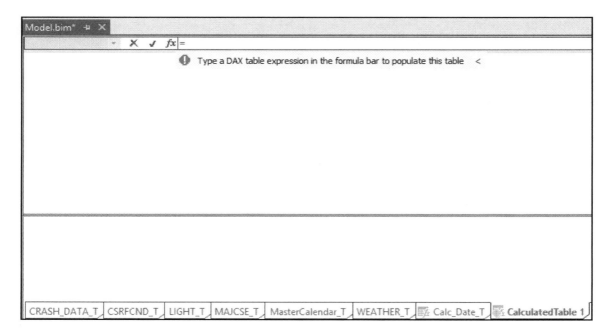

3. To create a row for each **CRASH_DATE**, use the SUMMARIZE function too return each row once:

```
=SUMMARIZE(CRASH_DATA_T,CRASH_DATA_T[CRASH_DATE])
```

4. Once you have done this, press *Enter* to complete the calculation.

5. In the **CRASH_DATA_T** table there are 93 records for the date **1/2/2006**. The new date table has only 1 row for **1/2/2006** and each other date found in the **CRASH_DATA_T** table:

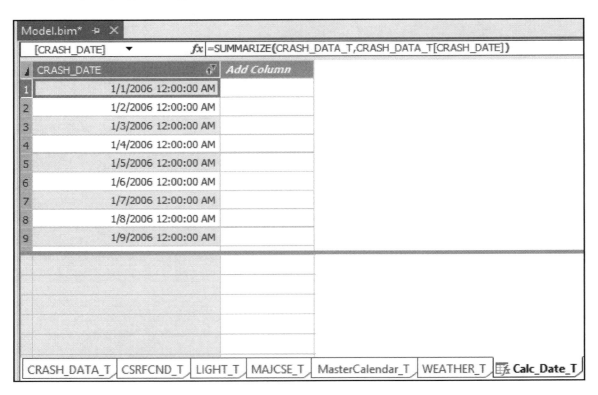

How it works...

This recipe uses the SUMMARIZE function to create a new date table. It uses the values from the **CRASH_DATA_T** table and **CRASH_DATE** column to return one row for each date on the table.

Using the CALENDAR function

You can also create a date table using the CALENDAR function in DAX. This function uses a begin date and end date in the arguments to create a table for all dates between the range given. If you need a complete table with all dates represented, using this method is quick and effective.

To demonstrate how this works, you will create a date table with 10 consecutive dates.

How to do it...

1. In Visual Studio, open the **Table** menu and then select **New Calculated Table**.
2. This creates a new table in the project that requires a DAX expression to populate the table.
3. To create a row for each row between 1/1/2006 and **1/10/2006**, use the CALENDAR function:

```
=CALENDAR("1/1/2006","1/10/2006")
```

4. Now mark this table as the date table in the model. Select the **Table** menu and then **Date** and **Mark As Date Table**:

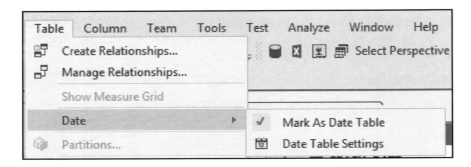

5. Create the relationship from the **Calc_Date_T** table to the **CRASH_DATA_T** on the **CRASH_DATE** table:

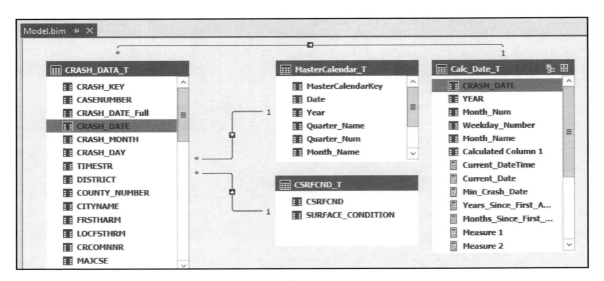

How it works...

The CALENDAR function is the best method to create a new calendar table for your model if required. Creating a table using this function returns one row for each day between the start date and end date passed to the function. Then you marked the new table as a date table and added a relationship from the **Calc_Date_T** table to the **CRASH_DATA_T** table.

Modifying the date table with the YEAR function

In order to make the date table easier to use in reporting, you will add new columns to the table created in the *Creating a date table in Visual Studio* recipe. In this recipe, you will create columns based on the date column such as year, month, and weekday.

Getting ready

Complete the steps in the *Creating a date table in Visual Studio* recipe.

How to do it...

1. Open the **Model.bim** to the **Calc_Date_T** table.
2. On the **Add Column** next to **CRASH_DATE**, select the first cell and enter the formula to return the year from the date:

   ```
   =YEAR(Calc_Date_T[CRASH_DATE])
   ```

3. Once you have done this, press *Enter*:

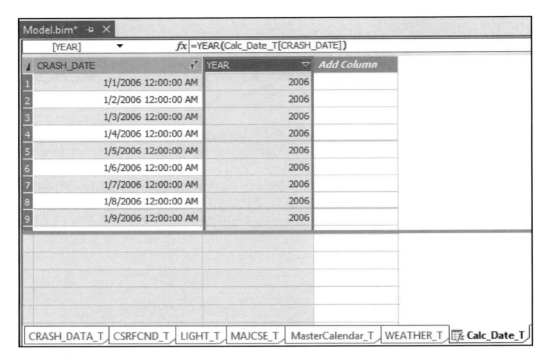

How it works...

In this recipe, you added a new calculated column to the **Calc_Date_T** table to show the year for each record. You passed the date to the YEAR function and it returned the 4-digit year as the output. Using this method, you can create the columns required to build a hierarchy for your uses to leverage.

Modifying the date table to include month data

This recipe is similar to the YEAR function recipe. You will create a calculated column to return the month number of the year. Then you will use the format function to convert the number returned to the name of the month.

How to do it...

1. Open the **Model.bim** to the **Calc_Date_T** table.
2. On the **Add Column** next to **CRASH_DATE**, select the first cell and enter the formula to return the month number from the date:

   ```
   =MONTH(Calc_Date_T[CRASH_DATE])
   ```

3. Once you have done this, press *Enter* to create the calculation. The calculation returns the number of the year, for example, January equals one:

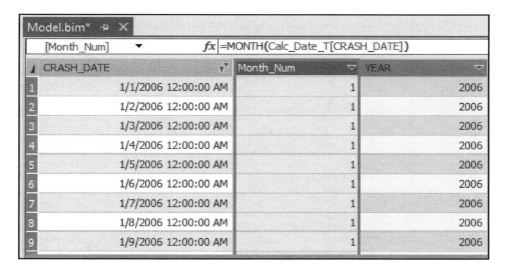

How it works...

In this recipe, you added a new calculated column to the **Calc_Date_T** table to show the month for each record. You passed the date to the MONTH function and it returns the month number as the output.

There's more...

To include a column that returns the month name, use the FORMAT function. To use the FORMAT function, pass in the date and the format argument. There are four options to change the information returned based on the arguments passed:

- "M": returns month number
- "MM": returns the 2-digit month number
- "MMM": returns the first three characters of the month name
- "MMMM": returns the full length of the month name

For example, to create a column that displays the first three characters of the month, click on the open cell on the next **Add Column**:

```
=FORMAT(Calc_Date_T[CRASH_DATE],"MMM")
```

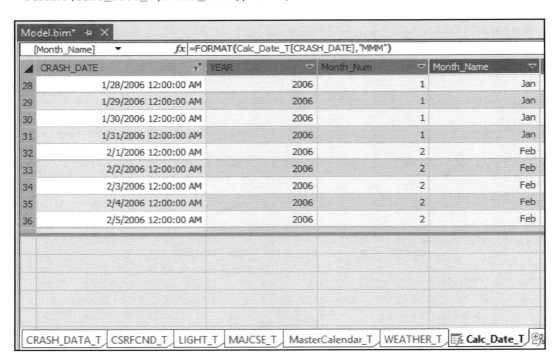

You can now use these fields to create a hierarchy in the **Calc_Date_T** table.

Using the NOW and TODAY functions

There are two functions to return the current datetime and date in the model. The TODAY function will return the current date with the time set to 12:00:00 AM. This function is useful when you need to use the current date as an input for your time calculations. The NOW function returns not only the current date, but also the exact time of when the function is executed. Depending on the time interval required, using the today function would allow you to calculate the number of sales over the last 6 or 12 hours.

How to do it...

1. Open the **Model.bim** to the **Calc_Date_T** table.
2. In the measure creation area, click on an empty cell to create a measure to return the current date and time:

   ```
   Current_DateTime:=NOW()
   ```

Model.bim*		
[Month_Name] ▼	*fx* Current_DateTime:=NOW()	

	CRASH_DATE	Month_Num	Month_Name
1	1/1/2006 12:00:00 AM	1	Jan
2	1/2/2006 12:00:00 AM	1	Jan
3	1/3/2006 12:00:00 AM	1	Jan
4	1/4/2006 12:00:00 AM	1	Jan
5	1/5/2006 12:00:00 AM	1	Jan
6	1/6/2006 12:00:00 AM	1	Jan
7	1/7/2006 12:00:00 AM	1	Jan
8	1/8/2006 12:00:00 AM	1	Jan
9	1/9/2006 12:00:00 AM	1	Jan

Current_DateTime: 11/27/2016 7:13:19 PM

3. Now that you can see the date and time, create a new measure under the **Current_DateTime** measure name **Current_Date** to return the current date with the time set to **12:00:00 AM**:

```
=Current_Date:=TODAY()
```

	CRASH_DATE	Month_Num	Month_Name
1	1/1/2006 12:00:00 AM	1	Jan
2	1/2/2006 12:00:00 AM	1	Jan
3	1/3/2006 12:00:00 AM	1	Jan
4	1/4/2006 12:00:00 AM	1	Jan
5	1/5/2006 12:00:00 AM	1	Jan
6	1/6/2006 12:00:00 AM	1	Jan
7	1/7/2006 12:00:00 AM	1	Jan
8	1/8/2006 12:00:00 AM	1	Jan
9	1/9/2006 12:00:00 AM	1	Jan

Current_DateTime: 11/27/2016 7:13:19 PM

Current_Date: 11/27/2016 12:00:00 AM

How it works...

In this recipe, you used two functions to add measures that return the current date and time. First you added the NOW function to return the exact date and time value. Then you added a new measure to determine the current date using the TODAY function. Both of these measures allow you to create calculations to determine the number of days between data in your model and the current date.

Using the DATEDIFF function

The DATEDIFF function returns the values between two dates given a specific date interval. You can use this function to determine the number of days between today and the first day of the year. You could also calculate the number of months between date values.

Available options for the date interval are:

- SECOND
- MINUTE
- HOUR
- DAY
- WEEK
- MONTH
- QUARTER
- YEAR

Getting ready

Create a new measure to calculate the minimum date in the **Calc_Date_T**. This value will be used to calculate the number of years from the first crash reported to today. In this case, 11/27/2016:

1. Open the **Model.bim** to the **Calc_Date_T** table.
2. In the measure creation area, click on an empty cell to create a measure to minimum date:

```
Min_Crash_Date:=MIN(Calc_Date_T[CRASH_DATE])
```

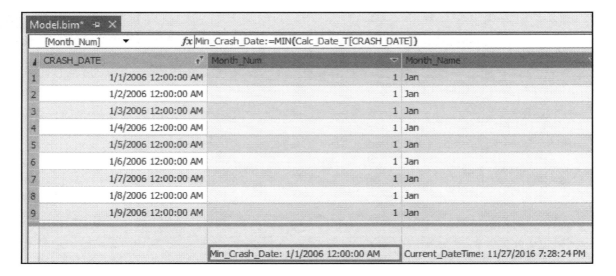

How to do it...

1. In the measure creation area, click on an empty cell to create a measure to return the current date and time:

```
Years_Since_First_Accident:=DATEDIFF(
[Min_Crash_Date],TODAY(), YEAR)
```

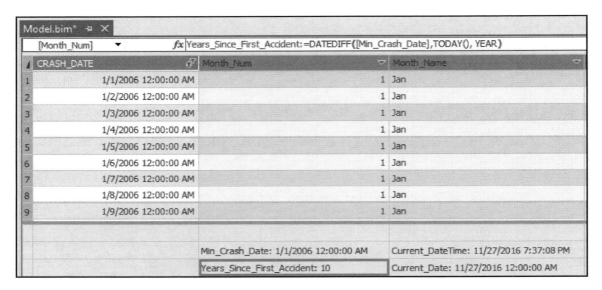

The result returns 10 as the number of years in this dataset.

How it works...

In this recipe, you created a measure to determine the minimum date value on the **CRASH_DATE_T** table. You then used this value in the DATEDIFF function to calculate the number of years between the **MIN_CRASH_DATE** and today.

There's more...

To change the date interval, you can replace YEAR in the preceding example to any of the predefined values. Often it is helpful to have commonly reported values pre-calculated in the model for your users and reporting tools. For example, to see the number of months between two values, change the YEAR argument to MONTH:

```
Months_Since_First_Accident:=
DATEDIFF([Min_Crash_Date], TODAY(), MONTH)
```

Using the WEEKDAY function

The WEEKDAY function returns the day of the week as an integer. The week starts with Sunday as 1. Using this function, you can include information in your model to indicate workdays and weekends. Also you can create analysis that reviews trends on performance based on the day of the week. For example, do more crashes occur on Fridays than Tuesdays?

How to do it...

1. Open the **Model.bim** to the **Calc_Date_T** table.
2. In the measure creation area, click on an empty cell to create a measure to return the day of the week as an integer:

```
DayofWeek:=WEEKDAY("1/1/2016")
```

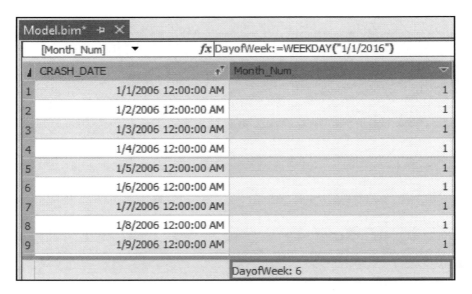

3. January 1st 2016 is a friday and the result returned is a 6.

4. To make this more beneficial to users, you can convert the number to the name of the day:

```
DayofWeekName:=FORMAT(WEEKDAY("1/1/2016"),"DDDD")
```

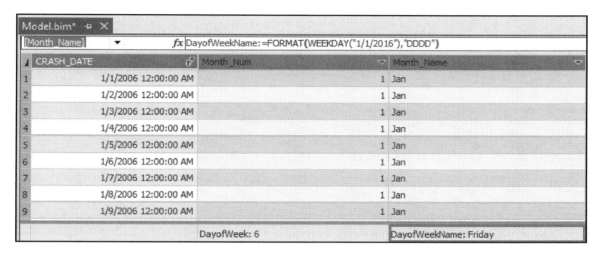

How it works...

This function takes a date as an argument and returns the day of the week as an integer. You can use this function to find dates that are weekday values (2-6) and weekend values (1 and 7).

There's more...

To determine the number of crashes that occur on Fridays and Tuesdays, create a new measure for each date:

```
Friday_Crashes:=CALCULATE(COUNT(CRASH_DATE_T[CASENUMBER]),
    WEEKDAY(CRASH_DATA_T[CRASH_DATE])=6)
Tuesday_Crashes:=CALCULATE(COUNT(CRASH_DATE_T[CASENUMBER]),
    WEEKDAY(CRASH_DATA_T[CRASH_DATE])=3)
```

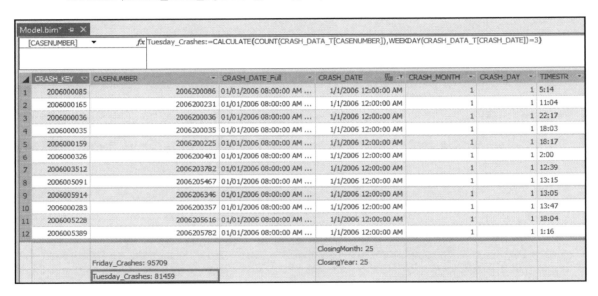

Once both are calculated, you can see that Fridays have approximately 14,000 crashes more than Tuesdays.

See also...

There are many common calculations that you will want to include in your tabular model to present data based on various time requirements. So far you have built time functions to return information based on a set date range or to calculate the time between two dates. Time intelligence functions make it easier to report on the data when comparing different time periods. For instance, a common way to view summary data is to look at the data in the current period compared to the last period. Another example is calculating year growth. The following recipes leverage the time intelligence functions to make the data easier to leverage and compare.

Using the FIRSTDATE function

This function returns the first date in the data column that you pass as an argument. You can use the FIRSTDATE function to find the first occurrence of a transaction or the first time an accident was reported that was associated to blowing sand.

How to do it...

1. Open the **Model.bim** to the **Calc_Date_T** table.
2. In the measure creation area, click on an empty cell to create a measure to return the first date found on the **Calc_Date_T** table:

```
First_Accident:=FIRSTDATE(Calc_Date_T[CRASH_DATE])
```

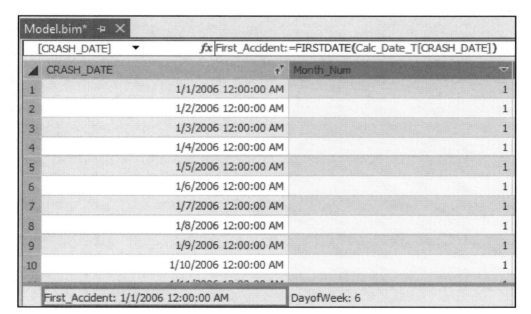

3. A more interesting date will be finding the first occurrence of an accident logged due to the weather condition of blowing sand. To do this you will use the CALCULATE function and FILTER to limit the results. Create a new measure under **First_Accident**:

```
First_Accident_Blowing_Sand:=CALCULATE (
  FIRSTDATE(CRASH_DATA_T[CRASH_DATE],
  FILTER(WEATHER_T,[WEATHER_CONDITION]="Blowing Sand"))
```

Based on the date in the table, the first time an accident was logged due to blowing sand was on **1/10/2006**.

How it works...

This recipe returns the first date found in a dataset. You passed in the crash date as the argument and found the first transaction record. Then you modified the function to look for a specific occurrence of an event using the FILTER function. In this recipe, you referenced the **WEATHER_T** table to look for the condition of blowing sand.

There's more...

You can also leverage the LASTDATE function to find the final entry in your table. LASTDATE works just like FIRSTDATE. This function is useful to locate the last occurrence of transactions, such as the last time a product was sold at a particular location.

Using the PARALLELPERIOD function

A common requirement for BI reporting is to show performance based on periods. Examples include reporting on this month versus last month, this quarter versus last quarter, or this year versus last year. In each of these instances you are calculating the totals based on the time frame required. DAX includes the PARALLELPERIOD function to create these types of comparisons.

How to do it...

1. Open the **Model.bim** to the **CRASH_DATA_T** table.
2. In the measure creation area, click on an empty cell to create a measure to return the number of accidents using year:

```
ParallelPeriod:=CALCULATE(
  COUNT(CRASH_DATA_T[CASENUMBER]),
  PARALLELPERIOD(Calc_Date_T[CRASH_DATE],
-1,YEAR))
```

Model.bim

[CASENUMBER] ▼   *fx* ParallelPeriod:=CALCULATE(COUNT(CRASH_DATA_T[CASENUMBER]),PARALLELPERIOD(Calc_Date_T[CRASH_DATE],-1,YEAR))

	CRASH_KEY	CASENUMBER	CRASH_DATE_Full	CRASH_DATE	CRASH_MONTH	CRASH_DAY	TIMESTR	DISTRICT
1	2006000085	2006200086	01/01/2006 08:00:00 AM ...	1/1/2006 12:00:00 AM	1	1	5:14	6
2	2006000165	2006200231	01/01/2006 08:00:00 AM ...	1/1/2006 12:00:00 AM	1	1	11:04	1
3	2006000036	2006200036	01/01/2006 08:00:00 AM ...	1/1/2006 12:00:00 AM	1	1	22:17	2
4	2006000035	2006200035	01/01/2006 08:00:00 AM ...	1/1/2006 12:00:00 AM	1	1	18:03	2
5	2006000159	2006200225	01/01/2006 08:00:00 AM ...	1/1/2006 12:00:00 AM	1	1	18:17	6
6	2006000326	2006200401	01/01/2006 08:00:00 AM ...	1/1/2006 12:00:00 AM	1	1	2:00	3
7	2006003512	2006203782	01/01/2006 08:00:00 AM ...	1/1/2006 12:00:00 AM	1	1	12:39	1
8	2006005091	2006205467	01/01/2006 08:00:00 AM ...	1/1/2006 12:00:00 AM	1	1	13:15	6
9	2006005914	2006206346	01/01/2006 08:00:00 AM ...	1/1/2006 12:00:00 AM	1	1	13:05	5
10	2006000283	2006200357	01/01/2006 08:00:00 AM ...	1/1/2006 12:00:00 AM	1	1	13:47	1

ParallelPeriod: 536670

3. This returns the total number of records in the table by year excluding the year 2006:

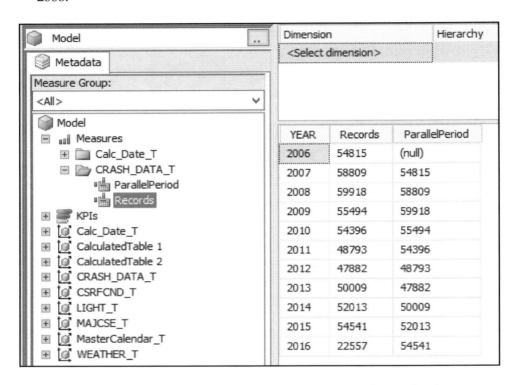

By looking at the total number of records per year in the **ParallelPeriod** column you can see how records were returned the prior year. For instance, in 2015 there were 52013 total records in the **ParallelPeriod** column. This matches with the total records from the year 2014.

How it works...

This recipe uses the PARALLELPERIOD function to compare total crashes from last year to the current year. The value of -1 passed to the function compares the context to the same period 1 year ago. If you used the value of -2 it would compare the context to two years ago.

There's more...

You can create other measures that use PARALLELPERIOD and a different time interval. By changing the interval, you can produce measures to return the prior quarter or month. For example, to see the number of crashes that occur in the prior month, you can copy the preceding formula and create a new measure. Then change the time interval to **MONTH**:

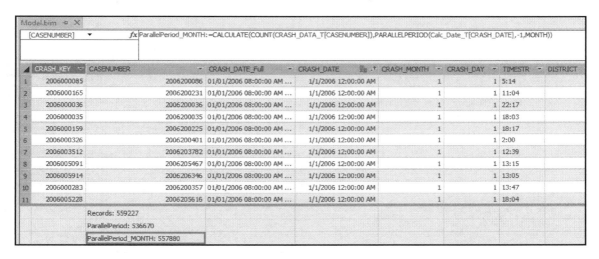

To see how that affects the model, deploy the model and view the results in SQL Server Management Studio.

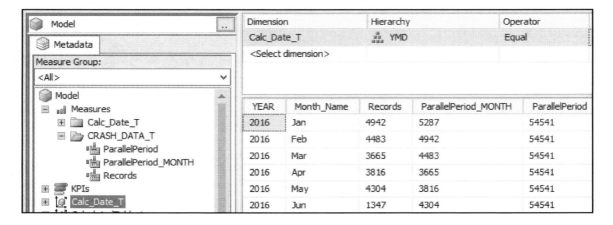

Calculating Year over Year Growth

You can leverage the measures you created that use PARALLELPERIOD function to calculate the growth over periods. In this recipe, you will create a measure to see if the number of crashes increased or decreased year by year.

How to do it...

1. Open the **Model.bim** to the **CRASH_DATA_T** table.
2. In the measure creation area, click on an empty cell to create a measure to return the number of accidents using year:

   ```
   YOY_Growth:=([Records]-[ParallelPeriod])/[ParallelPeriod]
   ```

3. Then press *Enter* to create the measure.

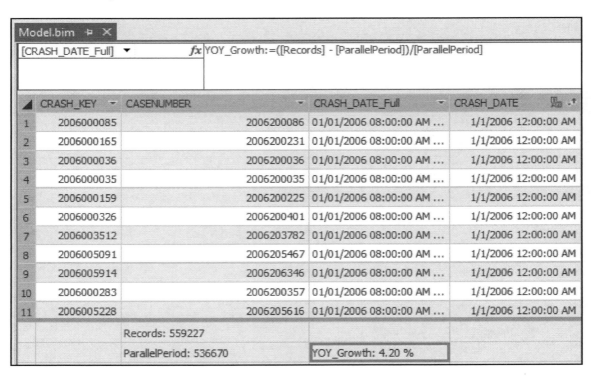

4. Now deploy the solution to the server and switch to SQL Server Management Studio to view the results. Browse the model and select the **YEAR**, **Records**, **ParallelPeriod**, and **YOY_Growth** columns:

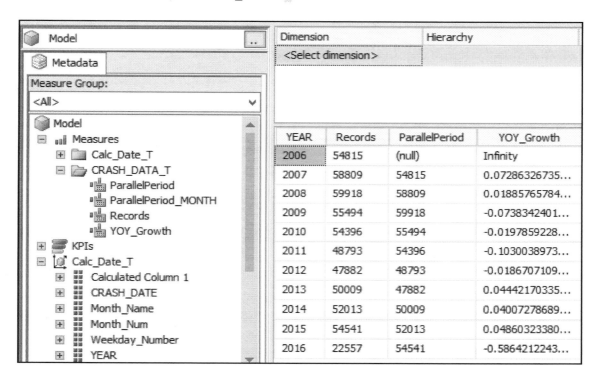

5. You will see the percentage growth for each year in the results. Notice that the first value for **YOY_Growth** is labeled **Infinity**. This is due to the formula not having a value for data prior to the year 2006. To correct this error, you need to modify the measure to account for blank values. Create a new measure named **YOY_Growth_New**:

```
YOY_Growth_New:= IF([ParallelPeriod],
([Records]- [ParallelPeriod])/[ParallelPeriod],BLANK())
```

6. Then press *Enter* to create the measure.

7. Once completed, deploy the model to view the data in SQL Server Management Studio. Refresh your view created in step 3 and add the new column, **YOY_Growth_New**, to see the results:

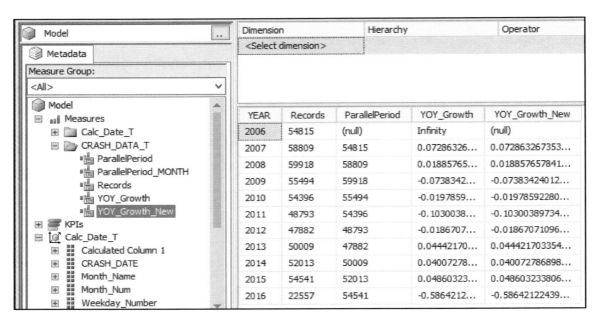

The value for the year **2006** is now set to null.

How it works...

In this recipe, you created a formula to calculate the Year over Year Growth in crashes. To accomplish this, you created a measure that calculates the **ParallelPeriod** for the prior year. To handle missing dates in the formula, you wrapped the function in an IF statement and passed BLANK() as the argument if no records were found.

Using the OPENINGBALANCEMONTH function

To determine the total number of crashes at the beginning of each month, you can use the built-in functions to calculate opening balances. In this recipe, you will create a semi-additive measure to calculate the number of crashes at the beginning of each month. This will enable you to find out the total number of crashes each month and determine trends.

How to do it...

1. Open the **Model.bim** to the **CRASH_DATA_T** table.
2. In the measure creation area, click on an empty cell to create a measure to return the opening month balance:

```
OpeningMonth:=OPENINGBALANCEMONTH( COUNT
    (CRASH_DATA_T[CASE_NUMBER]),
Calc_Date_T[CRASH_DATE])
```

3. Then press *Enter* to create the measure:

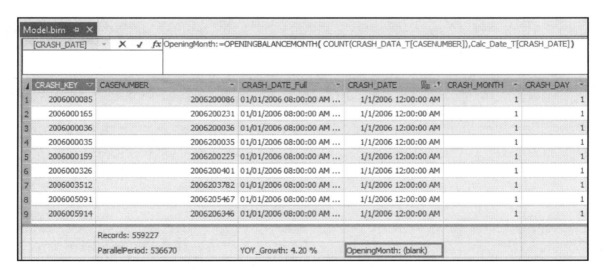

4. Now deploy the solution to the server and switch to SQL Server Management Studio to view the results. Browse the model and select the **YEAR, Month_Name, Records**, and **OpeningMonth**. Set the slicer to use the **Calc_Date_T** year equal to 2016 to limit the results:

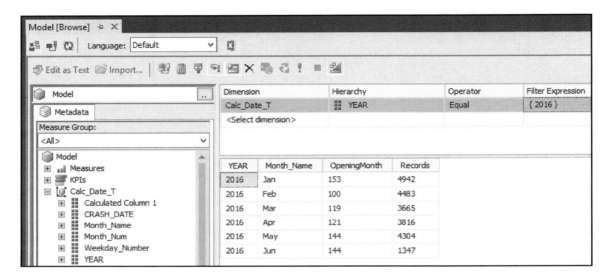

The results displayed in the **OpeningMonth** measure are the number of records on the first day of each month. January 2016 had 153 crashes out of a total 4942 recorded in the month of January.

How it works...

In this recipe, you passed in the date from the **Calc_Date_T** to count the number of crashes on the **CRASH_DATE_T** table. The OPENINGBALANCEMONTH function takes these arguments and calculates the count of crashes on the first day of each month.

Using the OPENINGBALANCEYEAR function

To determine the total number of crashes at the beginning of each year, you can use the built-in functions to calculate opening balances. In this recipe, you will create a semi-additive measure to calculate the number of crashes at the beginning of each year. This will enable you to find out the total number of crashes each year and determine trends.

How to do it...

1. Open the **Model.bim** to the **CRASH_DATA_T** table.

2. In the measure creation area, click on an empty cell to create a measure to return the opening year balance:

```
OpeningYear:=OPENINGBALANCEYEAR( COUNT
    (CRASH_DATA_T[CASE_NUMBER]),
Calc_Date_T[CRASH_DATE])
```

3. Then press *Enter* to create the measure:

Model.bim						
[CRASH_DATE] ▼		*fx* OpeningYear:=OPENINGBALANCEYEAR(COUNT(CRASH_DATA_T[CASENUMBER]),Calc_Date_T[CRASH_DATE])				
CRASH_KEY	CASENUMBER	CRASH_DATE_Full	CRASH_DATE	CRASH_MONTH	CRASH_DAY	
1	2006000085	2006200086	01/01/2006 08:00:00 AM ...	1/1/2006 12:00:00 AM	1	
2	2006000165	2006200231	01/01/2006 08:00:00 AM ...	1/1/2006 12:00:00 AM	1	
3	2006000036	2006200036	01/01/2006 08:00:00 AM ...	1/1/2006 12:00:00 AM	1	
4	2006000035	2006200035	01/01/2006 08:00:00 AM ...	1/1/2006 12:00:00 AM	1	
5	2006000159	2006200225	01/01/2006 08:00:00 AM ...	1/1/2006 12:00:00 AM	1	
6	2006000326	2006200401	01/01/2006 08:00:00 AM ...	1/1/2006 12:00:00 AM	1	
7	2006003512	2006203782	01/01/2006 08:00:00 AM ...	1/1/2006 12:00:00 AM	1	
8	2006005091	2006205467	01/01/2006 08:00:00 AM ...	1/1/2006 12:00:00 AM	1	
9	2006005914	2006206346	01/01/2006 08:00:00 AM ...	1/1/2006 12:00:00 AM	1	
	Records: 559227					
	ParallelPeriod: 536670		YOY_Growth: 4.20 %	OpeningMonth: (blank)		
	ParallelPeriod_MONTH: 557880		YOY_Growth_New: 4.20 %	OpeningYear: (blank)		

4. Now deploy the solution to the server and switch to SQL Server Management Studio to view the results. Browse the model and select the **YEAR, Month_Name, Records, OpeningMonth**, and **OpeningYear**. Set the slicer to use the **Calc_Date_T** year to include **2016** and **2015** to limit the results:

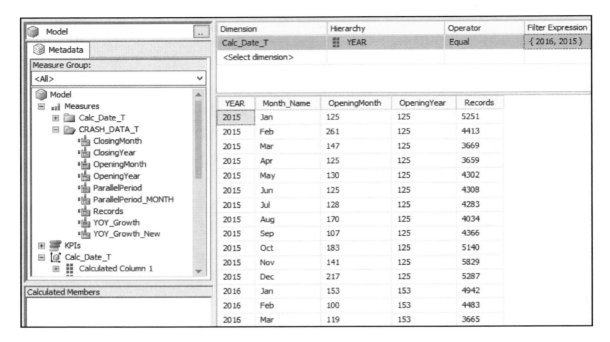

The results displayed in the **OpeningYear** measure are the number of records on the first day of the month for each year. January 2015 had 125 crashes out of a total 5251 recorded in the month of January. The **OpeningYear** measure stores this value regardless of the month in the year 2015. Then in the year 2016 it is set to the value of January 2016 of 153.

How it works...

Just like the OPENINGBALANCEMONTH function, this function returns the total records from the beginning of the year.

Using the CLOSINGBALANCEMONTH function

To determine the total number of crashes at the end of each month, you can use the built-in functions to calculate ending balances. In this recipe, you will create a semi-additive measure to calculate the number of crashes at the end of each month. This will enable you to find out the total number of crashes at the end of each month and determine trends.

How to do it...

1. Open the **Model.bim** to the **CRASH_DATA_T** table.
2. In the measure creation area, click on an empty cell to create a measure to return the closing month balance:

   ```
   ClosingMonth:=CLOSINGBALANCEMONTH( COUNT
       (CRASH_DATA_T[CASE_NUMBER]),
   Calc_Date_T[CRASH_DATE])
   ```

3. Then press *Enter* to create the measure:

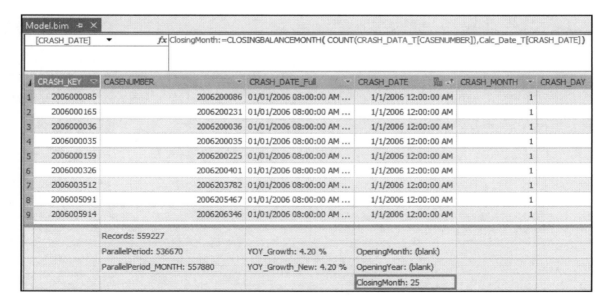

4. Now deploy the solution to the server and switch to SQL Server Management Studio to view the results. Browse the model and select the **YEAR, Month_Name, Records**, and **ClosingMonth**. Set the slicer to use the **Calc_Date_T** year equal to **2016** to limit the results:

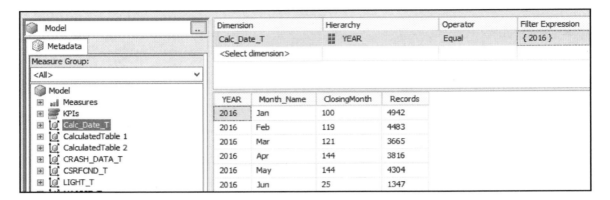

The results displayed in the **ClosingMonth** measure are the number of records on the first day of each month. January 2016 had 100 crashes out of a total 4942 recorded in the month of January.

How it works...

In this recipe, you passed in the date from the **Calc_Date_T** table to calculate the number of crashes at the end of each month. This measure, like the OPENINGBALANCEMONTH function, allows you to create a trend and see performance of the measure over time.

Using the CLOSINGBALANCEYEAR function

To determine the total number of crashes at the end of each year, you can use the built-in functions to calculate ending balances. In this recipe, you will create a semi-additive measure to calculate the number of crashes at the end of each year. This will enable you to find out the total number of crashes at the end of each year and determine trends.

How to do it...

1. Open the **Model.bim** to the **CRASH_DATA_T** table.
2. In the measure creation area, click on an empty cell to create a measure to return the closing year balance:

```
ClosingYear:=CLOSINGBALANCEYEAR( COUNT
    (CRASH_DATA_T[CASE_NUMBER]),
Calc_Date_T[CRASH_DATE])
```

3. Then press *Enter* to create the measure:

Model.bim ↗ ×						
[CRASH_DATE] ▼		*fx* ClosingYear:=CLOSINGBALANCEYEAR(COUNT(CRASH_DATA_T[CASENUMBER]),Calc_Date_T[CRASH_DATE])				

	CRASH_KEY	CASENUMBER	CRASH_DATE_Full	CRASH_DATE	CRASH_MONTH	CRASH_DAY
1	2006000085	2006200086	01/01/2006 08:00:00 AM ...	1/1/2006 12:00:00 AM	1	
2	2006000165	2006200231	01/01/2006 08:00:00 AM ...	1/1/2006 12:00:00 AM	1	
3	2006000036	2006200036	01/01/2006 08:00:00 AM ...	1/1/2006 12:00:00 AM	1	
4	2006000035	2006200035	01/01/2006 08:00:00 AM ...	1/1/2006 12:00:00 AM	1	
5	2006000159	2006200225	01/01/2006 08:00:00 AM ...	1/1/2006 12:00:00 AM	1	
6	2006000326	2006200401	01/01/2006 08:00:00 AM ...	1/1/2006 12:00:00 AM	1	
7	2006003512	2006203782	01/01/2006 08:00:00 AM ...	1/1/2006 12:00:00 AM	1	
8	2006005091	2006205467	01/01/2006 08:00:00 AM ...	1/1/2006 12:00:00 AM	1	
9	2006005914	2006206346	01/01/2006 08:00:00 AM ...	1/1/2006 12:00:00 AM	1	
		Records: 559227				
		ParallelPeriod: 536670	YOY_Growth: 4.20 %	OpeningMonth: (blank)		
		ParallelPeriod_MONTH: 557880	YOY_Growth_New: 4.20 %	OpeningYear: (blank)		
				ClosingMonth: 25		
				ClosingYear: 25		

4. Now deploy the solution to the server and switch to SQL Server Management Studio to view the results. Browse the model and select the **YEAR, Month_Name, Records, OpeningMonth,** and **OpeningYear**. Set the slicer to use the **Calc_Date_T** year to include 2016 and 2015. Include another filter to limit the results to the **Month_Num** of {3,4,5,6, 12}:

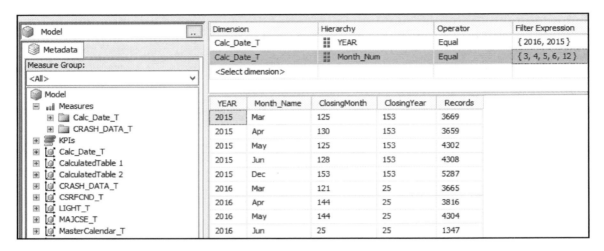

The results displayed in the **ClosingYear** measure are the number of records on the last day of the month for each year. December 31st 2015 had 153 crashes out of a total 5287 recorded in the month of January. The **ClosingYear** measure stores this value regardless of the month in the year 2015. Then in the year 2016 it is set to the value of the last day of the dataset, in this case, June 2016 with 25 recorded crashes.

How it works...

In this recipe, you passed in the date from the **Calc_Date_T** table to calculate the number of crashes at the end of each year. This measure, like the OPENINGBALANCEYEAR, allows you to create a trend and see performance of the measure over time.

Using the TOTALYTD function

The TOTALYTD function is an additive measure that returns the total records from the beginning of the year to the date in the context. For example, you can use this function to calculate the total number of crashes from 1/1/2016 to the date that you selected in the filter context. You can quickly calculate the number of records at any point in the year.

How to do it…

1. Open the **Model.bim** to the **CRASH_DATA_T** table.

2. In the measure creation area, click on an empty cell to create a measure to return the year to date cumulative total for the number of crashes:

```
YTDTotals:=TOTALYTD( COUNT
    (CRASH_DATA_T[CASE_NUMBER]),
Calc_Date_T[CRASH_DATE])
```

3. Then press *Enter* to create the measure:

Model.bim ⊕ ×					
[CRASH_MONTH] ▼		*fx* YTDTotals:=TOTALYTD(COUNT(CRASH_DATA_T[CASENUMBER]),Calc_Date_T[CRASH_DATE])			
CRASH_KEY ▼	CASENUMBER ▼	CRASH_DATE_Full ▼	CRASH_DATE ▼	CRASH_MONTH ▼	
1	2006000085	2006200086	01/01/2006 08:00:00 AM …	1/1/2006 12:00:00 AM	1
2	2006000165	2006200231	01/01/2006 08:00:00 AM …	1/1/2006 12:00:00 AM	1
3	2006000036	2006200036	01/01/2006 08:00:00 AM …	1/1/2006 12:00:00 AM	1
4	2006000035	2006200035	01/01/2006 08:00:00 AM …	1/1/2006 12:00:00 AM	1
5	2006000159	2006200225	01/01/2006 08:00:00 AM …	1/1/2006 12:00:00 AM	1
6	2006000326	2006200401	01/01/2006 08:00:00 AM …	1/1/2006 12:00:00 AM	1
7	2006003512	2006203782	01/01/2006 08:00:00 AM …	1/1/2006 12:00:00 AM	1
8	2006005091	2006205467	01/01/2006 08:00:00 AM …	1/1/2006 12:00:00 AM	1
9	2006005914	2006206346	01/01/2006 08:00:00 AM …	1/1/2006 12:00:00 AM	1
	Records: 559227				
	ParallelPeriod: 536670	YOY_Growth: 4.20 %	OpeningMonth: (blank)	YTDTotals: 22557	

4. Now deploy the solution to the server and switch to SQL Server Management Studio to view the results. Browse the model and select the **YEAR, Month_Name, CRASH_DATE, Records,** and **YTDTotals**:

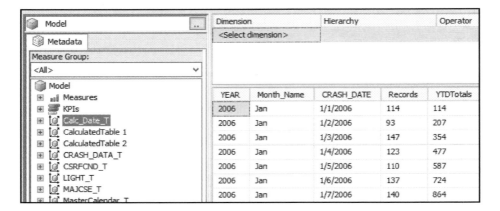

5. The results displayed in the **YTDTotals** measure are the number of records from the first date records. Then each day the total gets added to the next day's total to product a running total. On January 1st there were 114 records and the YTD total is **114**. Then on January 2nd the records total is 93. However, the YTD total is the sum of **114** from the 1st plus the 93 from the 2nd to equal 207.

6. By changing the view to remove the individual date, the function continues to calculate the totals by month:

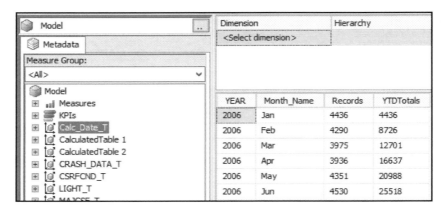

The total records for each month are calculated and then added to the next month to create the YTD total for the year.

How it works...

The TOTALYTD function uses the **Calc_Date_T** date column to calculate the crashes from the beginning of each year. The ending value of the context is set by the value you select in a filter. In this recipe, you see that the aggregated total from January 2006 to June 2006 is **25,518**.

11
Using Power BI for Analysis

In this chapter, we will cover the following recipes:

- Getting started with Power BI desktop
- Adding data to Power BI reports
- Using the SSAS tabular model as a source
- Visualizing the crash data with Power BI
- Adding additional visualizations to Power BI
- Editing visualization properties in Power BI
- Using analytics in Power BI

Introduction

Power BI is Microsoft's data analysis and visualization tool. Power BI allows users to create rich reporting, dashboards, and analytics by connecting to one or many data sources. There are several components that make up the Power BI environment. First you connect or manually add data to your report to create a dataset. The dataset is then available to be used for visualizations in the report. Each visualization which includes items, such as graphs, data tables, treemaps, or slicers, are represented in a tile that can be modified and edited independently. Visualizations are added to a page in a report. Each report can have from one to many pages that are connected to the data.

In this section you will install Power BI desktop and connect to your tabular model. Then you will create an initial graph and go through the steps to edit the visualization. Next you will enhance the report by adding more visualizations and a slicer to filter the data. Finally, you will create a new page in the report and create a line graph, and you will use the Analytics feature to add the average to the graph.

Getting started with Power BI desktop

In this recipe you will download and install the Power BI desktop 64 bit edition. Once installed you will be ready to continue with the remaining recipes in the chapter to visualize the Iowa crash data.

How to do it...

1. This software is available to download from
   `https://powerbi.microsoft.com/en-us/desktop/`.
2. Download the 32 or 64 bit version depending upon your environment.
3. Double-click the downloaded `PBIDesktop_x64.msi` file and install the software.
4. Launch the application from the desktop shortcut:

5. A blank report will be shown as follows:

How it works...

In this recipe you downloaded Microsoft's Power BI desktop. You then installed and launched the application to ensure it is working.

Adding data to Power BI reports

Power BI can currently connect to a wide variety of data sources. Your reports begin by connecting to the data you want to explore and visualize. For example, you can connect to file data sources like Excel, csv, txt or xml file types. You can also connect databases like SQL Server, Oracle, MySQL, PostgresSQL or Hadoop HDFS. In addition, you can get data from Azure datastores such as HDInsight, SQL Data Warehouse, and DocumentDB. In this recipe you will connect Power BI to the SQL Server Analysis Services Tabular model.

How to do it...

1. Open Power BI desktop and select**Get Data** from the opening screen:

2. On the **Get Data** window, select the data source you want to connect to. In this recipe you connect to the completed crash data database:

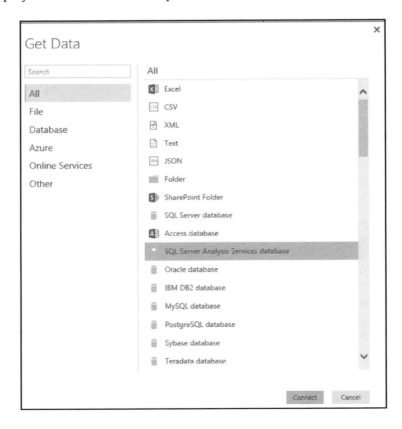

3. Select **SQL Server Analysis Services Database** and then**Connect**.

4. Type in your server name for the SSAS tabular model and make sure the **Connect live** radio button is selected and click **OK**:

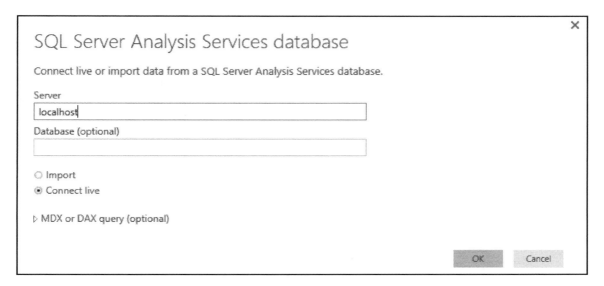

5. In the **Navigator** window, select the **Crash_Data_Model_Complete** and the model to establish the connection:

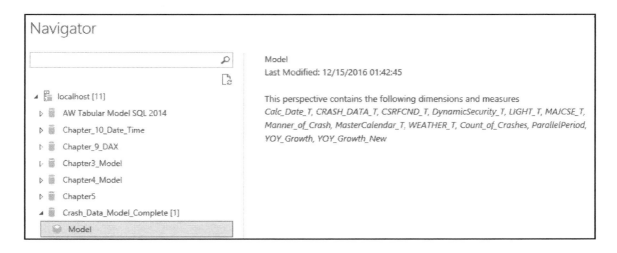

6. Then click **OK**.
7. A new Power BI report is ready with all visible fields from your tabular model. You should be able to see the tables in the **Fields** window:

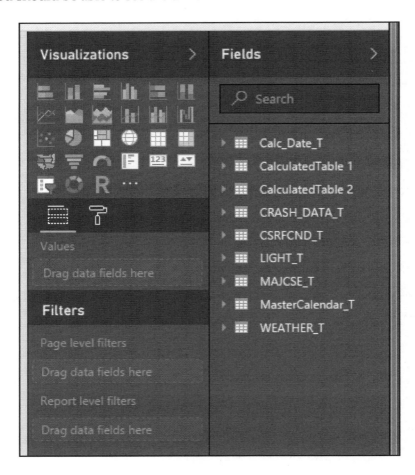

8. As models become larger with more fields it can be difficult for users to keep track of the available fields. Users can use the **Search** field to type in a word and all tables or columns that match the term will be shown.

9. Type `light` into the search field to return all columns and tables with the word `light`:

How it works...

Power BI is a reporting tool that can connect to a wide variety of data sources. Before you can use Power BI, you must connect it to the data you want to use. In this recipe you started a new Power BI desktop report and connected to the SSAS tabular model. Power BI established the connection and has the schema loaded. You are now ready to start building reports.

There's more...

Once you are working on a report you can also retrieve data by selecting the **Get Data** menu on the **Home** tab. This is the method that will enable you to add more connections:

Visualizing the crash data with Power BI

Once you have data connected to Power BI you can create visualizations. Each visualization is designed and built independently. Once the basic visualization is completed you can format it to make it easier to read. Formatting allows you modify settings like showing label values, changing the color of the charts, or changing the title. By creating several visualizations, you can combine them on a report page. In this recipe you will create a stacked bar graph and then format it to change the default settings.

Getting ready

The **Visualizations** window in Power BI gives you over 26 out of the box graphs that you can use on your data. To begin creating reports you select the type of visualization you want and then the fields used to build the graphic.

How to do it...

1. Connect to your data source and create a new report.
2. Select the first icon–**Stacked Bar Chart** from the **Visualizations** window:

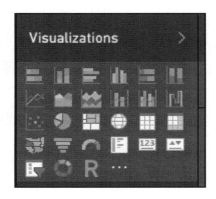

3. A new blank chart is added to the report tab as a tile:

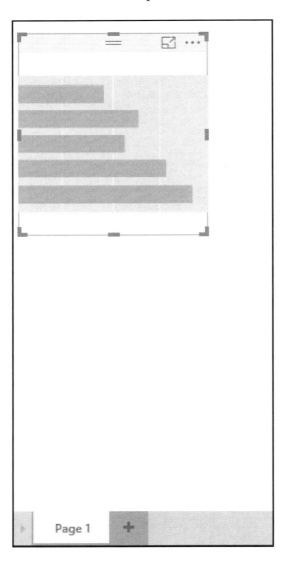

4. Select **Count_of_Crashes** from the **CRASH_DATA_T** table and the **Light_Description** from the **LIGHT_T** table. A chart will be created with the data from the tabular model:

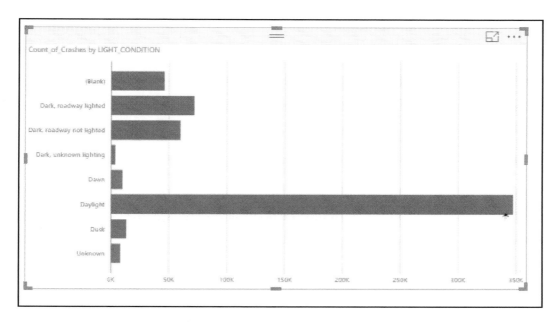

5. To format the chart select the ellipse to see the options:

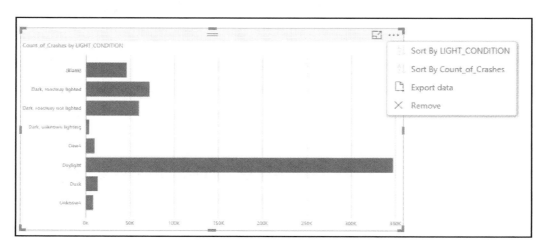

6. Then select**Sort by Count_of_Crashes** to reorder the graph:

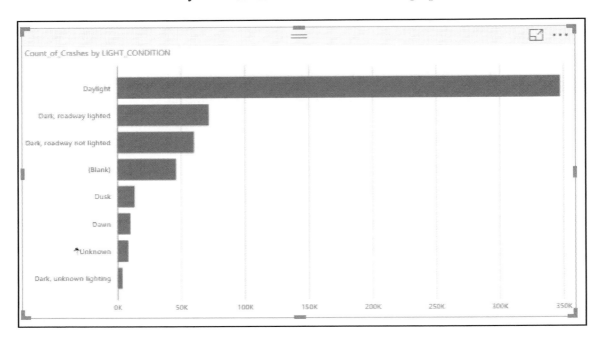

How it works...

In this recipe you added a stacked bar chart to the Power BI canvas. Then, using the data connection to your tabular model, you created a bar graph that shows the number of crashes that occurred by recorded light condition. To make the data easier to read, you then sorted the chart based on the highest number of crashes from top to bottom. You now have a completed visualization on page 1 of your report.

Editing visualization properties in Power BI

There are many properties that you can modify to change the appearance of your visualizations. These properties allow you to modify properties such as background, title, borders, and colors. In this recipe you will modify the stacked bar chart to understand how properties affect the visualization.

Getting ready

Complete the initial visualization in the recipe Visualizing the crash data in Power BI.

How to do it...

1. Select the graph and click on the paint roller icon under the **Visualization** to bring up the **Properties** window:

2. Select the data colors and click the down arrow to show the available properties to change. On the **Default color** select the drop down and change the color to purple to change the bar graph colors:

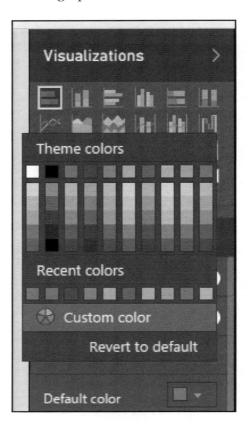

3. The chart is now updated to reflect the new color:

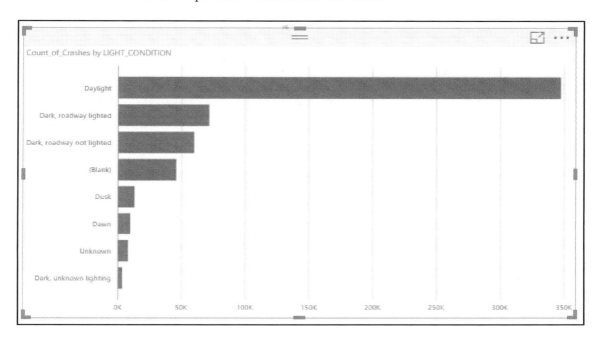

4. Next expand the **Title** property to change the **Title Text** to **Total Crashes based on Reported Light Condition** and increase the **Text Size** to **12**:

5. Now to show the values of each bar chart, change the **Data Labels** slider from **Off** to **On**.

6. Finally, to add a border to the graph, change the **Border** slider from **Off** to **On**:

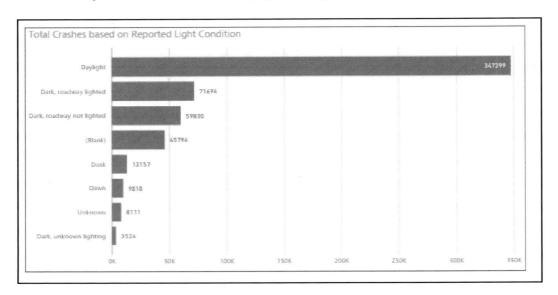

7. The graph will now reflect all of these changes on the report.

How it works...

There are many properties you can change on a graph. In this recipe you changed the default data color to purple. You then updated the title text and font size. Finally, you added a border to the selected graph. By selecting the format icon, you will see a list of properties that are available for you to modify. Experiment with the different properties to ensure you understand what is available and how they work.

Adding additional visualizations to Power BI

Reports normally contain multiple tables and visualizations designed to solve business problems. A report page can contain many separate visualization tiles on the canvas. In the prior recipe you worked with a single stacked bar chart visualization on a single page. In this recipe you will add two more visualizations to the report to fill out your canvas.

Getting ready

Complete the initial visualization in the recipe *Visualizing the crash data in Power BI*.

How it to do it...

1. Select an area of the page canvas and not the existing graph. Then select a new treemap visualization to add to the report page:

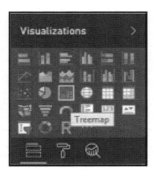

2. A new blank treemap will be added to the report:

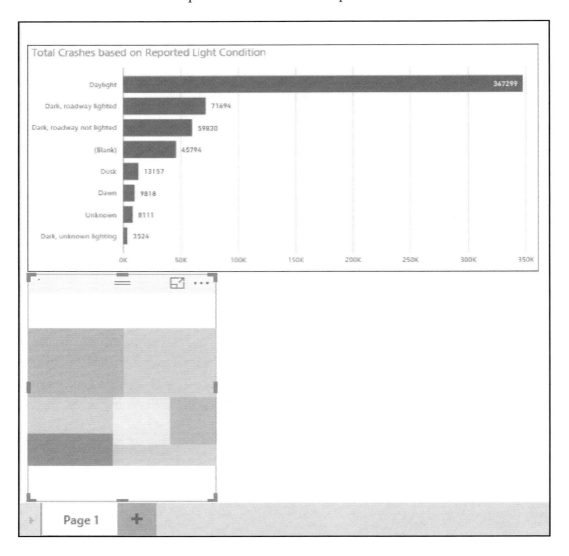

3. Select the **Count_of_Crashes** from the **CRASH_DATA_T** table and the **Weather_Condition** from the **Weather_T** table. This will create the default treemap:

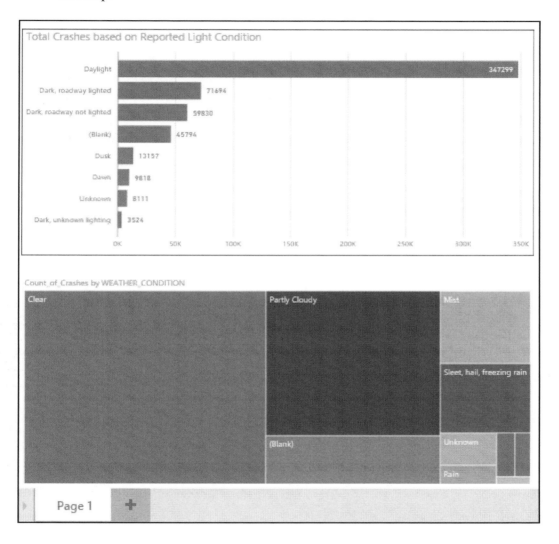

4. Select the roller brush to edit the properties and change the **Title Text** to **Heatmap of Crashes by Weather Condition** and change the **Text** to size **12**:

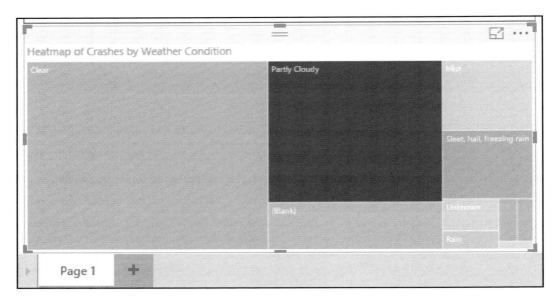

5. Since the data is related, you can interact with the charts to filter the results in real time. Based on all the records, most crashes occur in clear conditions because it has the largest of the squares in the treemap. To see the number of crashes caused by a specific light condition, select the square with sleet, hail, freezing rain in the treemap. The top graph is filtered to show the number of crashes related to this condition:

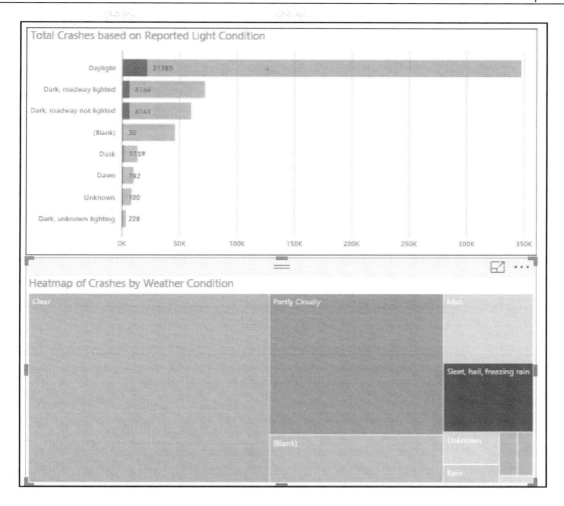

6. There were 21,385 crashes in **Daylight** that were recorded in sleet, hail, or freezing rain. Notice the total bar length did not change. You can see the impact relative to the total number of records.

7. Finally, add a data table to the report to see the total crashes by weather condition. Select a blank area on the report and then the table icon from **Visualizations**:

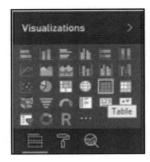

8. Add the **Count_of_Crashes** and the **Weather_Condition** to populate the table:

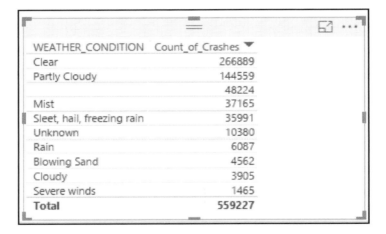

WEATHER_CONDITION	Count_of_Crashes ▼
Clear	266889
Partly Cloudy	144559
	48224
Mist	37165
Sleet, hail, freezing rain	35991
Unknown	10380
Rain	6087
Blowing Sand	4562
Cloudy	3905
Severe winds	1465
Total	**559227**

How it works...

In this recipe you added a treemap and data table to the report canvas. The treemap helps you visualize the impact of weather on crashes. By adding the data table, you can see the exact number of crashes. Because all of the data is related in the model, when you select a value in a visualization the other visualizations are filtered based on the selection. This allows for quick analysis and data exploration in your report.

Adding a slicer to Power BI

Slicers are a way to filter the data in your report. Slicers create a checkbox list of available values to limit the dataset. For commonly used filters, slicers are a great choice to enable users to easily interact and analyze data. In this recipe you will add a slicer tile to the report and use it to limit the data shown in the report.

Getting ready

Complete the steps in the recipe *Adding additional visualizations to Power BI*.

How to do it...

1. Select an open area of the report canvas and then select the slicer icon from the bottom left under **Visualizations**:

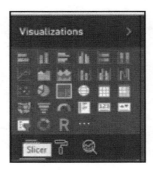

2. A new blank slicer will be added to the report page:

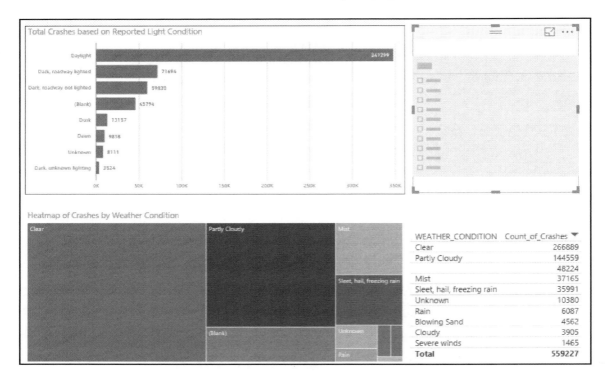

3. To enable slicing by the manner of crash, select the **Manner_of_Crash** from the **Manner_of_Crash** table. The slicer will now be populated with all values from this field:

4. Next select **Rear-end** as the manner of crash to filter the bar graph, the treemap, and the data table to only show data related to rear-end crashes:

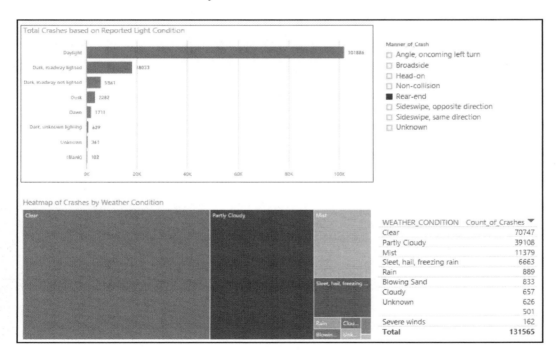

5. Rename the page to `Crash Overview` by double-clicking **Page1** on the bottom tab:

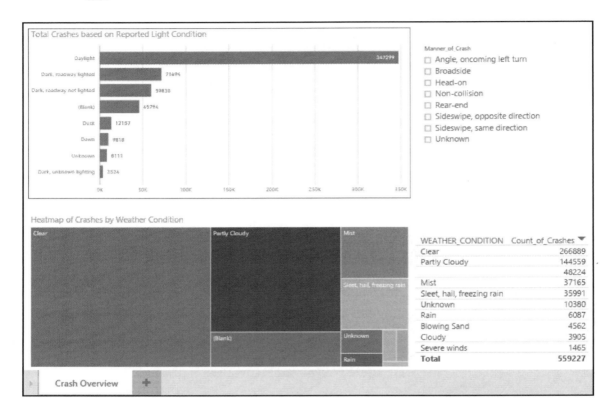

How it works...

The slicer tile acts as a filter on the other visualizations on the report page. When you select one or more values in the slicer, the other visualizations are automatically limited based on the selected values.

Using analytics in Power BI

Getting ready

Complete the steps in the recipe *Adding additional visualizations to Power BI.*

How to do it...

1. Add a new page to the report and rename it `Analytics`.
2. Add a line chart to the report and add the **count_of_crashes** from the **CRASH_DATA_T** table and the **Light_Condition** from the **LIGHT_T** table:

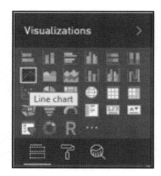

3. Select the ellipse and change the sort order to **Sort by Count_of_Crashes**:

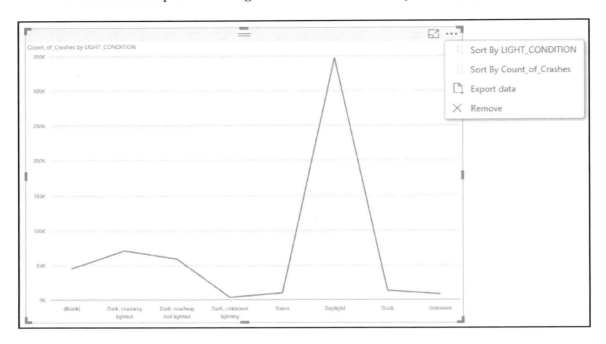

4. While the chart is selected, select the spyglass icon next to the paint roller to see the available analytics. The available choices vary based on the visualization that you select:

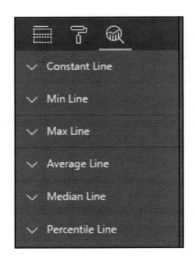

5. To add an **Average** line, click on the down arrow next to Average Line. Then click
    + Add to create an average line and rename it `Average`. Then change the color to
    red and change the data label slider to **On**. Finally, change the color to red and
    change the **Text** drop down to **Name and Value**:

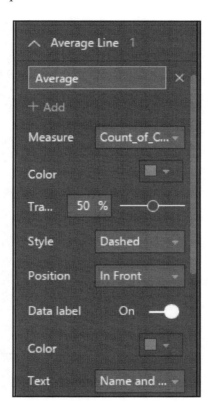

6. The graph now has a horizontal line that shows the average of all value:

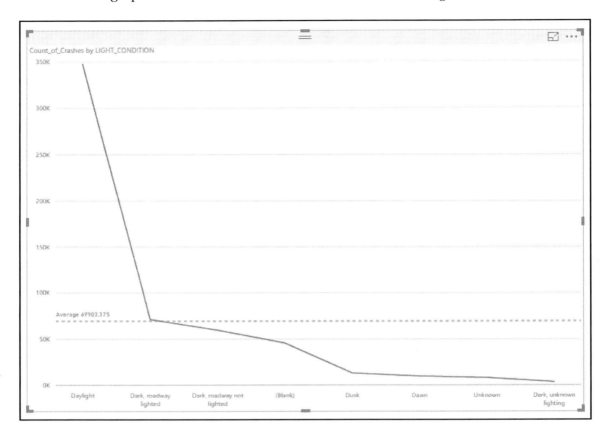

7. The average is 69903. This average is calculated based on any filters that you have. Therefore, if you add a slicer the average will be recalculated based on the slicer or filter.

8. Add a slicer and **SURFACE_CONDITION** from the **CSRFCND_T** table and select **Snow**. The Average line is now 5383 and calculated based on all values related to **Snow**:

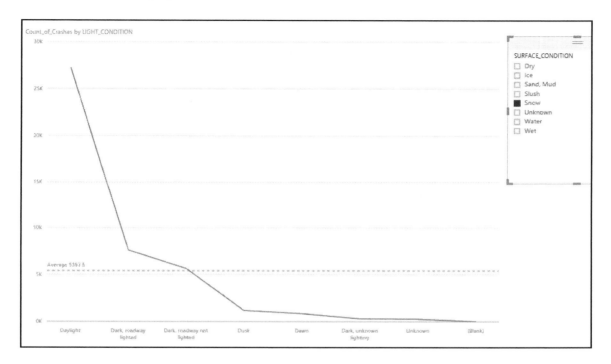

How it works...

The average line is calculated based on all of the displayed data in the report. You modified the properties to make it easy to see by changing the color and displaying the name and value on the report. Since the average is calculated within Power BI, as you filter the data, the average will be automatically recalculated to reflect the data being shown.

Index

Year over Year Growth

calculating 302, 303, 304